JOURNEY TO STAR WARS: THE FORCE AWAKENS

STAR WARS

SHATTERED EMPIRE

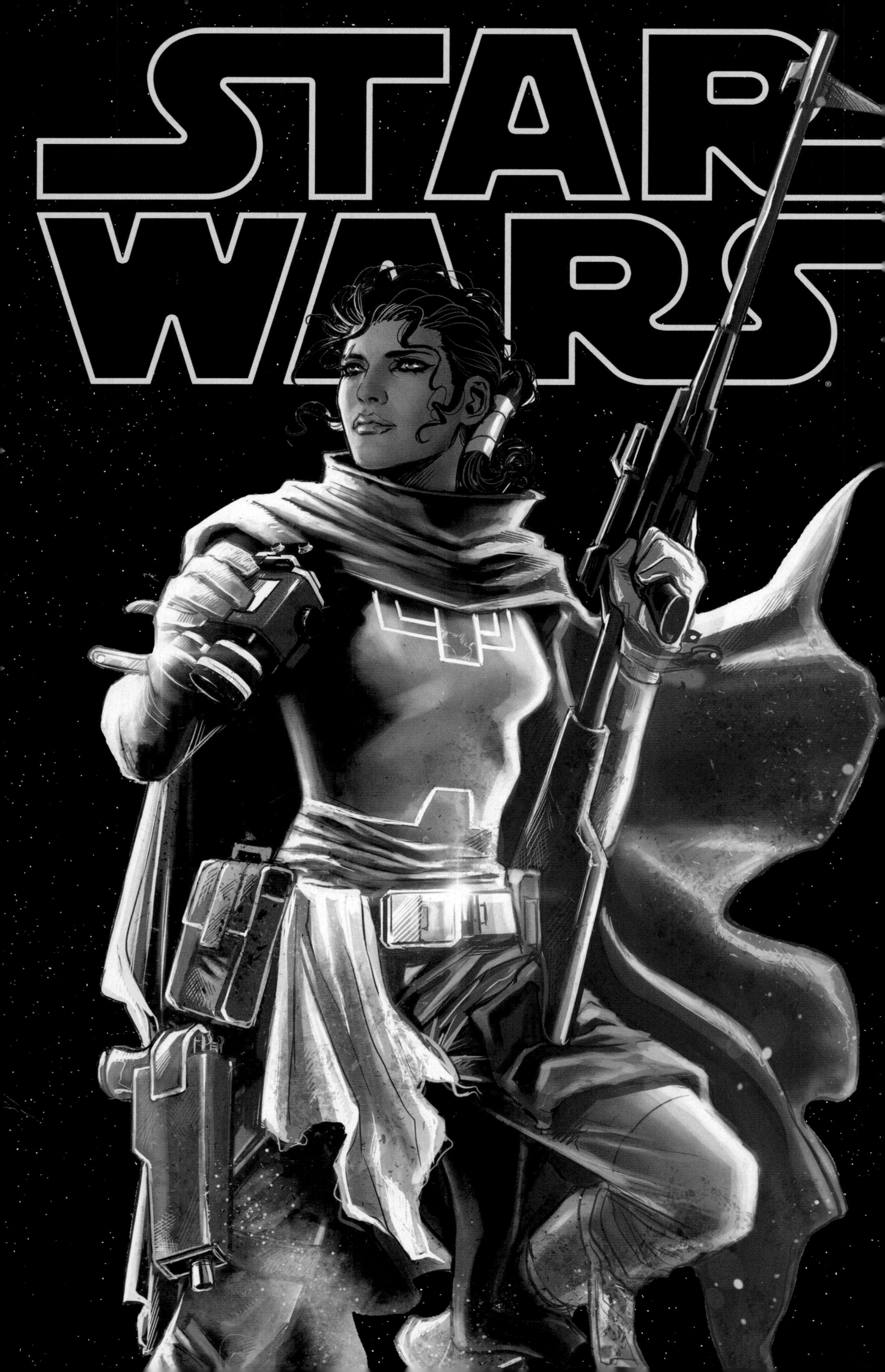
STAR WARS

JOURNEY TO **STAR WARS: THE FORCE AWAKENS**

SHATTERED EMPIRE

Writer	**GREG RUCKA**
Artists	**MARCO CHECCHETTO (#1-4), ANGEL UNZUETA (#2-3) & EMILIO LAISO (#2)**
Colorist	**ANDRES MOSSA**
Cover Art	**PHIL NOTO (#1) & MARCO CHECCHETTO (#2-4)**

STAR WARS SPECIAL: C-3PO 1

Writer	**JAMES ROBINSON**
Artist/Cover	**TONY HARRIS**

Letterer	**VC's JOE CARAMAGNA**
Assistant Editor	**HEATHER ANTOS**
Editor	**JORDAN D. WHITE**
Executive Editor	**C.B. CEBULSKI**

Editor in Chief	**AXEL ALONSO**
Chief Creative Officer	**JOE QUESADA**
Publisher	**DAN BUCKLEY**

For Lucasfilm:

Creative Director	**MICHAEL SIGLAIN**
Senior Editor	**FRANK PARISI**
Lucasfilm Story Group	**RAYNE ROBERTS, PABLO HIDALGO, LELAND CHEE, MATT MARTIN**

Collection Editor	**JENNIFER GRÜNWALD**
Associate Editor	**SARAH BRUNSTAD**
Editor, Special Projects	**MARK D. BEAZLEY**
VP, Production & Special Projects	**JEFF YOUNGQUIST**
SVP Print, Sales & Marketing	**DAVID GABRIEL**
Book Designer	**ADAM DEL RE**

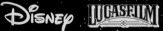

STAR WARS: JOURNEY TO STAR WARS: THE FORCE AWAKENS — SHATTERED EMPIRE. Contains material originally published in magazine form as JOURNEY TO STAR WARS: THE FORCE AWAKENS — SHATTERED EMPIRE #1-4 and STAR WARS SPECIAL: C-3PO #1. First printing 2016. ISBN# 978-1-302-90210-0. Published by MARVEL WORLDWIDE, INC., a subsidiary of MARVEL ENTERTAINMENT, LLC. OFFICE OF PUBLICATION: 135 West 50th Street, New York, NY 10020. STAR WARS and related text and illustrations are trademarks and/or copyrights, in the United States and other countries, of Lucasfilm Ltd. and/or its affiliates. © & TM Lucasfilm Ltd. No similarity between any of the names, characters, persons, and/or institutions in this magazine with those of any living or dead person or institution is intended, and any such similarity which may exist is purely coincidental. Marvel and its logos are TM Marvel Characters, Inc. **Printed in the U.S.A.** ALAN FINE, President, Marvel Entertainment; DAN BUCKLEY, President, TV, Publishing & Brand Management; JOE QUESADA, Chief Creative Officer; TOM BREVOORT, SVP of Publishing; DAVID BOGART, SVP of Business Affairs & Operations, Publishing & Partnership; C.B. CEBULSKI, VP of Brand Management & Development, Asia; DAVID GABRIEL, SVP of Sales & Marketing, Publishing; JEFF YOUNGQUIST, VP of Production & Special Projects; DAN CARR, Executive Director of Publishing Technology; ALEX MORALES, Director of Publishing Operations; SUSAN CRESPI, Production Manager; STAN LEE, Chairman Emeritus. For information regarding advertising in Marvel Comics or on Marvel.com, please contact Vit DeBellis, Integrated Sales Manager, at vdebellis@marvel.com. For Marvel subscription inquiries, please call 888-511-5480. **Manufactured between 6/20/2016 and 8/1/2016 by R.R. DONNELLEY, INC., SALEM, VA, USA.**

0 9 8 7 6 5 4 3 2 1

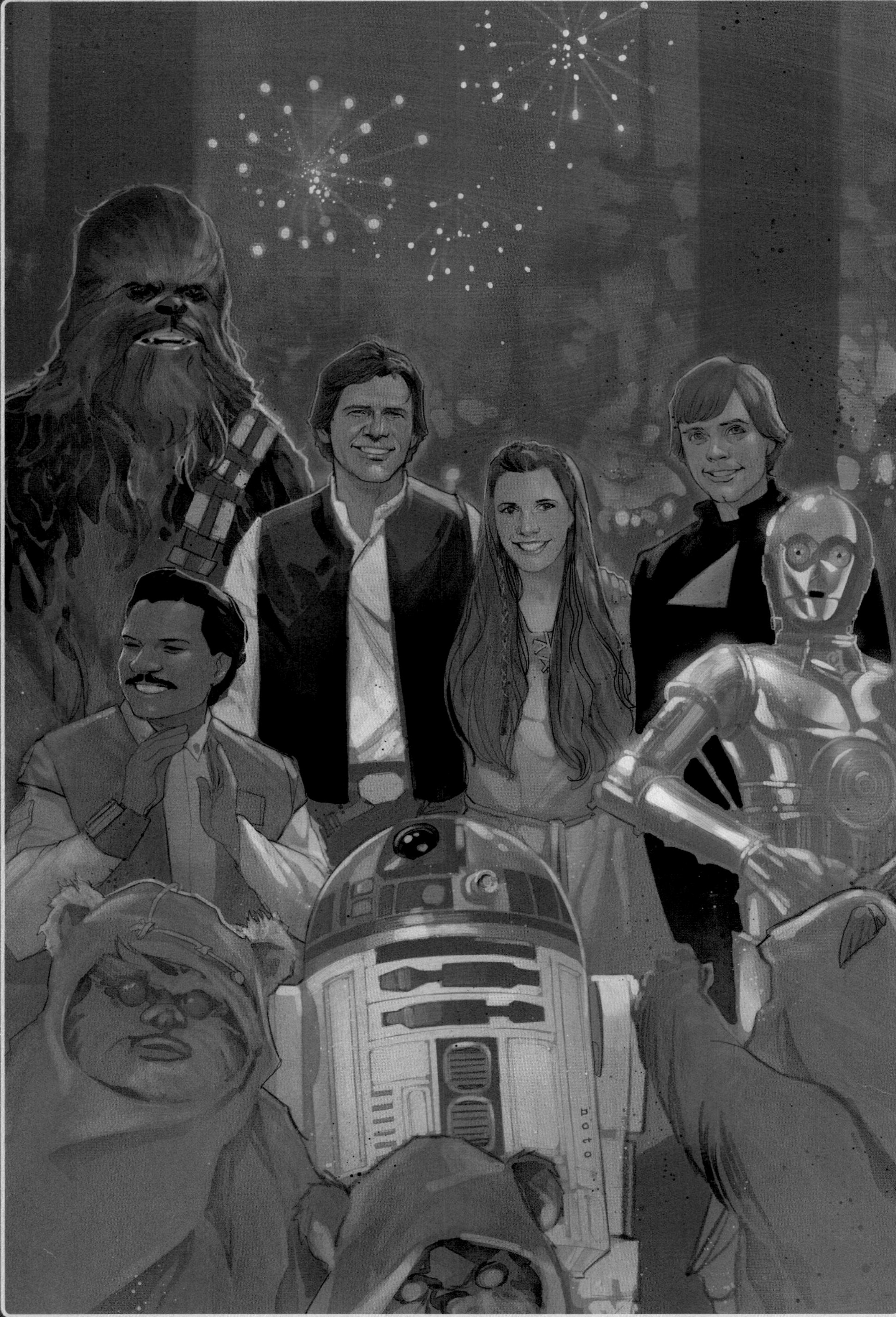
noto

1

SHATTERED EMPIRE

It is the final moments of the BATTLE OF ENDOR. Amidst the stars above the Forest Moon, Rebel forces have engaged the evil Galactic Empire in a desperate, final confrontation, hoping to end the tyrannical rule of Emperor Palpatine and bring peace to a wearied and battered galaxy.

But the Rebel Fleet has fallen into a trap. The second DEATH STAR is fully operational, and on Endor's moon, the energy shield protecting it still stands. What was to be a moment of triumph now teeters on the brink of disaster.

Now, rebel pilots have engaged Imperial forces in furious dogfights, frantically trying to protect the Rebellion's capital ships, and to buy enough time to rescue victory from the jaws of defeat....

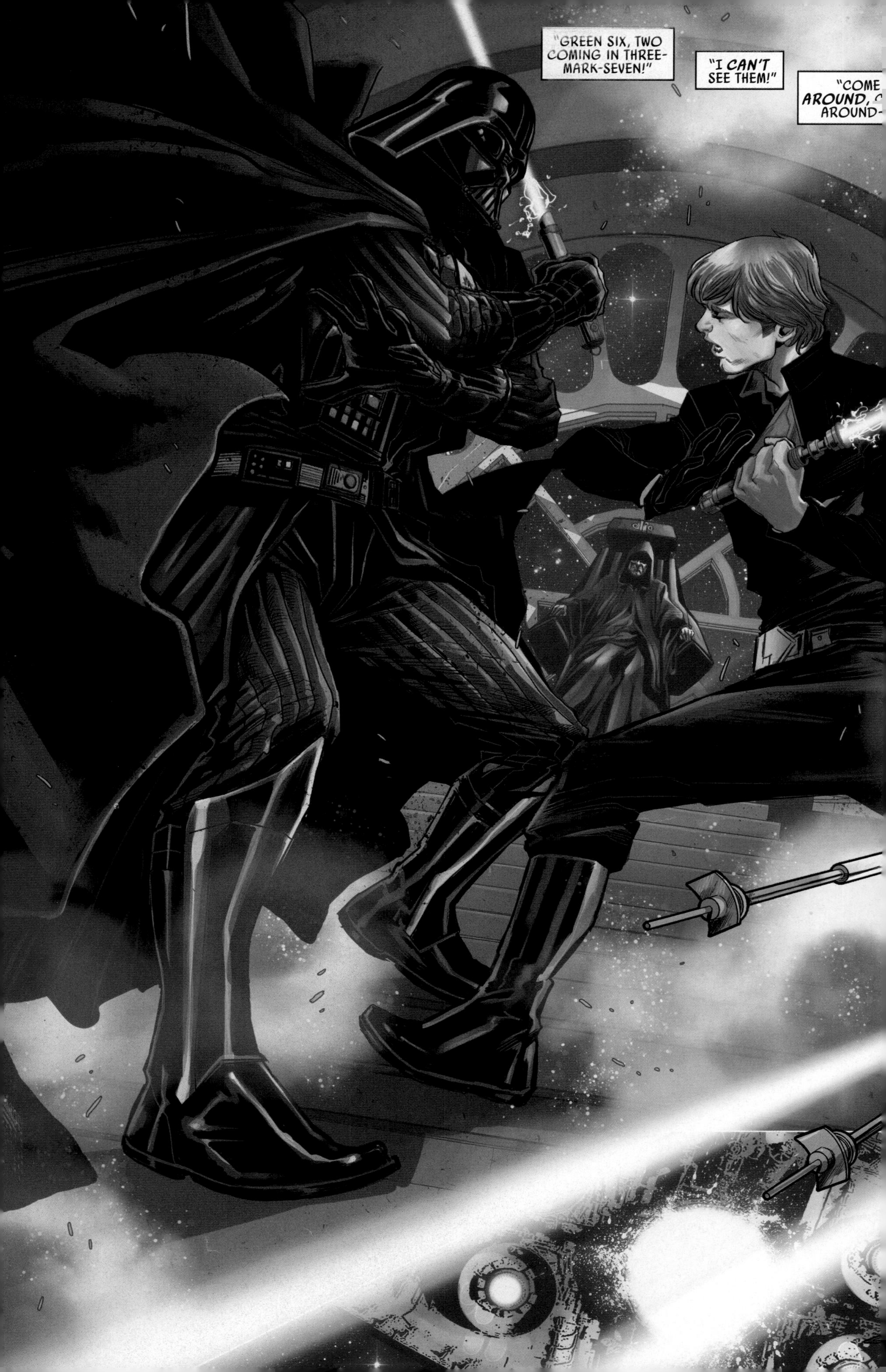
"GREEN SIX, TWO COMING IN THREE-MARK-SEVEN!"
"I CAN'T SEE THEM!"
"COME AROUND, AROUND-

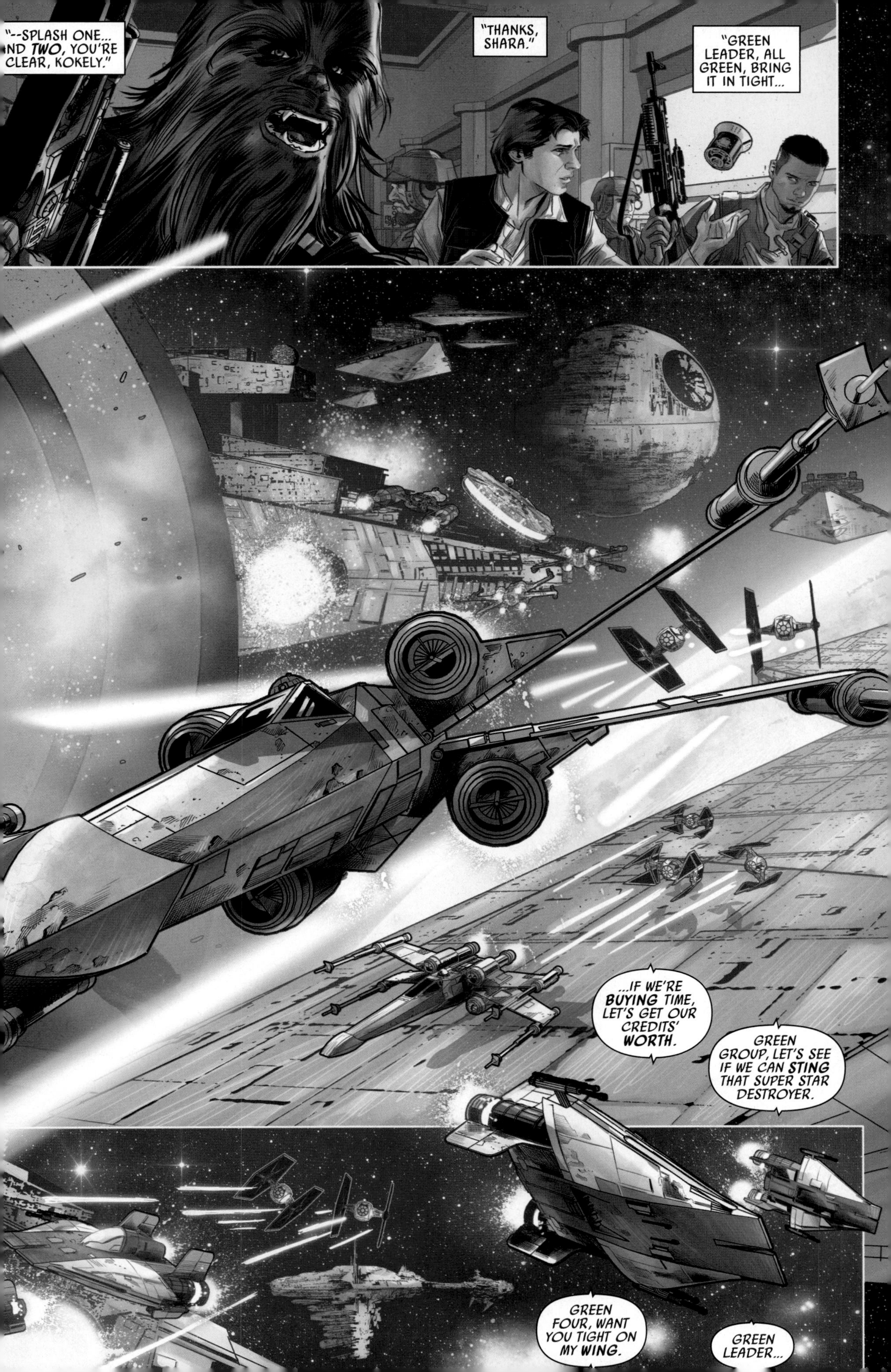
"--SPLASH ONE...
ND TWO, YOU'RE CLEAR, KOKELY."
"THANKS, SHARA."
"GREEN LEADER, ALL GREEN, BRING IT IN TIGHT...
...IF WE'RE BUYING TIME, LET'S GET OUR CREDITS' WORTH.
GREEN GROUP, LET'S SEE IF WE CAN STING THAT SUPER STAR DESTROYER.
GREEN FOUR, WANT YOU TIGHT ON MY WING.
GREEN LEADER...

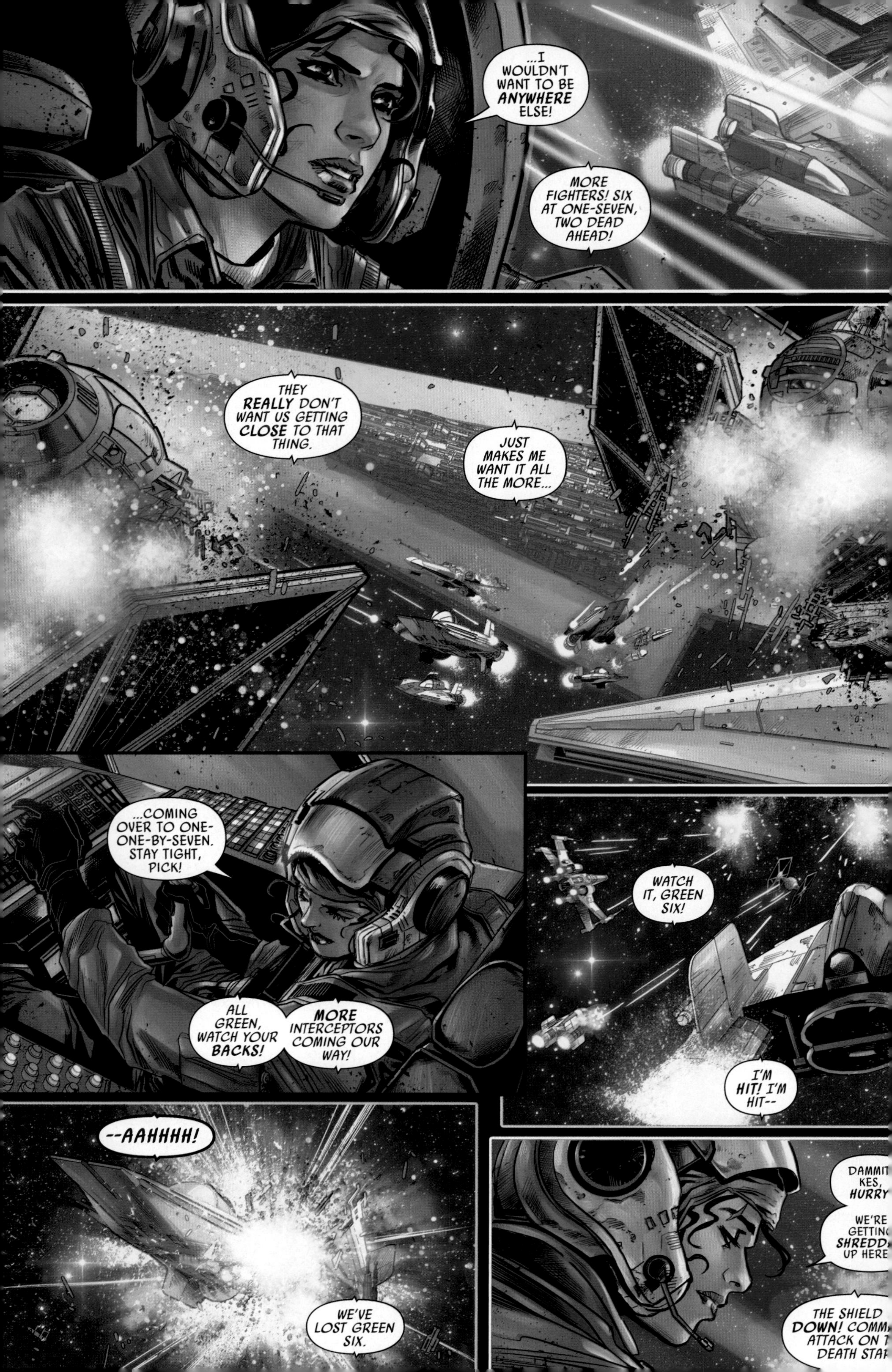
...I WOULDN'T WANT TO BE ANYWHERE ELSE!
MORE FIGHTERS! SIX AT ONE-SEVEN, TWO DEAD AHEAD!
THEY REALLY DON'T WANT US GETTING CLOSE TO THAT THING.
JUST MAKES ME WANT IT ALL THE MORE...
...COMING OVER TO ONE-ONE-BY-SEVEN. STAY TIGHT, PICK!
ALL GREEN, WATCH YOUR BACKS!
MORE INTERCEPTORS COMING OUR WAY!
WATCH IT, GREEN SIX!
I'M HIT! I'M HIT--
--AAHHHH!
WE'VE LOST GREEN SIX.
DAMMIT KES, HURRY
WE'RE GETTIN SHREDD UP HERE
THE SHIELD DOWN! COMM ATTACK ON T DEATH STA

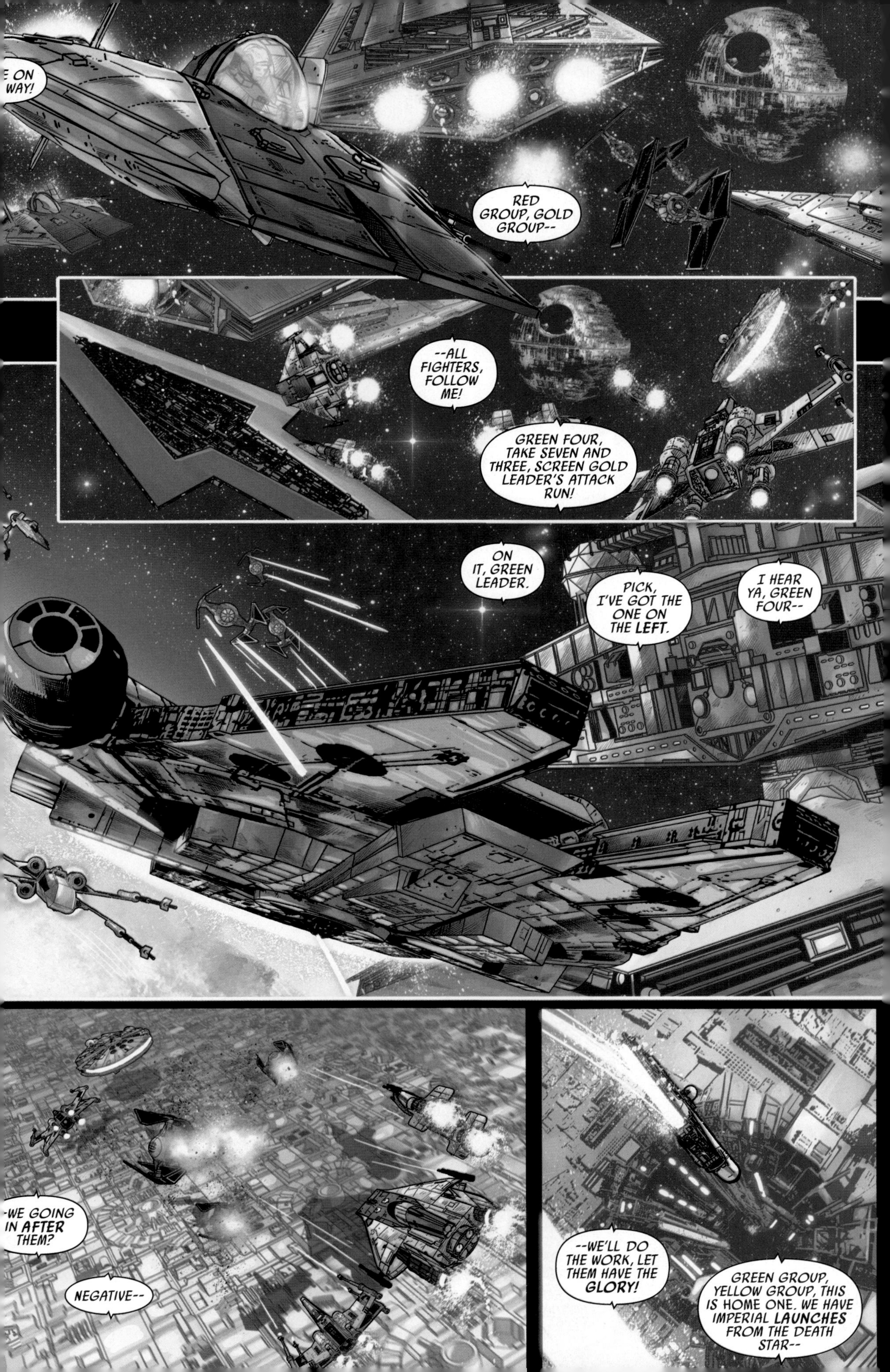
E ON WAY!
RED GROUP, GOLD GROUP--
--ALL FIGHTERS, FOLLOW ME!
GREEN FOUR, TAKE SEVEN AND THREE, SCREEN GOLD LEADER'S ATTACK RUN!
ON IT, GREEN LEADER.
PICK, I'VE GOT THE ONE ON THE LEFT.
I HEAR YA, GREEN FOUR--
-WE GOING IN AFTER THEM?
NEGATIVE--
--WE'LL DO THE WORK, LET THEM HAVE THE GLORY!
GREEN GROUP, YELLOW GROUP, THIS IS HOME ONE. WE HAVE IMPERIAL LAUNCHES FROM THE DEATH STAR--

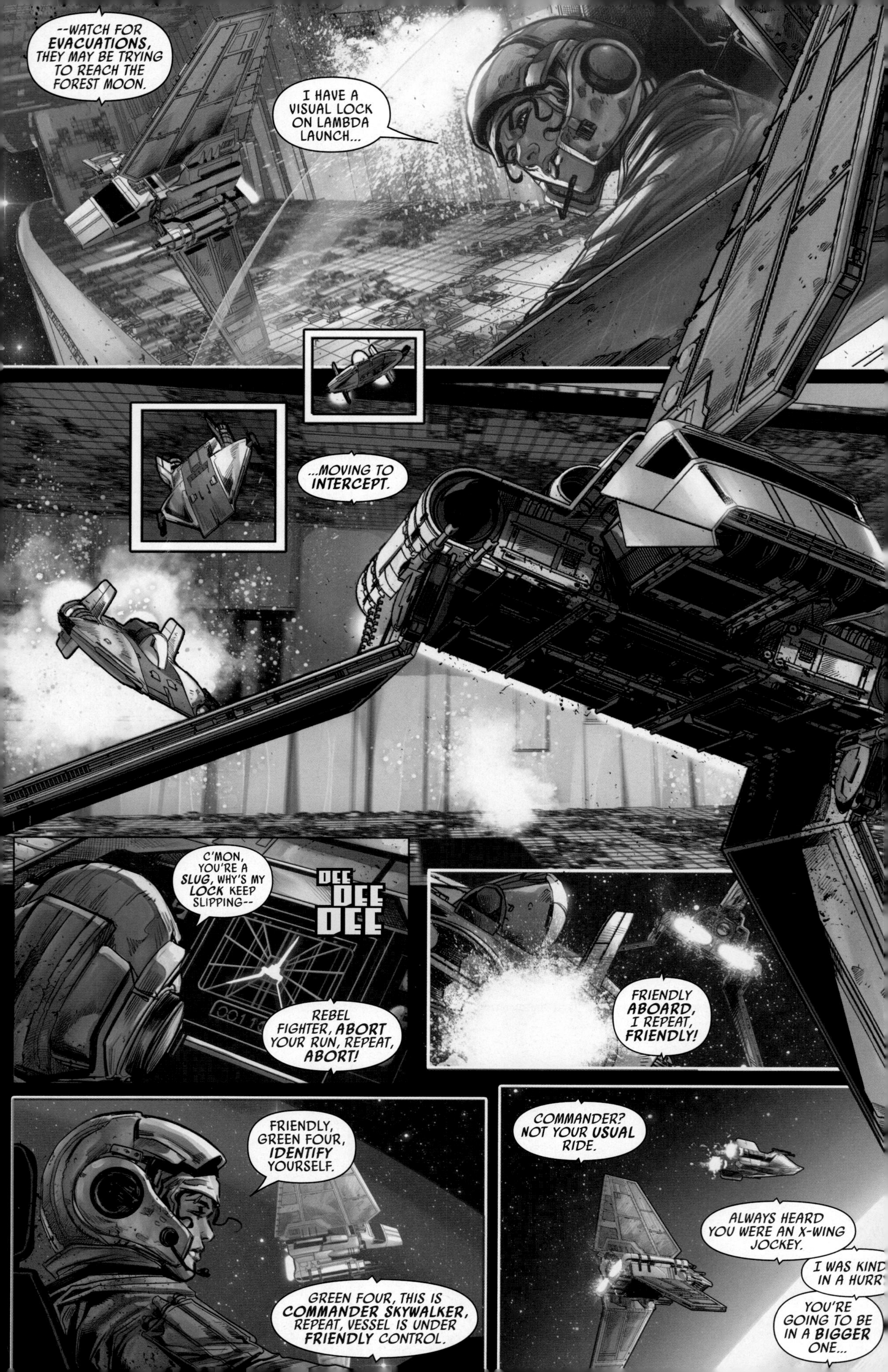
--WATCH FOR EVACUATIONS, THEY MAY BE TRYING TO REACH THE FOREST MOON.
I HAVE A VISUAL LOCK ON LAMBDA LAUNCH...
...MOVING TO INTERCEPT.
C'MON, YOU'RE A SLUG, WHY'S MY LOCK KEEP SLIPPING--
DEE DEE DEE
REBEL FIGHTER, ABORT YOUR RUN, REPEAT, ABORT!
FRIENDLY ABOARD, I REPEAT, FRIENDLY!
FRIENDLY, GREEN FOUR, IDENTIFY YOURSELF.
GREEN FOUR, THIS IS COMMANDER SKYWALKER, REPEAT, VESSEL IS UNDER FRIENDLY CONTROL.
COMMANDER? NOT YOUR USUAL RIDE.
ALWAYS HEARD YOU WERE AN X-WING JOCKEY.
YOU'RE GOING TO BE IN A BIGGER ONE...

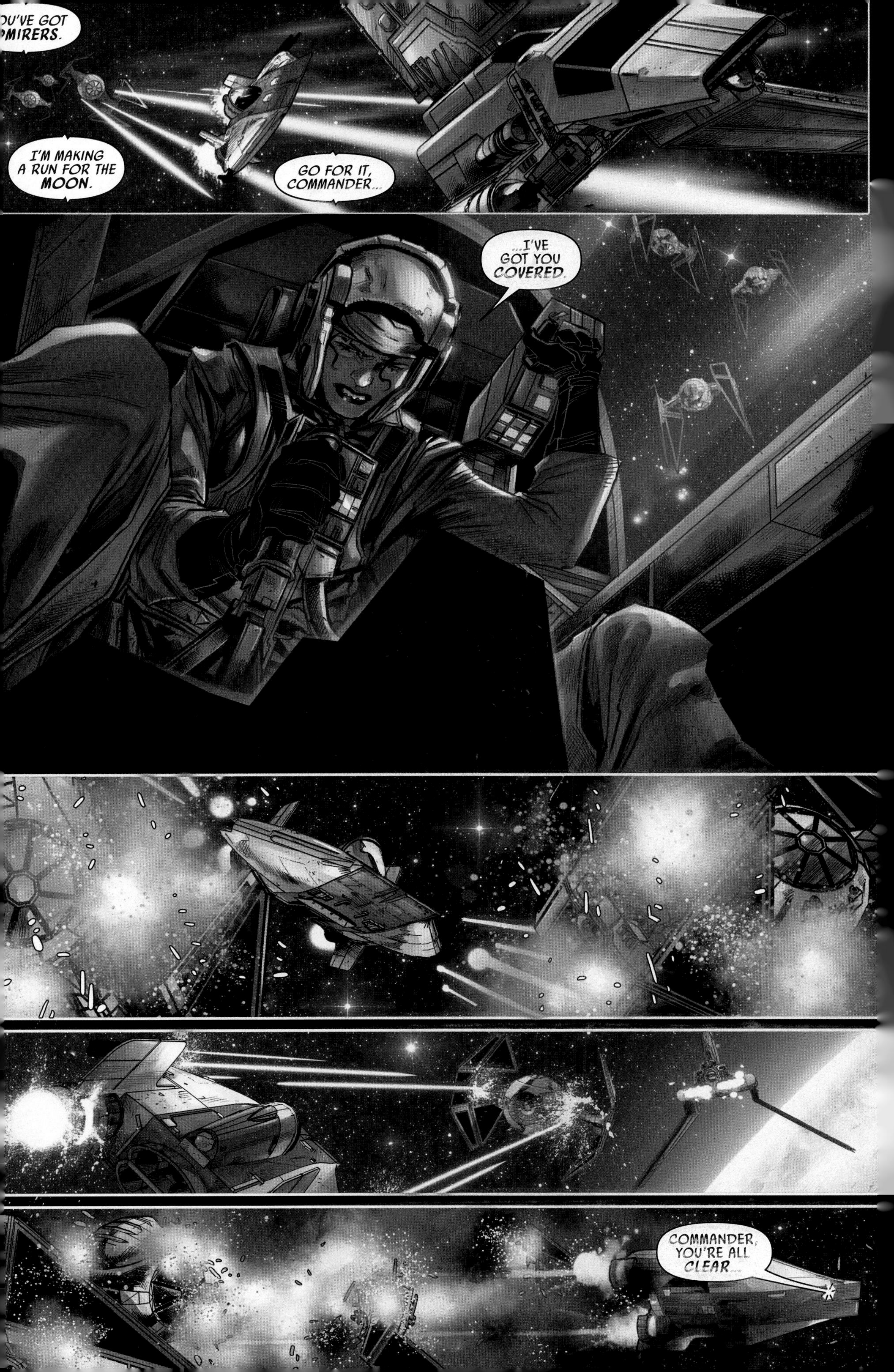
OU'VE GOT
MIRERS.
I'M MAKING A RUN FOR THE MOON.
GO FOR IT, COMMANDER...
...I'VE GOT YOU COVERED.
COMMANDER, YOU'RE ALL CLEAR...

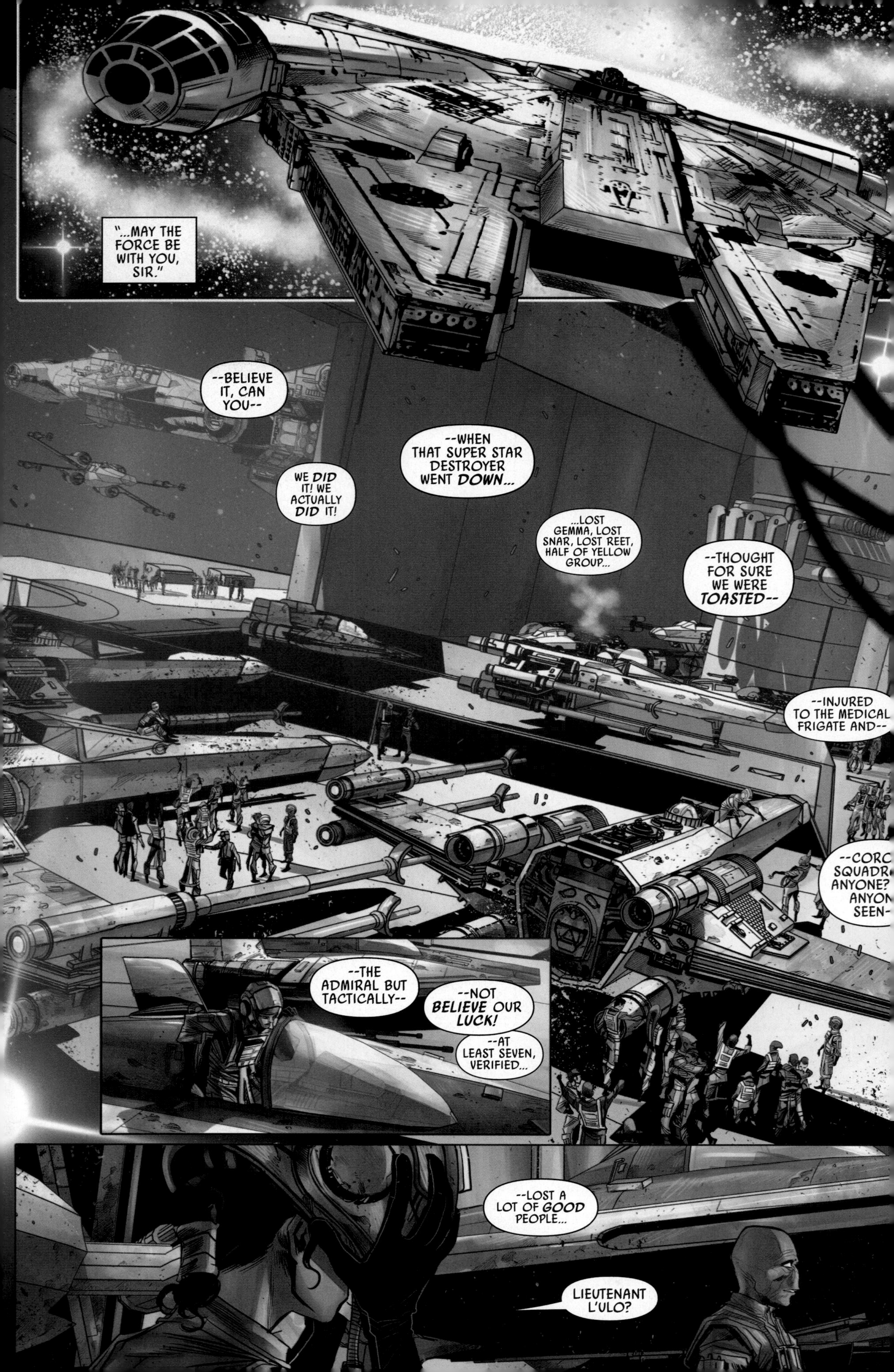
"...MAY THE FORCE BE WITH YOU, SIR."
--BELIEVE IT, CAN YOU--
WE DID IT! WE ACTUALLY DID IT!
--WHEN THAT SUPER STAR DESTROYER WENT DOWN...
...LOST GEMMA, LOST SNAR, LOST REET, HALF OF YELLOW GROUP...
--THOUGHT FOR SURE WE WERE TOASTED--
--INJURED TO THE MEDICAL FRIGATE AND--
--CORC SQUADR ANYONE? ANYON SEEN-
--THE ADMIRAL BUT TACTICALLY--
--NOT BELIEVE OUR LUCK!
--AT LEAST SEVEN, VERIFIED...
--LOST A LOT OF GOOD PEOPLE...
LIEUTENANT L'ULO?

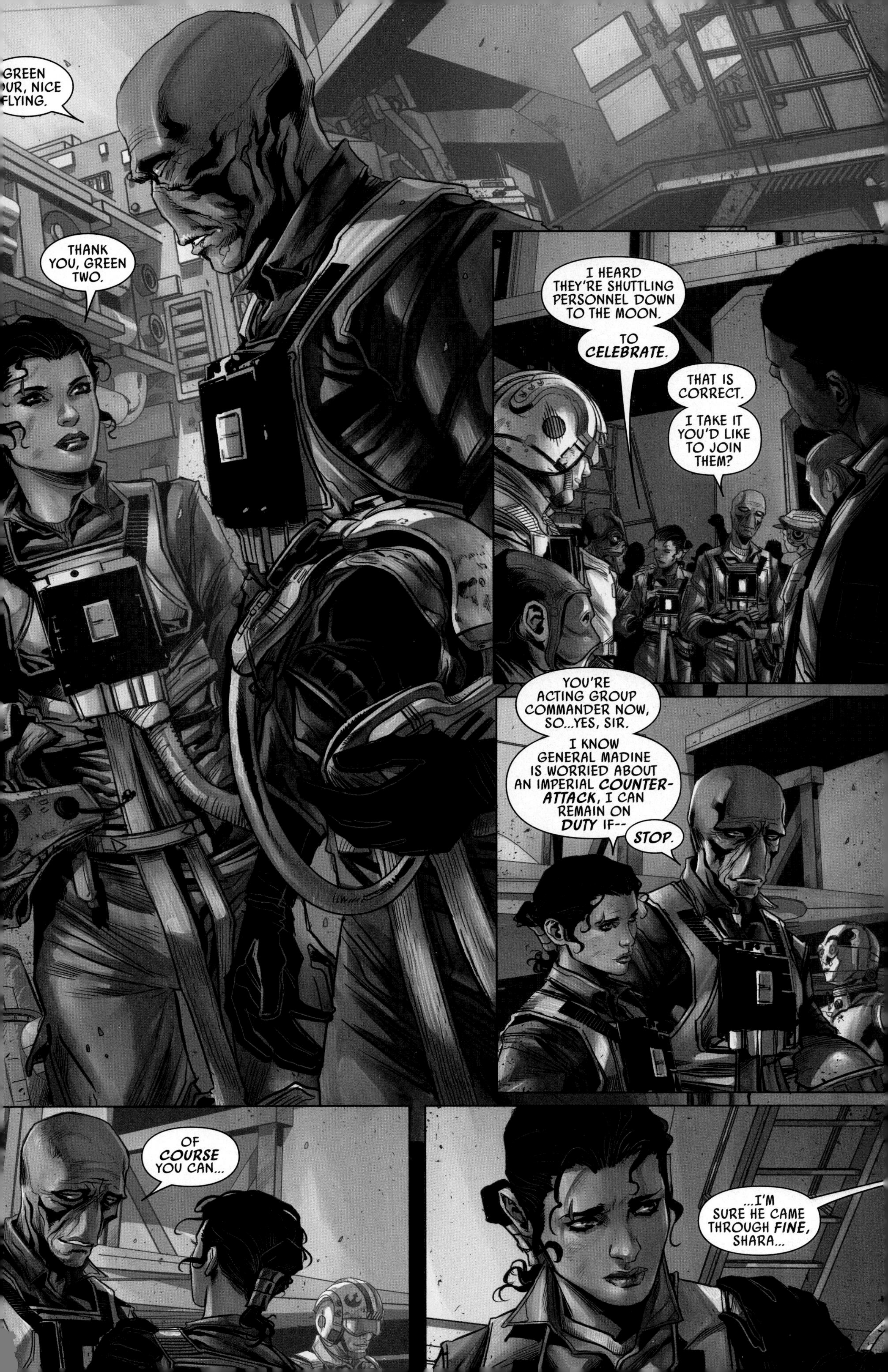
GREEN
OUR, NICE
FLYING.
THANK YOU, GREEN TWO.
I HEARD THEY'RE SHUTTLING PERSONNEL DOWN TO THE MOON.
TO CELEBRATE.
THAT IS CORRECT.
I TAKE IT YOU'D LIKE TO JOIN THEM?
YOU'RE ACTING GROUP COMMANDER NOW, SO...YES, SIR.
I KNOW GENERAL MADINE IS WORRIED ABOUT AN IMPERIAL COUNTER-ATTACK, I CAN REMAIN ON DUTY IF--
STOP.
OF COURSE YOU CAN...
...I'M SURE HE CAME THROUGH FINE, SHARA...

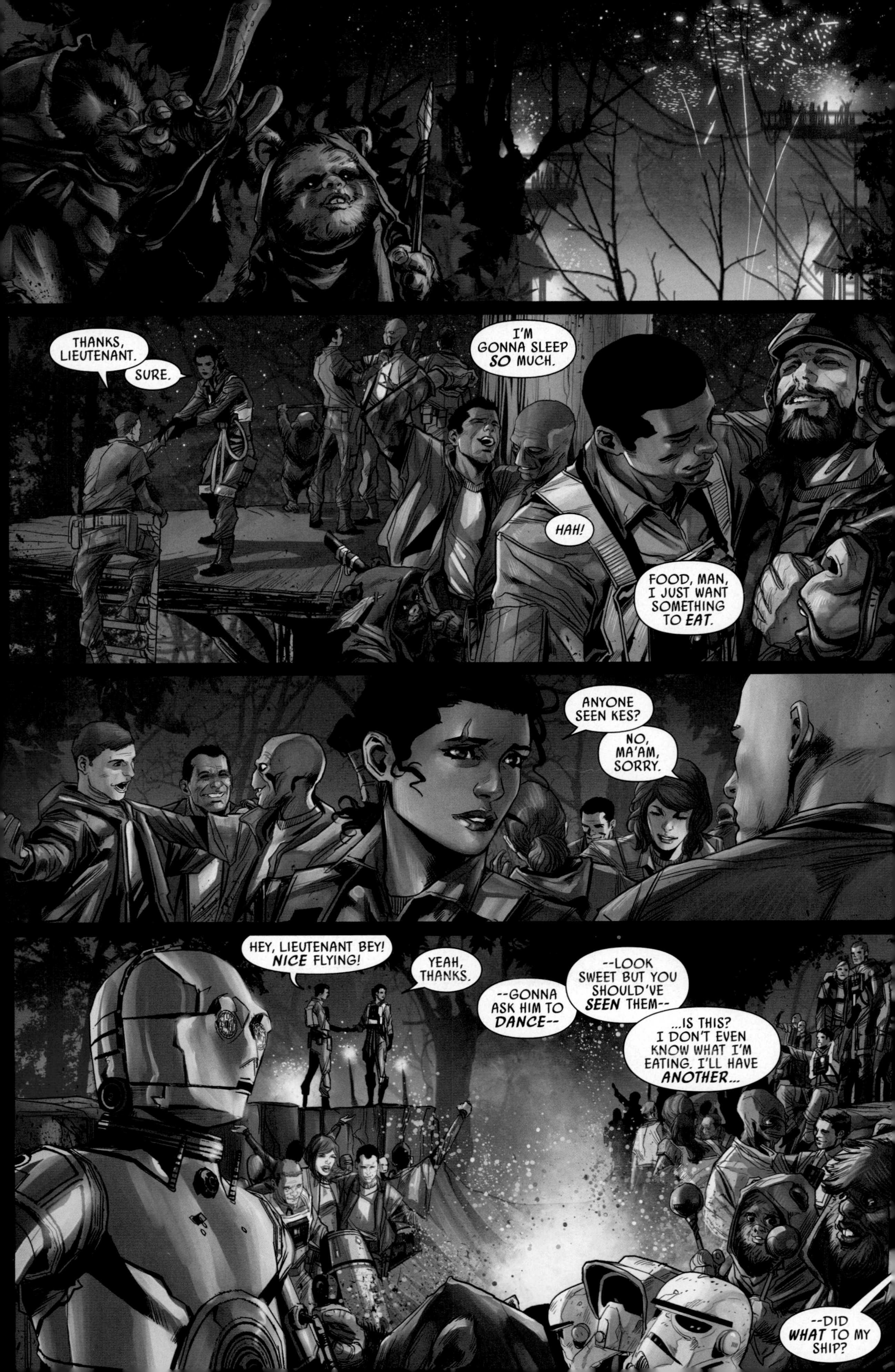
THANKS, LIEUTENANT.
SURE.
I'M GONNA SLEEP SO MUCH.
HAH!
FOOD, MAN, I JUST WANT SOMETHING TO EAT.
ANYONE SEEN KES?
NO, MA'AM, SORRY.
HEY, LIEUTENANT BEY! NICE FLYING!
YEAH, THANKS.
--GONNA ASK HIM TO DANCE--
--LOOK SWEET BUT YOU SHOULD'VE SEEN THEM--
...IS THIS? I DON'T EVEN KNOW WHAT I'M EATING. I'LL HAVE ANOTHER...
--DID WHAT TO MY SHIP?

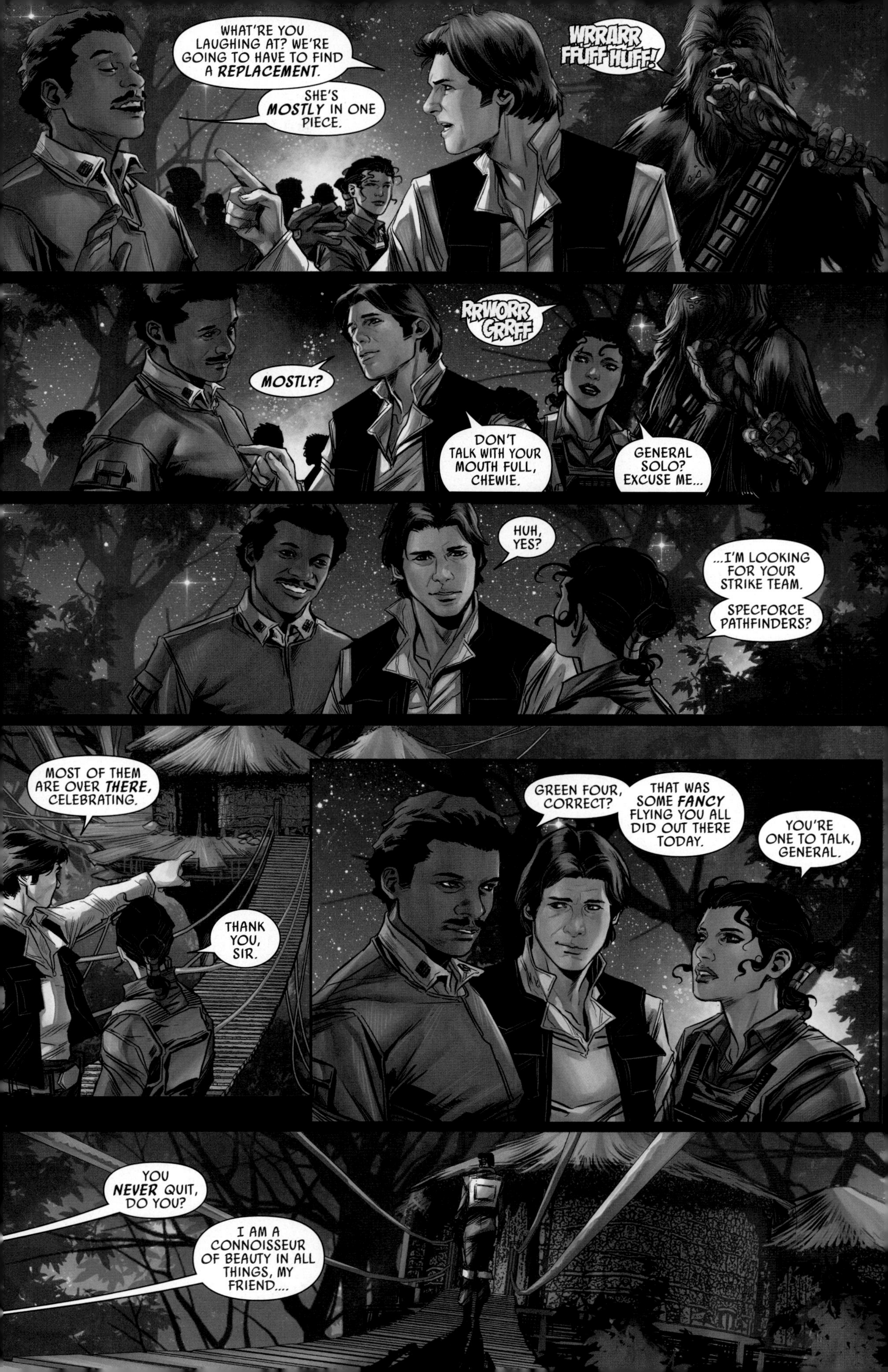
WHAT'RE YOU LAUGHING AT? WE'RE GOING TO HAVE TO FIND A REPLACEMENT.
SHE'S MOSTLY IN ONE PIECE.
WRRARR FFUFF HUFF!
MOSTLY?
RRWORR GRRFF
DON'T TALK WITH YOUR MOUTH FULL, CHEWIE.
GENERAL SOLO? EXCUSE ME...
HUH, YES?
...I'M LOOKING FOR YOUR STRIKE TEAM.
SPECFORCE PATHFINDERS?
MOST OF THEM ARE OVER THERE, CELEBRATING.
THANK YOU, SIR.
GREEN FOUR, CORRECT?
THAT WAS SOME FANCY FLYING YOU ALL DID OUT THERE TODAY.
YOU'RE ONE TO TALK, GENERAL.
YOU NEVER QUIT, DO YOU?
I AM A CONNOISSEUR OF BEAUTY IN ALL THINGS, MY FRIEND....

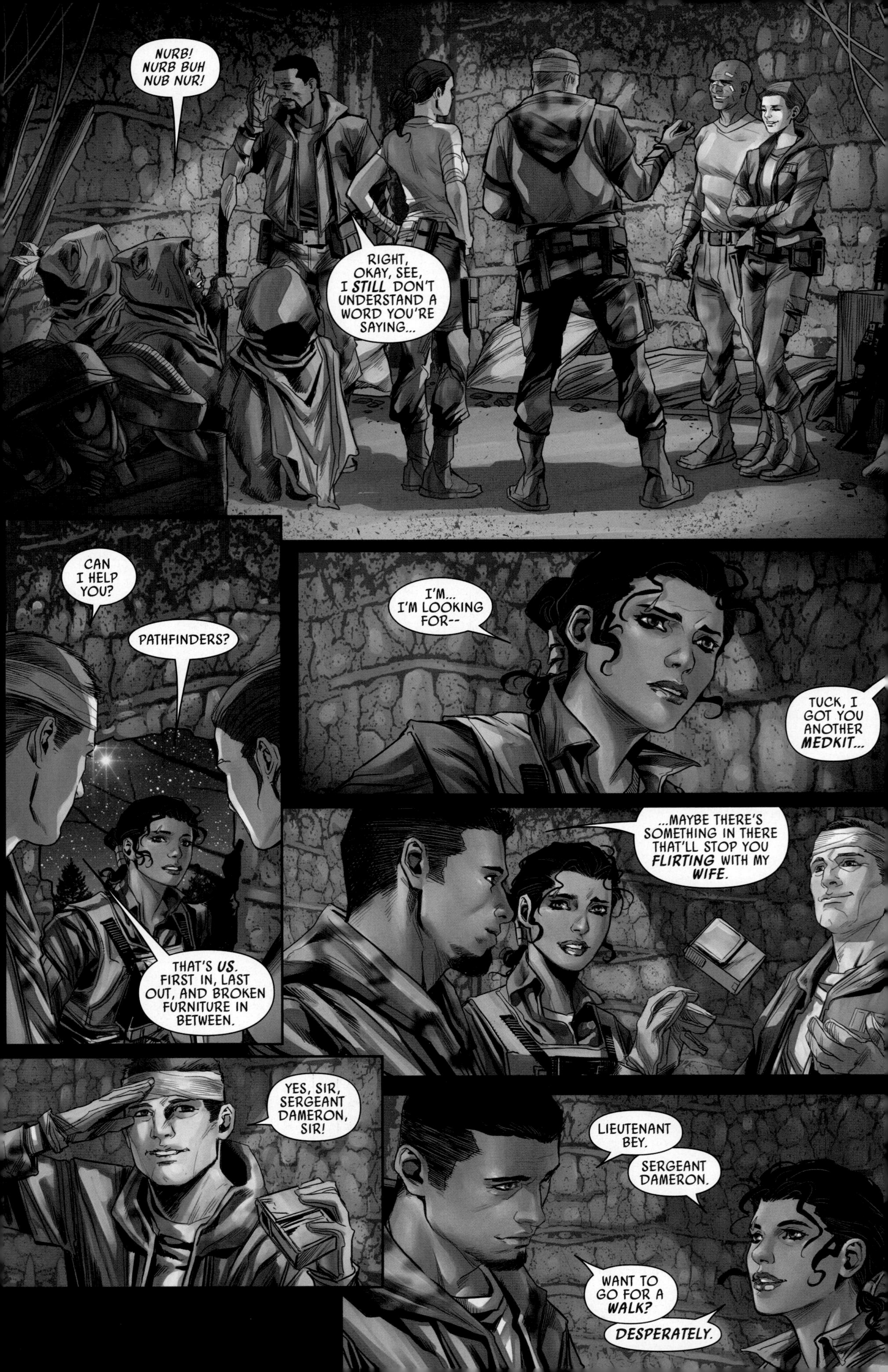
NURB! NURB BUH NUB NUR!
RIGHT, OKAY, SEE, I STILL DON'T UNDERSTAND A WORD YOU'RE SAYING...
CAN I HELP YOU?
PATHFINDERS?
THAT'S US. FIRST IN, LAST OUT, AND BROKEN FURNITURE IN BETWEEN.
I'M... I'M LOOKING FOR--
TUCK, I GOT YOU ANOTHER MEDKIT...
...MAYBE THERE'S SOMETHING IN THERE THAT'LL STOP YOU FLIRTING WITH MY WIFE.
YES, SIR, SERGEANT DAMERON, SIR!
LIEUTENANT BEY.
SERGEANT DAMERON.
WANT TO GO FOR A WALK?
DESPERATELY.

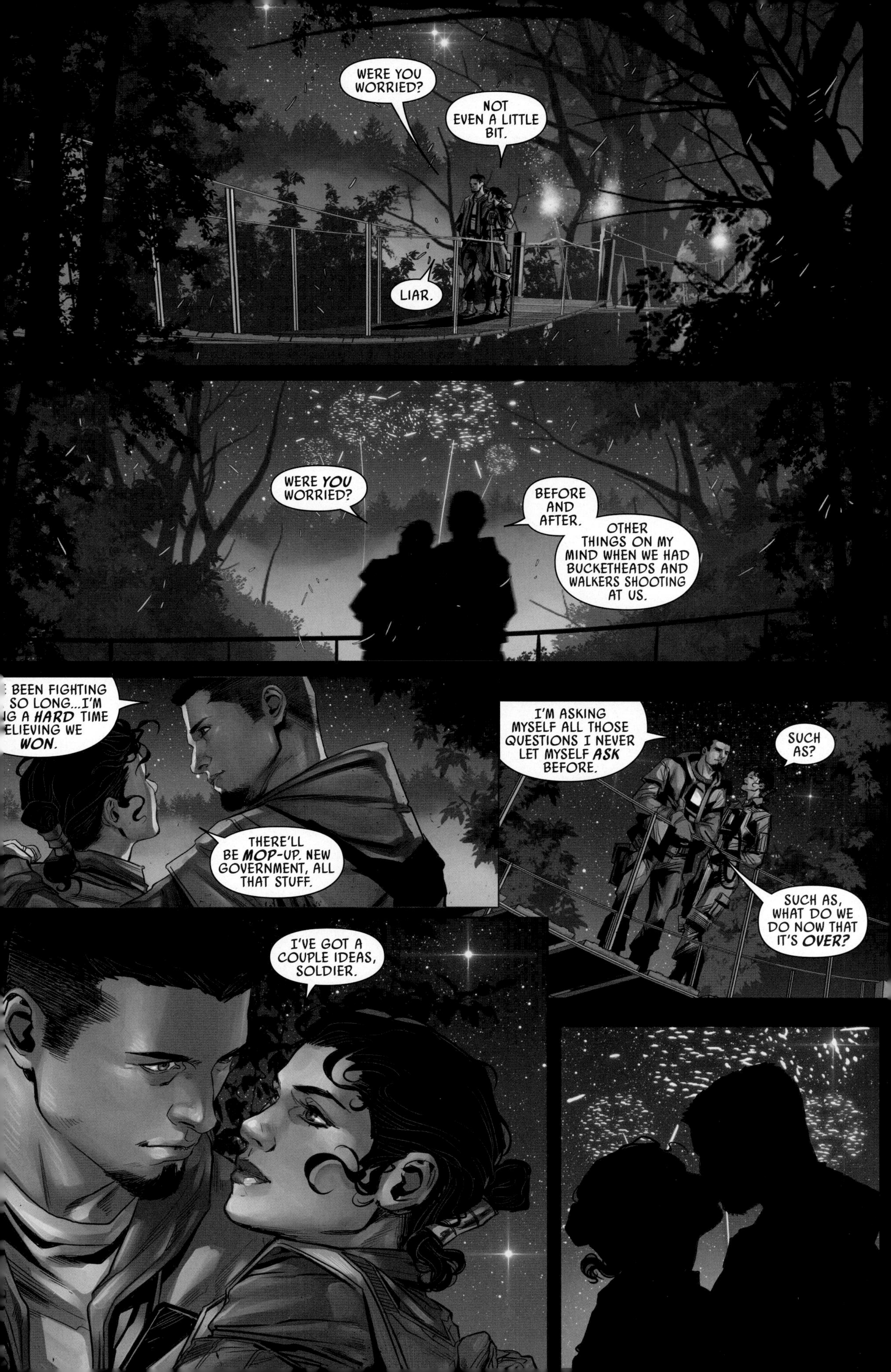

WERE YOU WORRIED?
NOT EVEN A LITTLE BIT.
LIAR.
WERE YOU WORRIED?
BEFORE AND AFTER.
OTHER THINGS ON MY MIND WHEN WE HAD BUCKETHEADS AND WALKERS SHOOTING AT US.
E BEEN FIGHTING SO LONG...I'M G A HARD TIME ELIEVING WE WON.
THERE'LL BE MOP-UP. NEW GOVERNMENT, ALL THAT STUFF.
I'M ASKING MYSELF ALL THOSE QUESTIONS I NEVER LET MYSELF ASK BEFORE.
SUCH AS?
SUCH AS, WHAT DO WE DO NOW THAT IT'S OVER?
I'VE GOT A COUPLE IDEAS, SOLDIER.

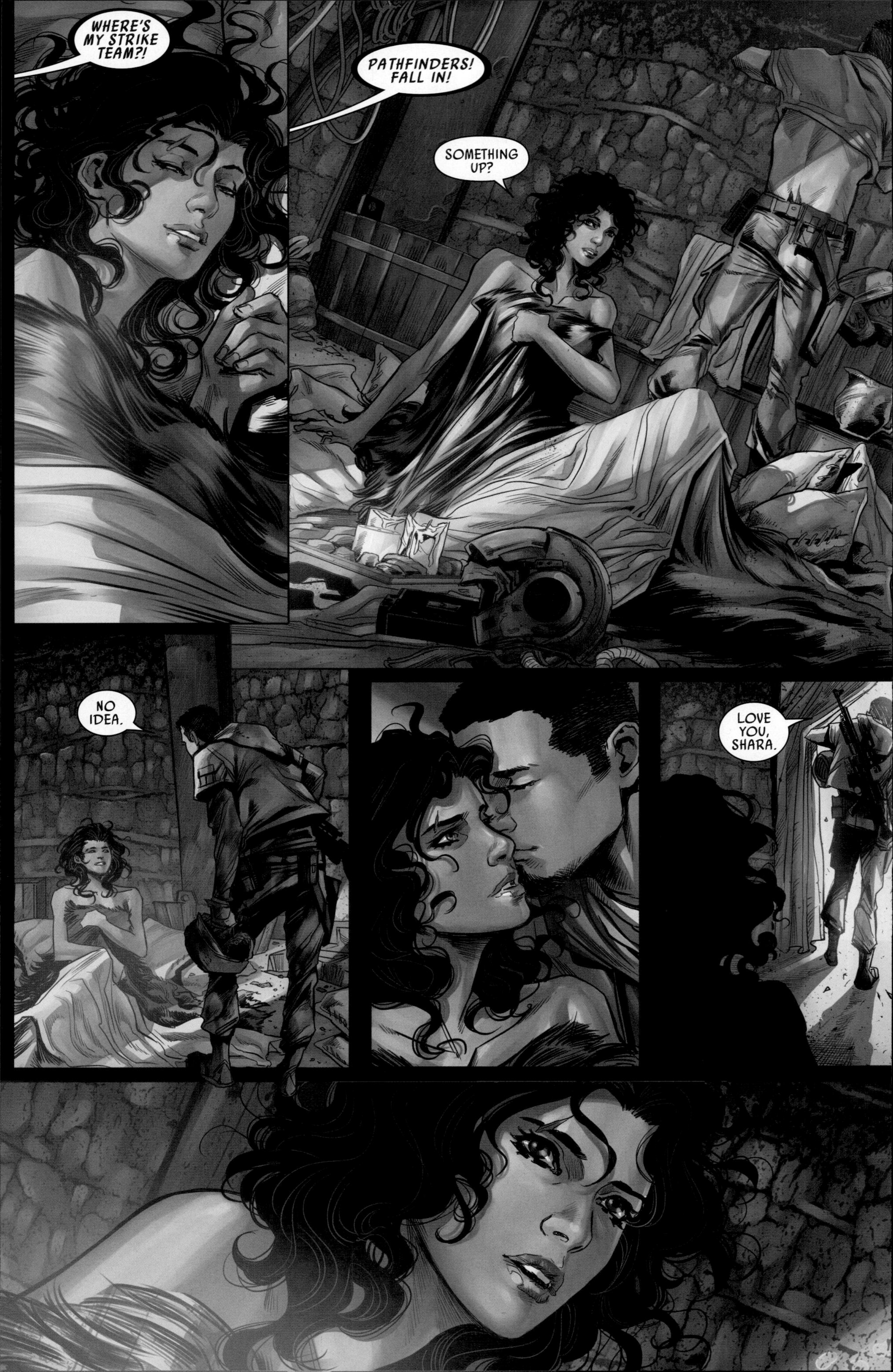
WHERE'S MY STRIKE TEAM?!
PATHFINDERS! FALL IN!
SOMETHING UP?
NO IDEA.
LOVE YOU, SHARA.

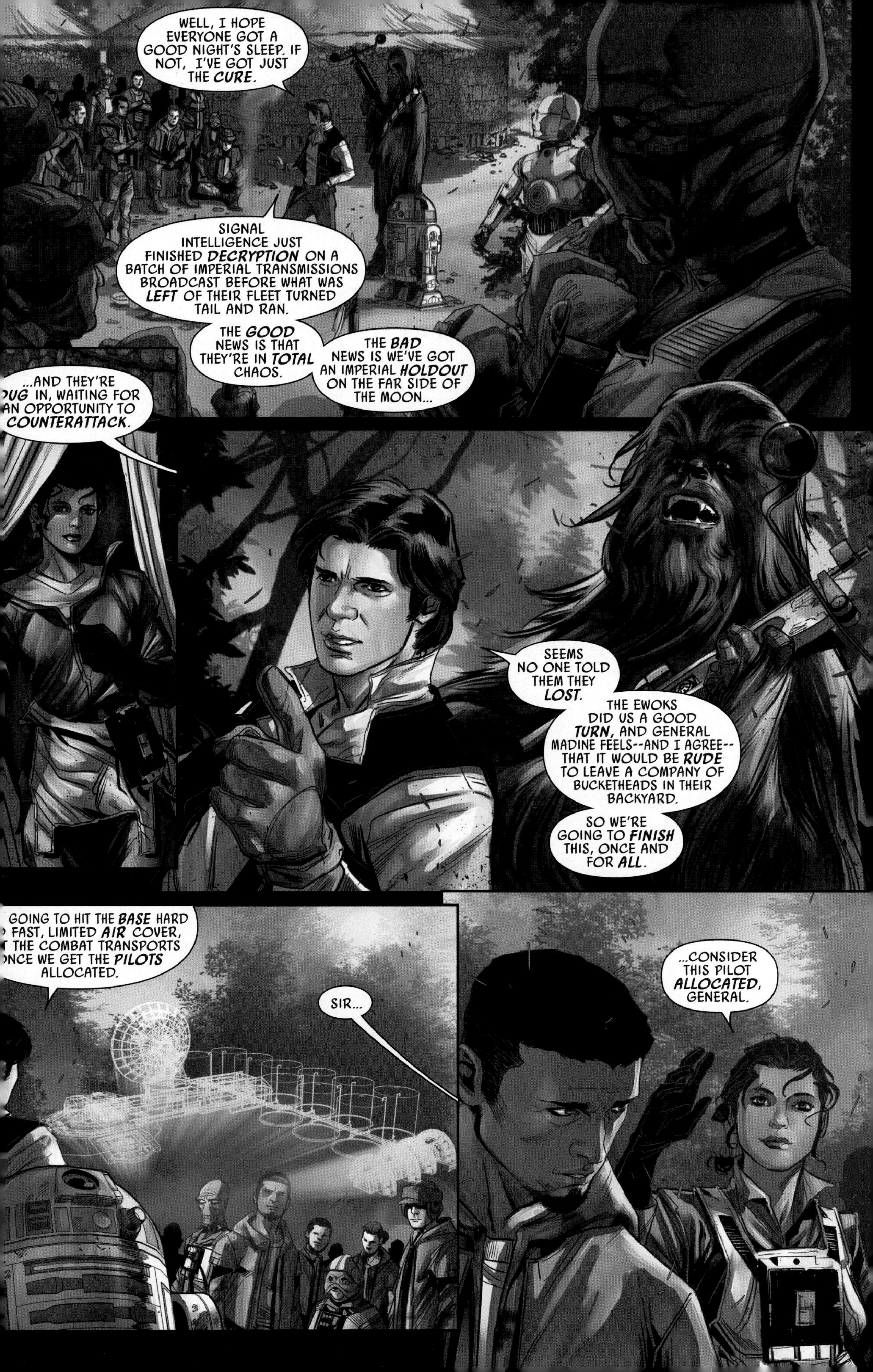
WELL, I HOPE EVERYONE GOT A GOOD NIGHT'S SLEEP. IF NOT, I'VE GOT JUST THE CURE.
SIGNAL INTELLIGENCE JUST FINISHED DECRYPTION ON A BATCH OF IMPERIAL TRANSMISSIONS BROADCAST BEFORE WHAT WAS LEFT OF THEIR FLEET TURNED TAIL AND RAN.
THE GOOD NEWS IS THAT THEY'RE IN TOTAL CHAOS.
THE BAD NEWS IS WE'VE GOT AN IMPERIAL HOLDOUT ON THE FAR SIDE OF THE MOON...
...AND THEY'RE DUG IN, WAITING FOR AN OPPORTUNITY TO COUNTERATTACK.
SEEMS NO ONE TOLD THEM THEY LOST.
THE EWOKS DID US A GOOD TURN, AND GENERAL MADINE FEELS--AND I AGREE--THAT IT WOULD BE RUDE TO LEAVE A COMPANY OF BUCKETHEADS IN THEIR BACKYARD.
SO WE'RE GOING TO FINISH THIS, ONCE AND FOR ALL.
GOING TO HIT THE BASE HARD FAST, LIMITED AIR COVER, THE COMBAT TRANSPORTS ONCE WE GET THE PILOTS ALLOCATED.
SIR...
...CONSIDER THIS PILOT ALLOCATED, GENERAL.

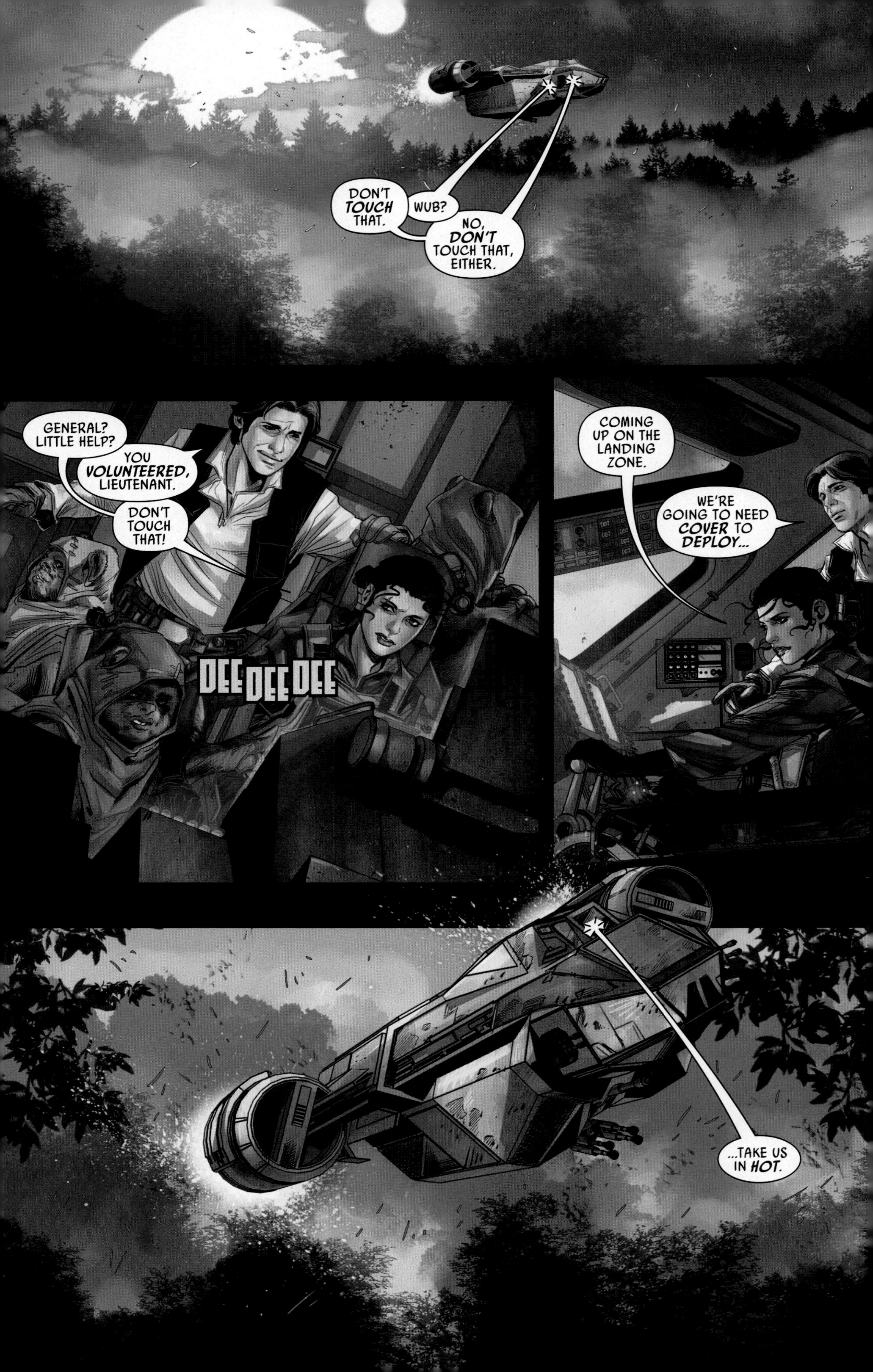
DON'T TOUCH THAT.
WUB?
NO, DON'T TOUCH THAT, EITHER.
GENERAL? LITTLE HELP?
YOU VOLUNTEERED, LIEUTENANT.
DON'T TOUCH THAT!
DEE DEE DEE
COMING UP ON THE LANDING ZONE.
WE'RE GOING TO NEED COVER TO DEPLOY...
...TAKE US IN HOT.

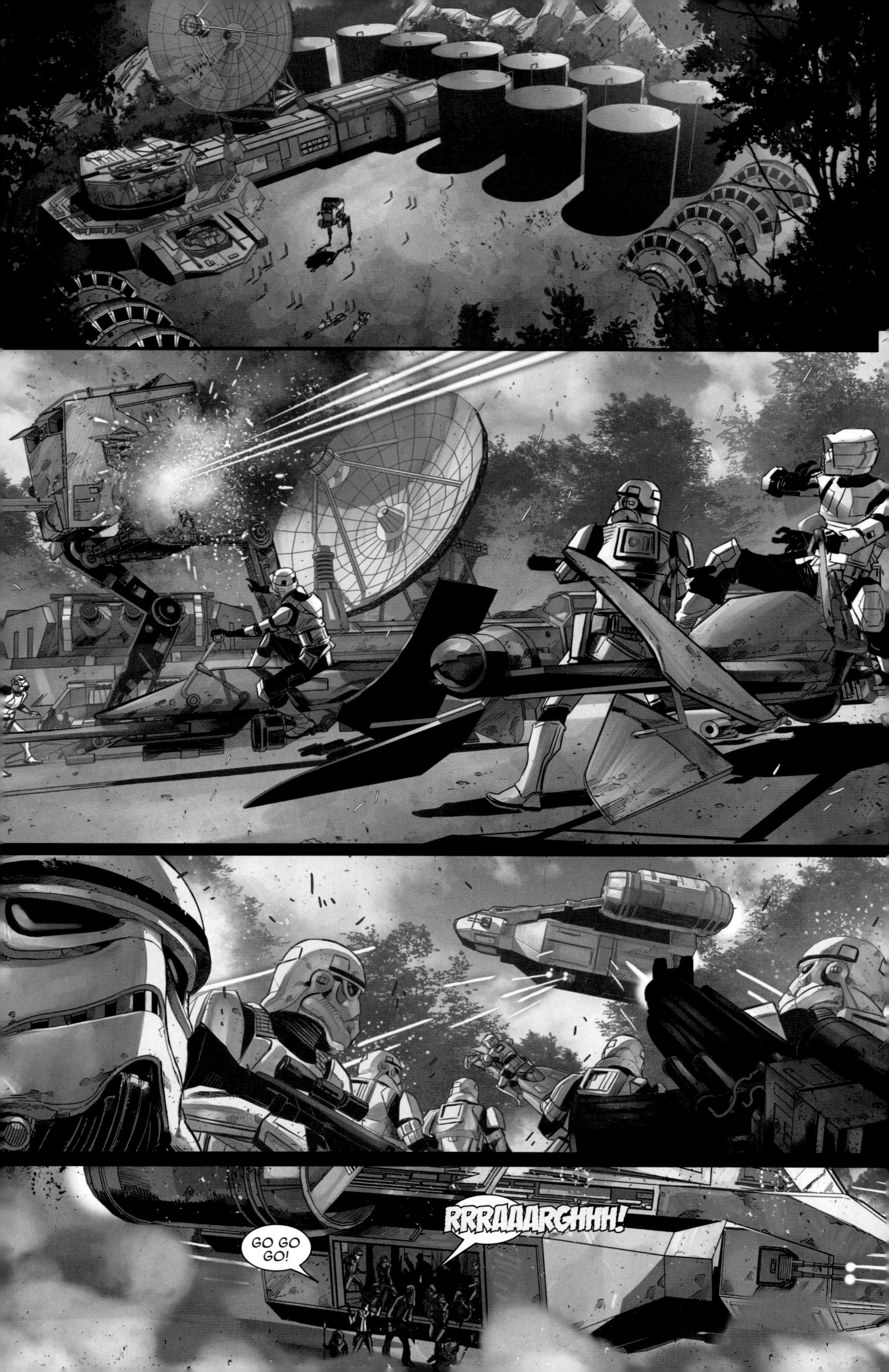
RRRAAARGHHH!
GO GO GO!

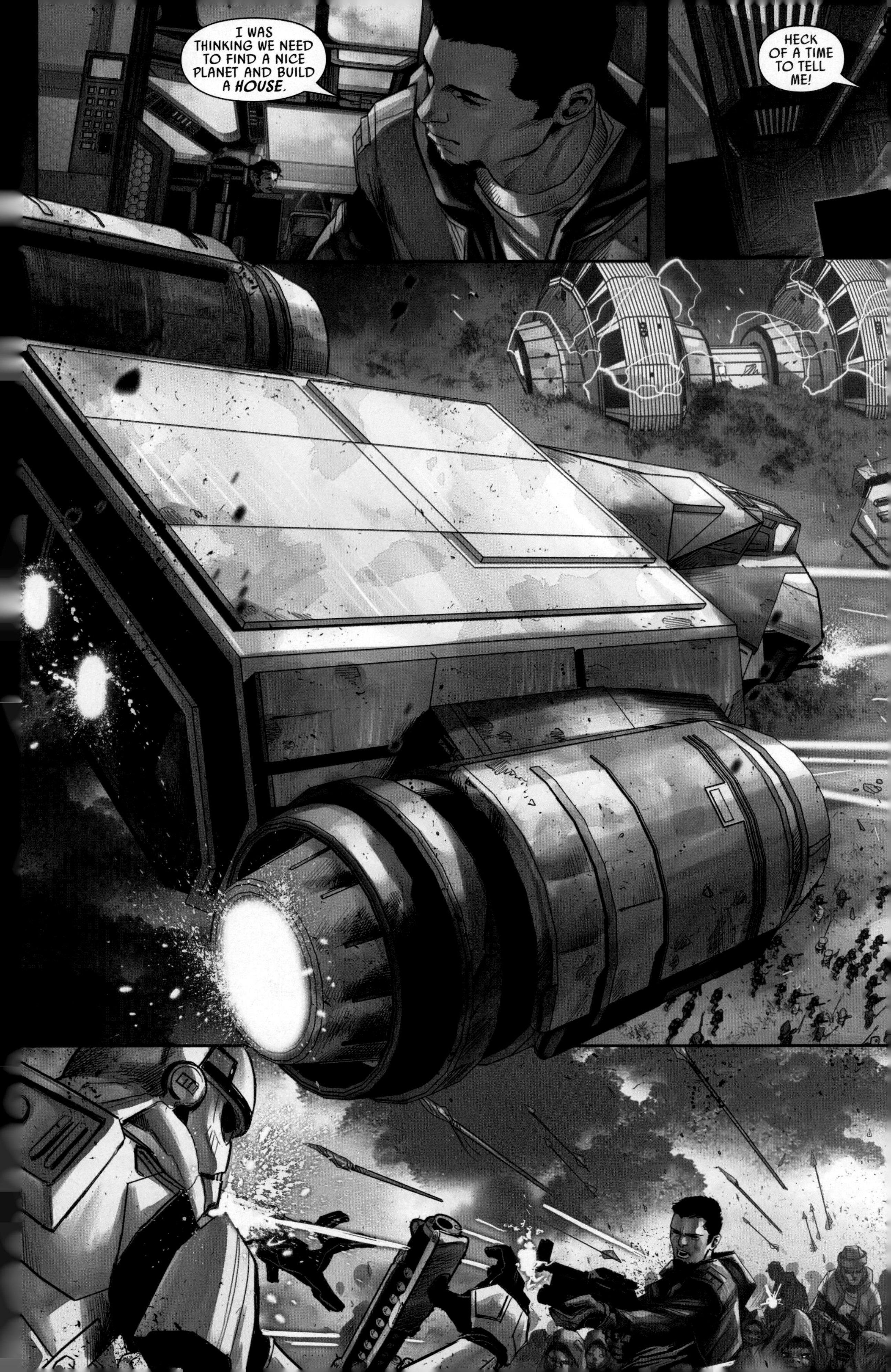
I WAS THINKING WE NEED TO FIND A NICE PLANET AND BUILD A HOUSE.
HECK OF A TIME TO TELL ME!

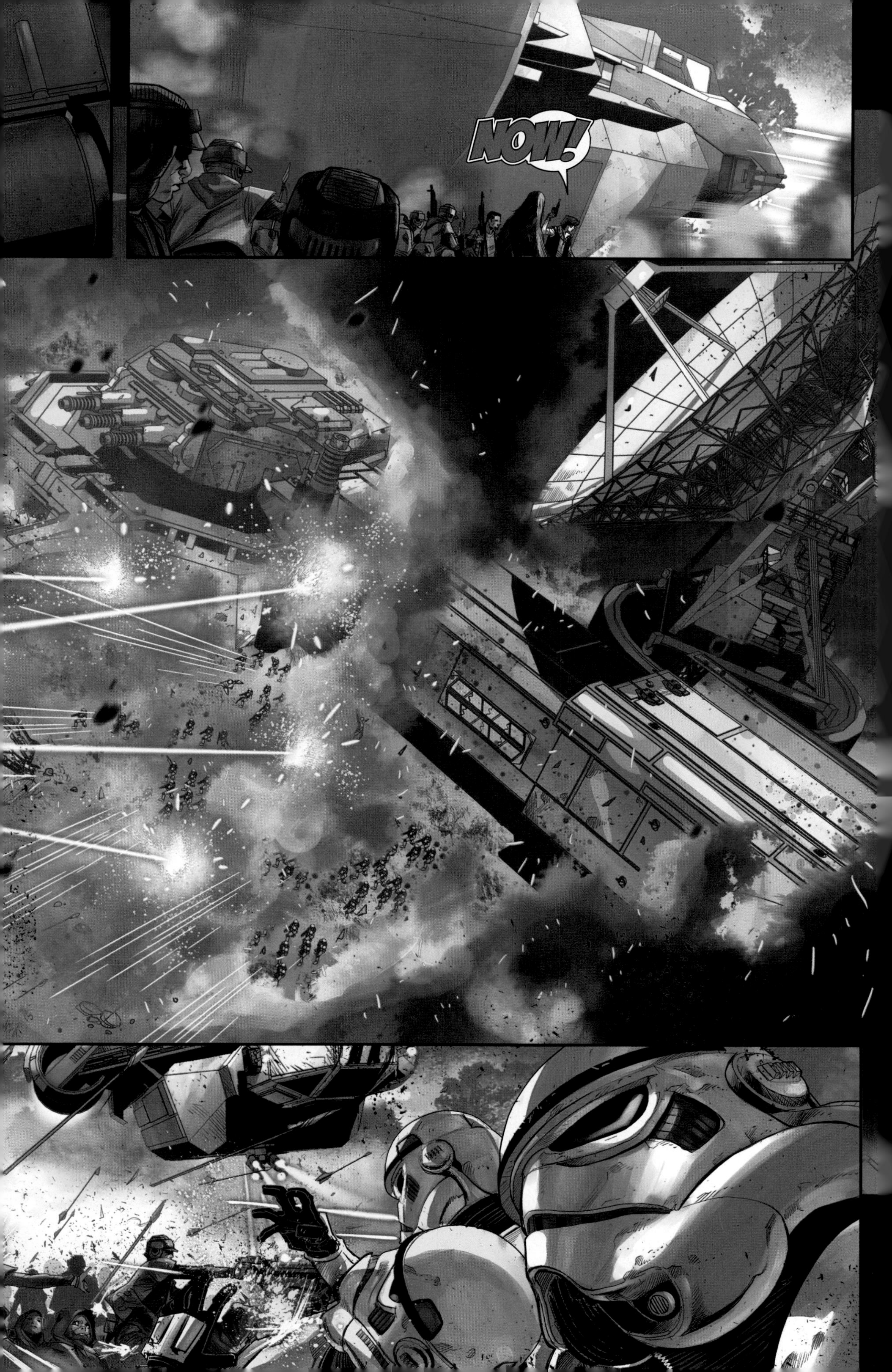
NOW!

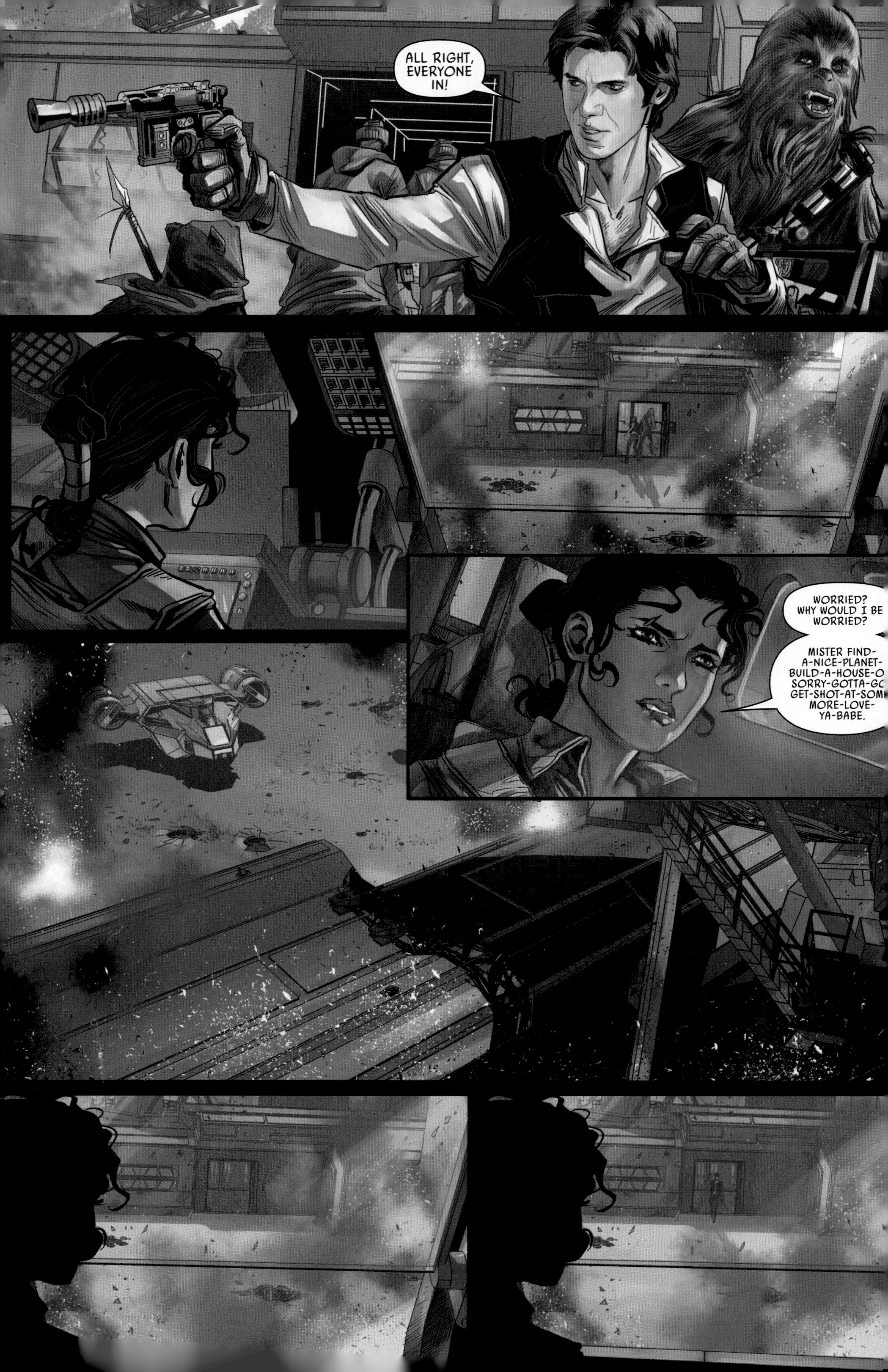
ALL RIGHT, EVERYONE IN!
WORRIED? WHY WOULD I BE WORRIED?
MISTER FIND-
A-NICE-PLANET-
BUILD-A-HOUSE-O
SORRY-GOTTA-G
GET-SHOT-AT-SOM
MORE-LOVE-
YA-BABE.

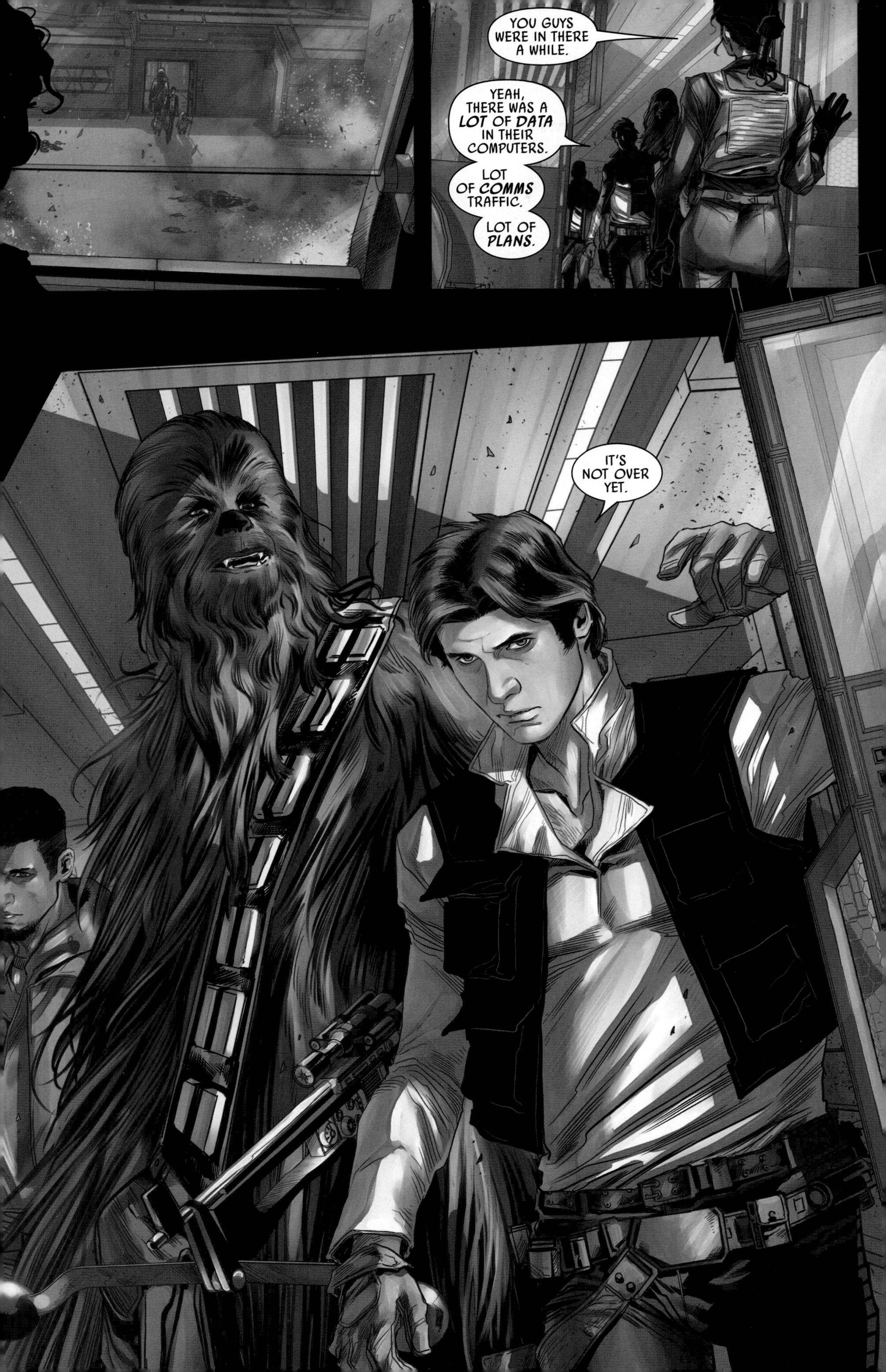
YOU GUYS WERE IN THERE A WHILE.
YEAH, THERE WAS A LOT OF DATA IN THEIR COMPUTERS.
LOT OF COMMS TRAFFIC.
LOT OF PLANS.
IT'S NOT OVER YET.

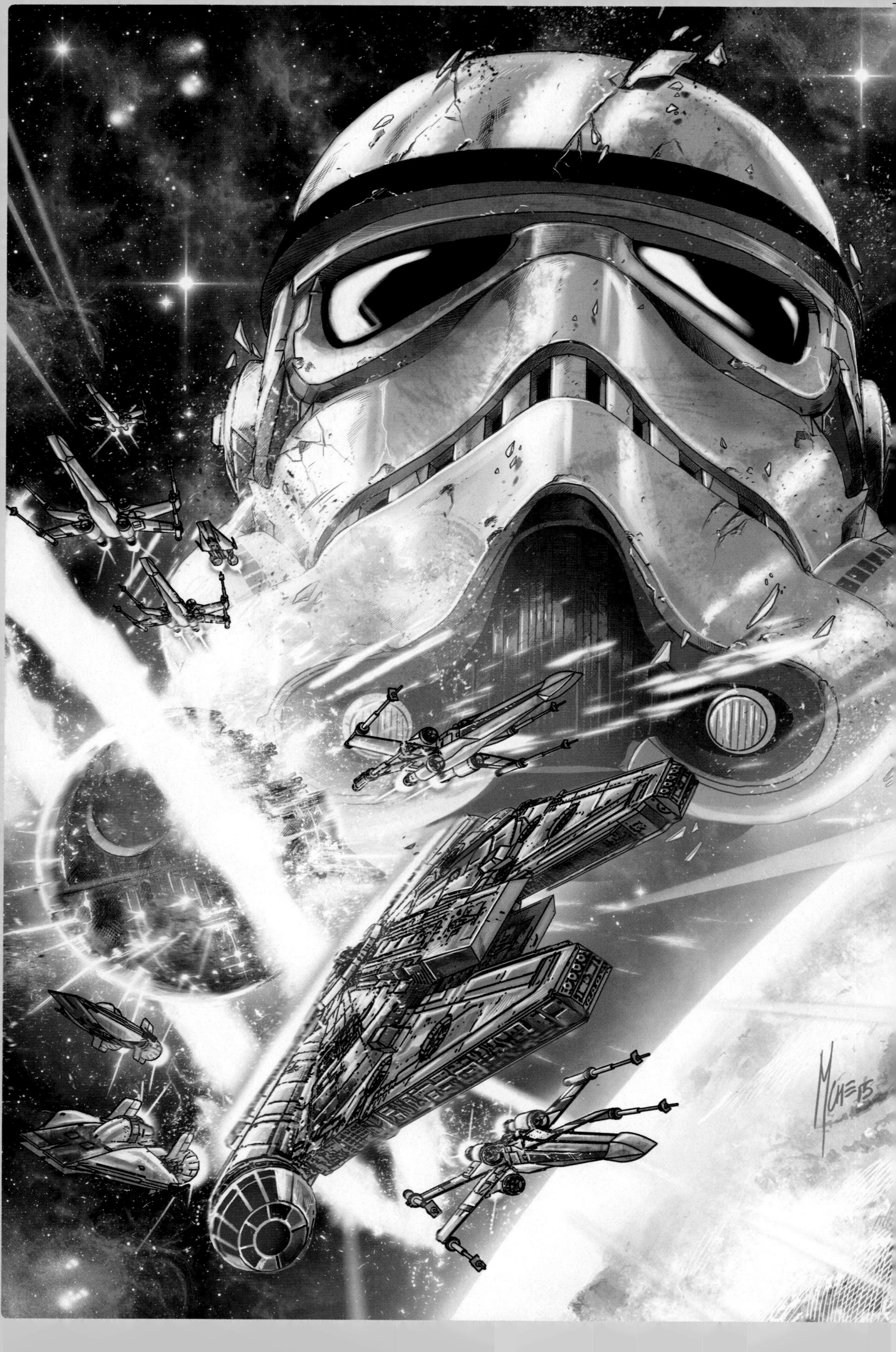

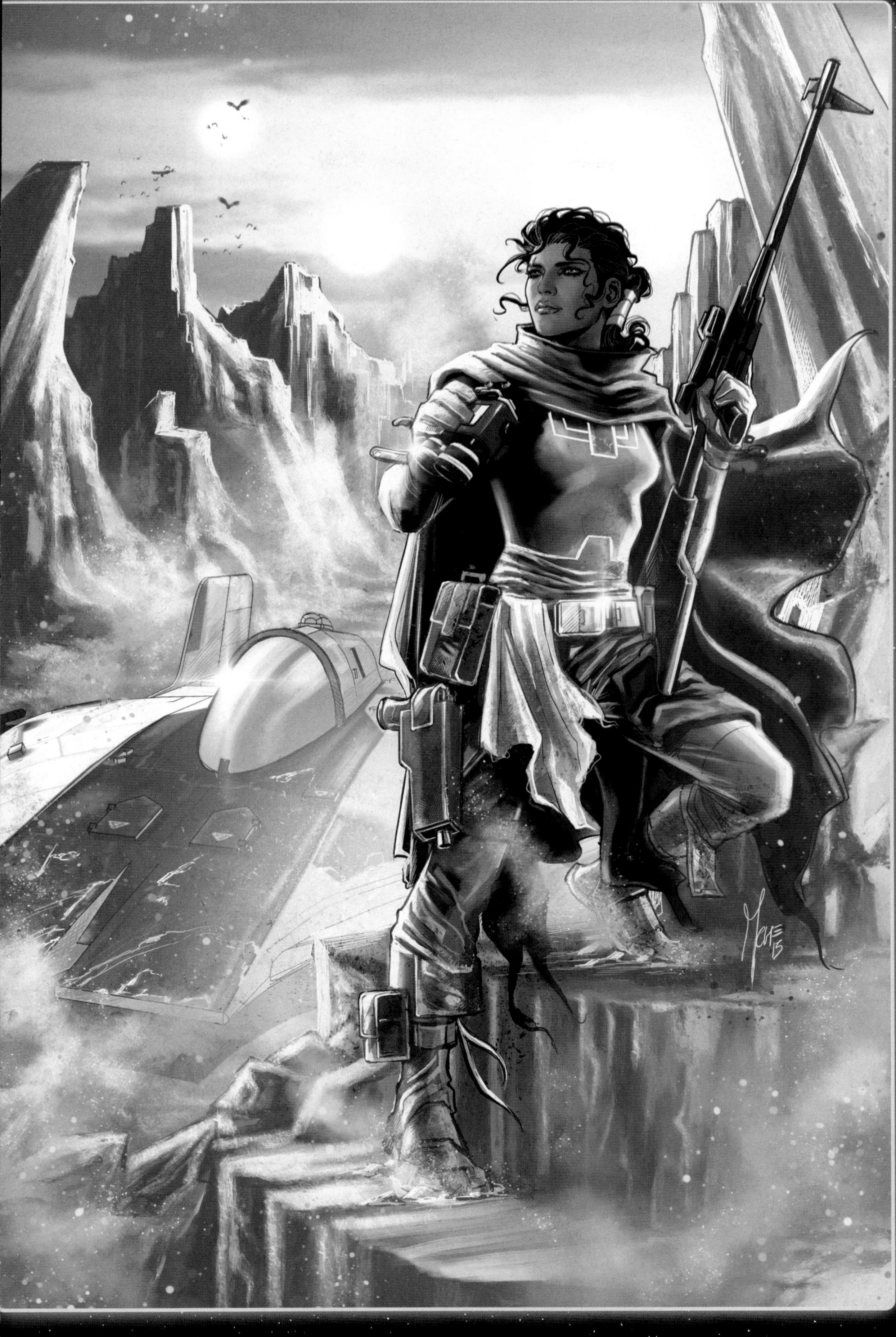

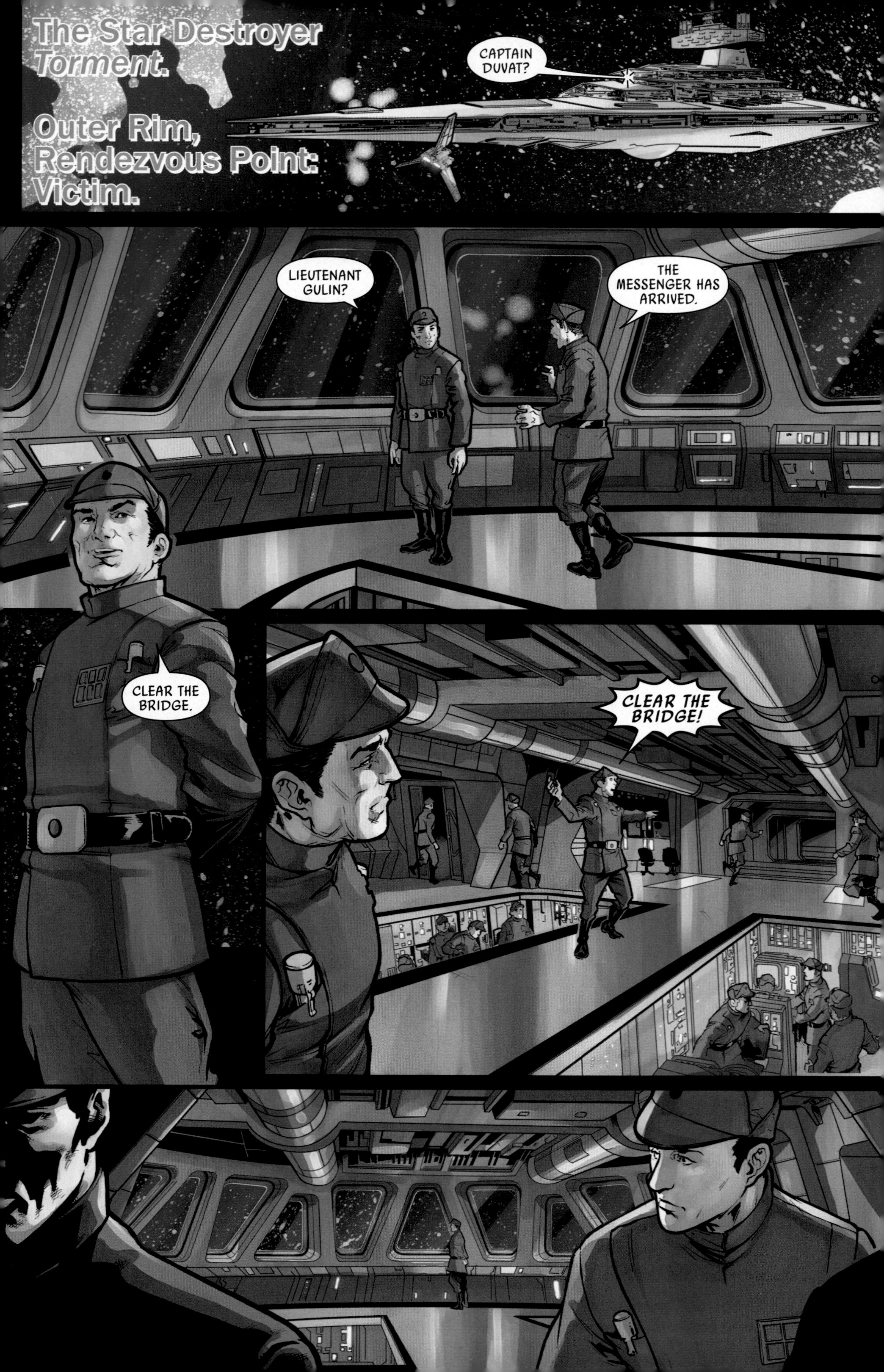
The Star Destroyer *Torment*.
Outer Rim, Rendezvous Point: Victim.
CAPTAIN DUVAT?
LIEUTENANT GULIN?
THE MESSENGER HAS ARRIVED.
CLEAR THE BRIDGE.
CLEAR THE BRIDGE!

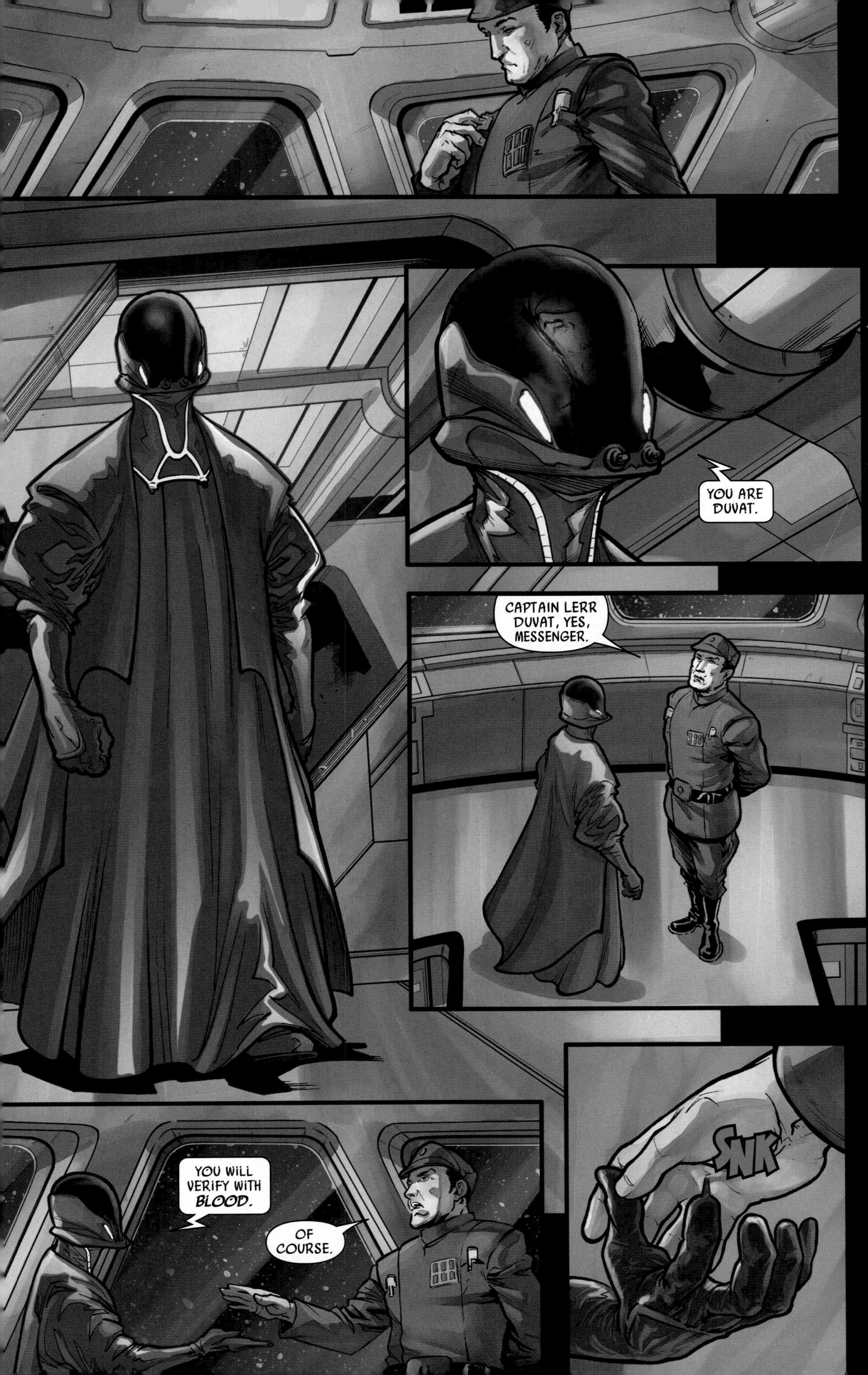
YOU ARE DUVAT.
CAPTAIN LERR DUVAT, YES, MESSENGER.
YOU WILL VERIFY WITH BLOOD.
OF COURSE.
SNK

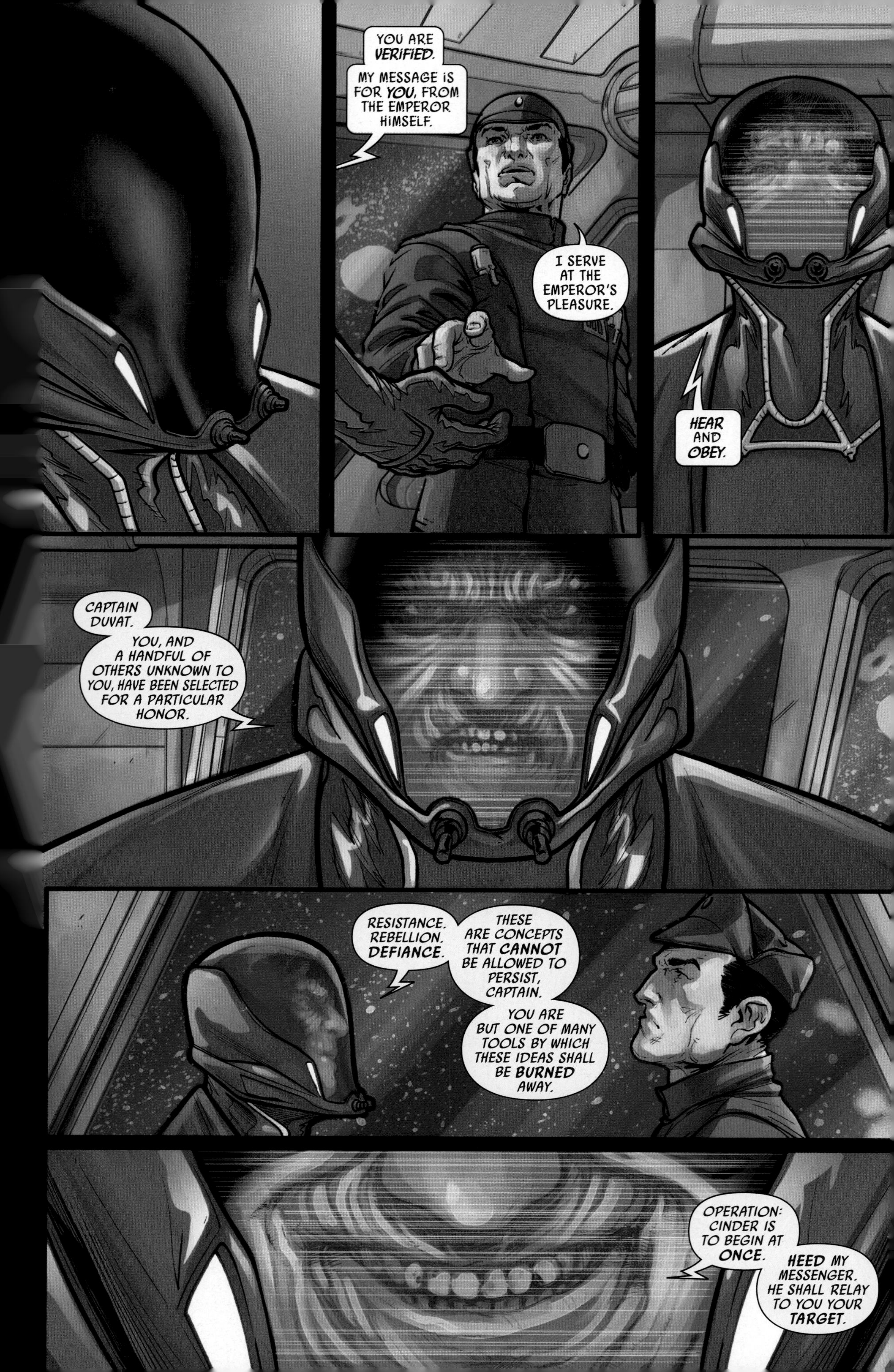
YOU ARE VERIFIED.
MY MESSAGE IS FOR YOU, FROM THE EMPEROR HIMSELF.
I SERVE AT THE EMPEROR'S PLEASURE.
HEAR AND OBEY.
CAPTAIN DUVAT.
YOU, AND A HANDFUL OF OTHERS UNKNOWN TO YOU, HAVE BEEN SELECTED FOR A PARTICULAR HONOR.
RESISTANCE. REBELLION. DEFIANCE.
THESE ARE CONCEPTS THAT CANNOT BE ALLOWED TO PERSIST, CAPTAIN.
YOU ARE BUT ONE OF MANY TOOLS BY WHICH THESE IDEAS SHALL BE BURNED AWAY.
OPERATION: CINDER IS TO BEGIN AT ONCE.
HEED MY MESSENGER. HE SHALL RELAY TO YOU YOUR TARGET.

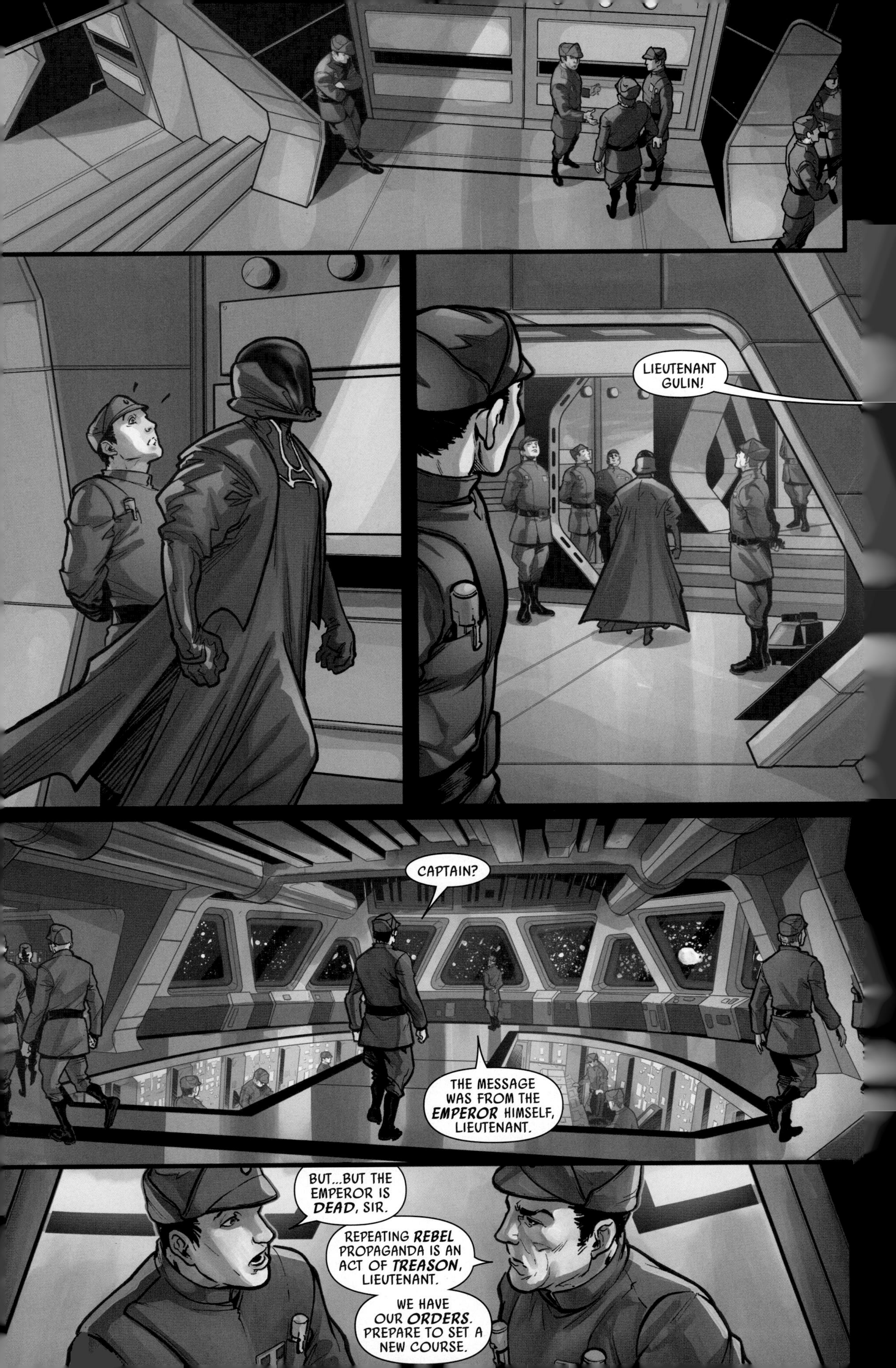
LIEUTENANT GULIN!
CAPTAIN?
THE MESSAGE WAS FROM THE EMPEROR HIMSELF, LIEUTENANT.
BUT...BUT THE EMPEROR IS DEAD, SIR.
REPEATING REBEL PROPAGANDA IS AN ACT OF TREASON, LIEUTENANT.
WE HAVE OUR ORDERS. PREPARE TO SET A NEW COURSE.

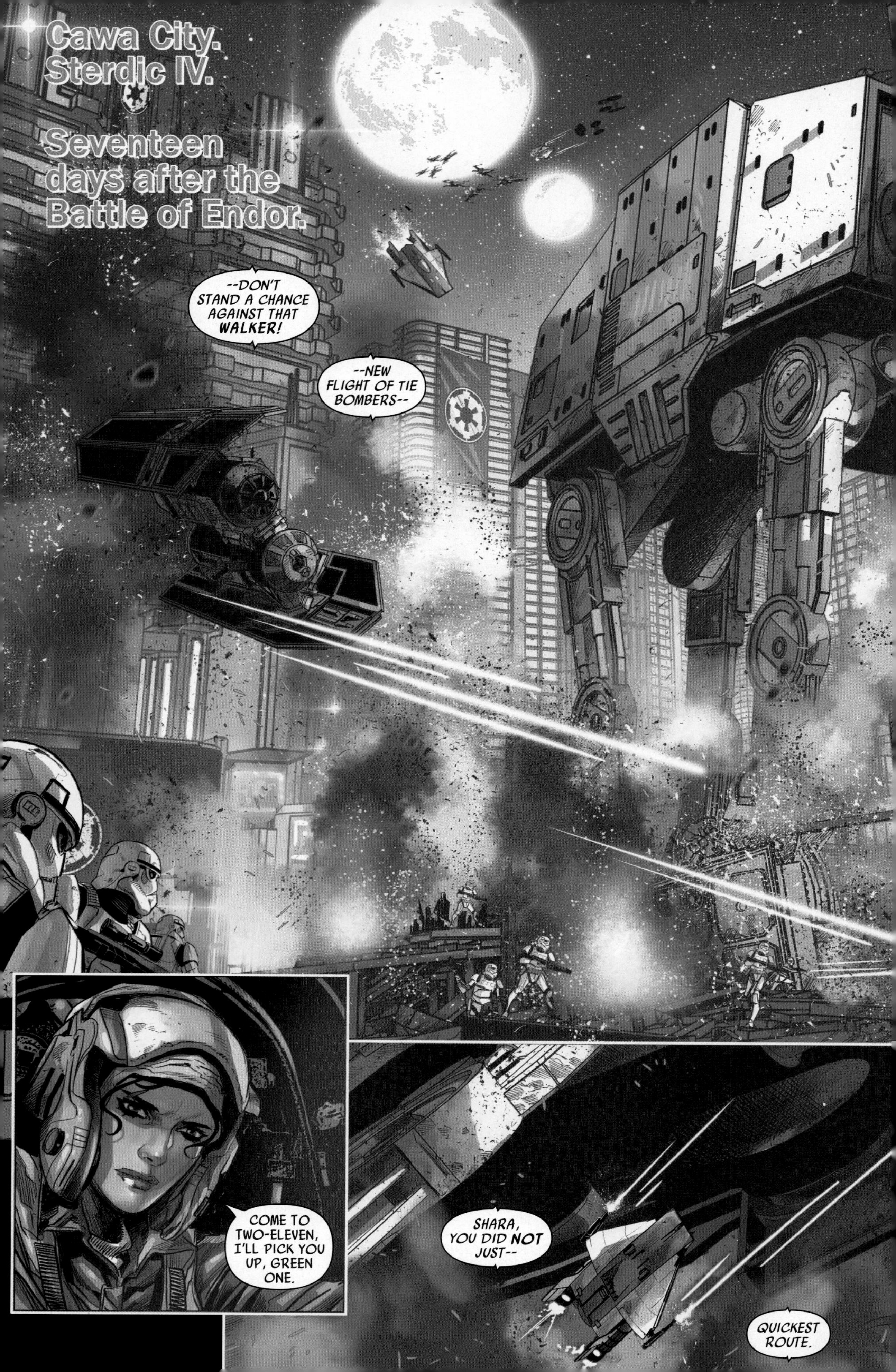
Cawa City. Sterdic IV.
Seventeen days after the Battle of Endor.
--DON'T STAND A CHANCE AGAINST THAT WALKER!
--NEW FLIGHT OF TIE BOMBERS--
COME TO TWO-ELEVEN, I'LL PICK YOU UP, GREEN ONE.
SHARA, YOU DID NOT JUST--
QUICKEST ROUTE.

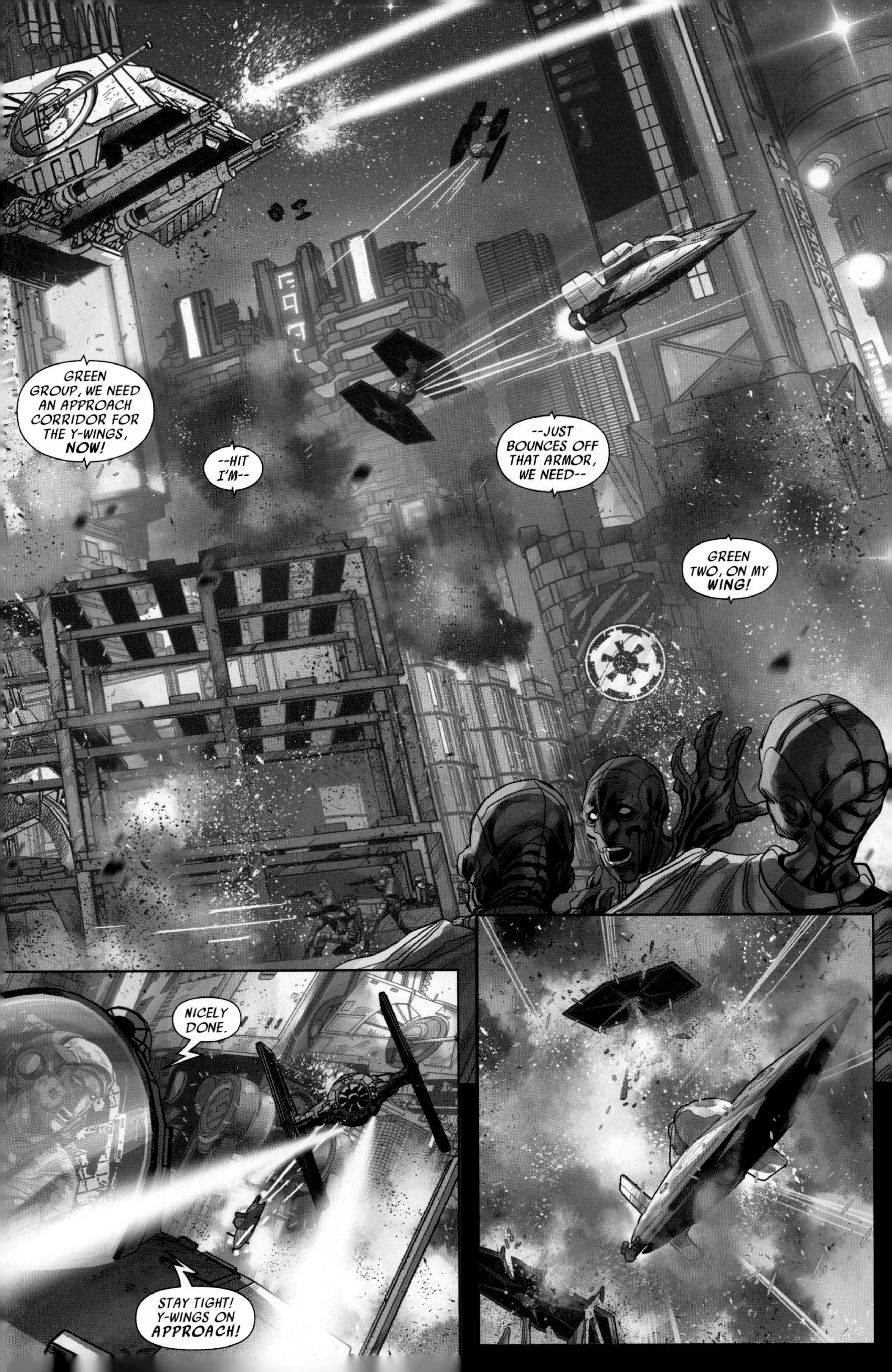
GREEN GROUP, WE NEED AN APPROACH CORRIDOR FOR THE Y-WINGS, NOW!
--HIT I'M--
--JUST BOUNCES OFF THAT ARMOR, WE NEED--
GREEN TWO, ON MY WING!
NICELY DONE.
STAY TIGHT! Y-WINGS ON APPROACH!

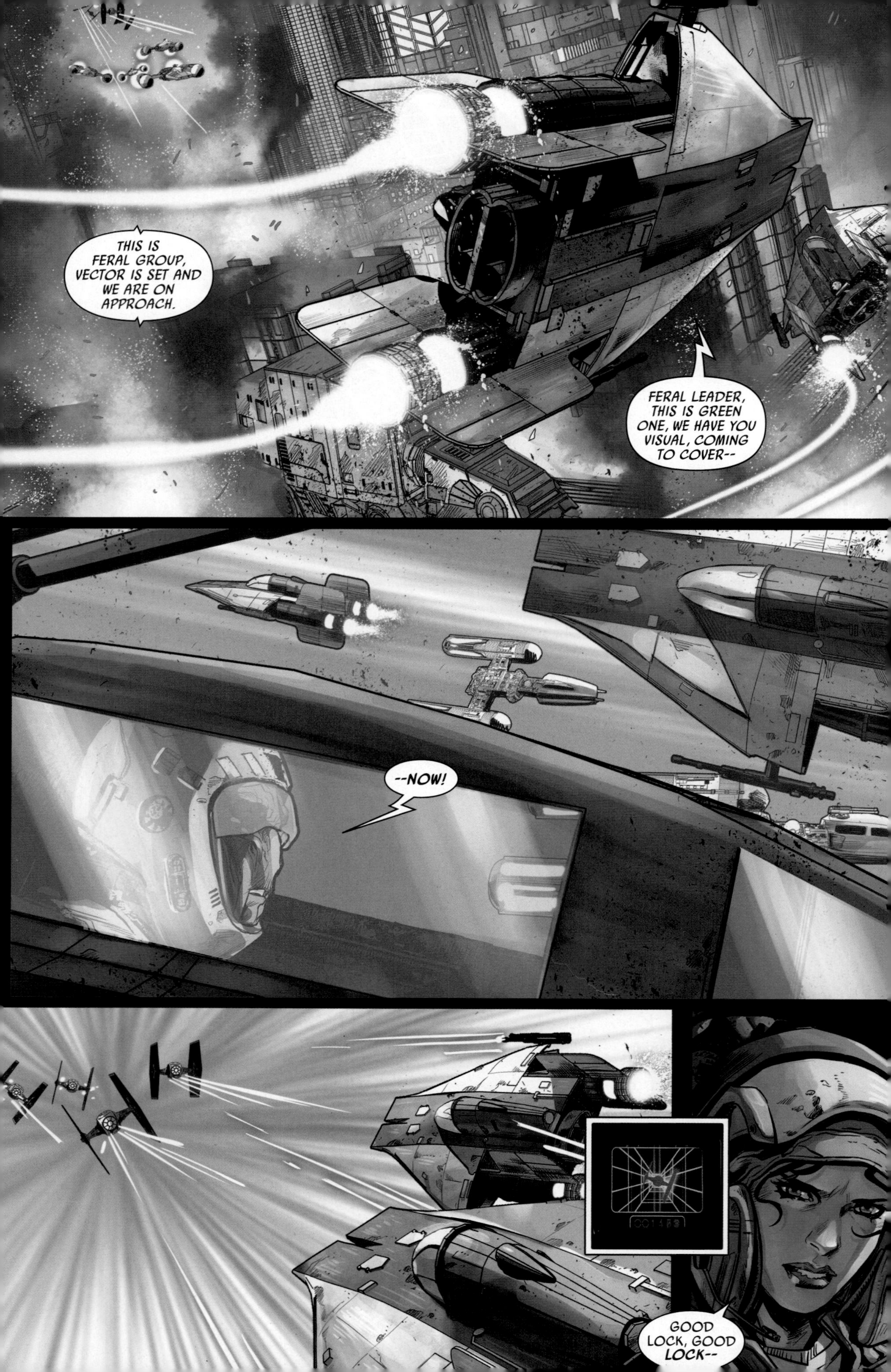
THIS IS FERAL GROUP, VECTOR IS SET AND WE ARE ON APPROACH.
FERAL LEADER, THIS IS GREEN ONE, WE HAVE YOU VISUAL, COMING TO COVER--
--NOW!
GOOD LOCK, GOOD LOCK--

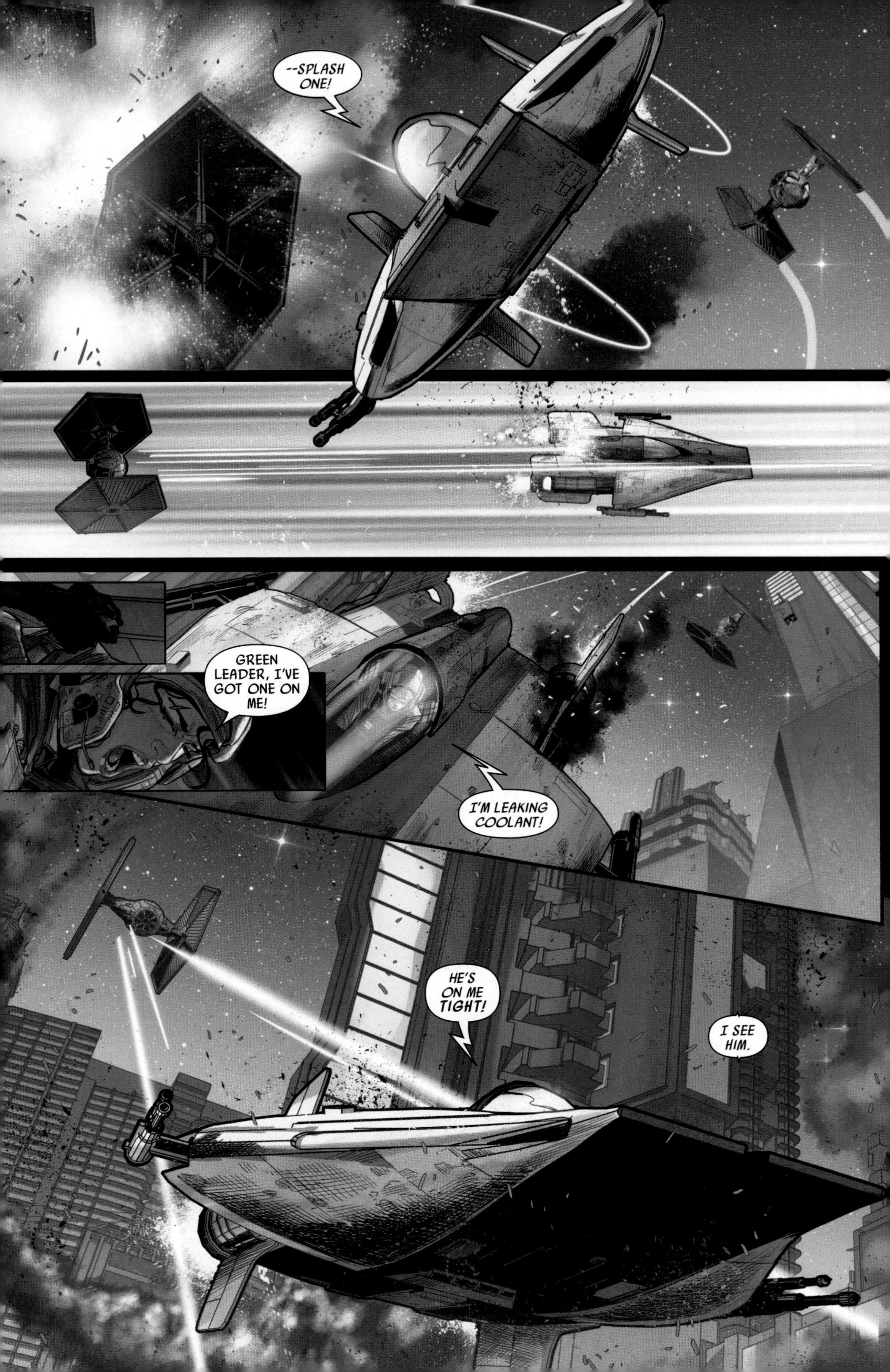
--SPLASH ONE!
GREEN LEADER, I'VE GOT ONE ON ME!
I'M LEAKING COOLANT!
HE'S ON ME TIGHT!
I SEE HIM.

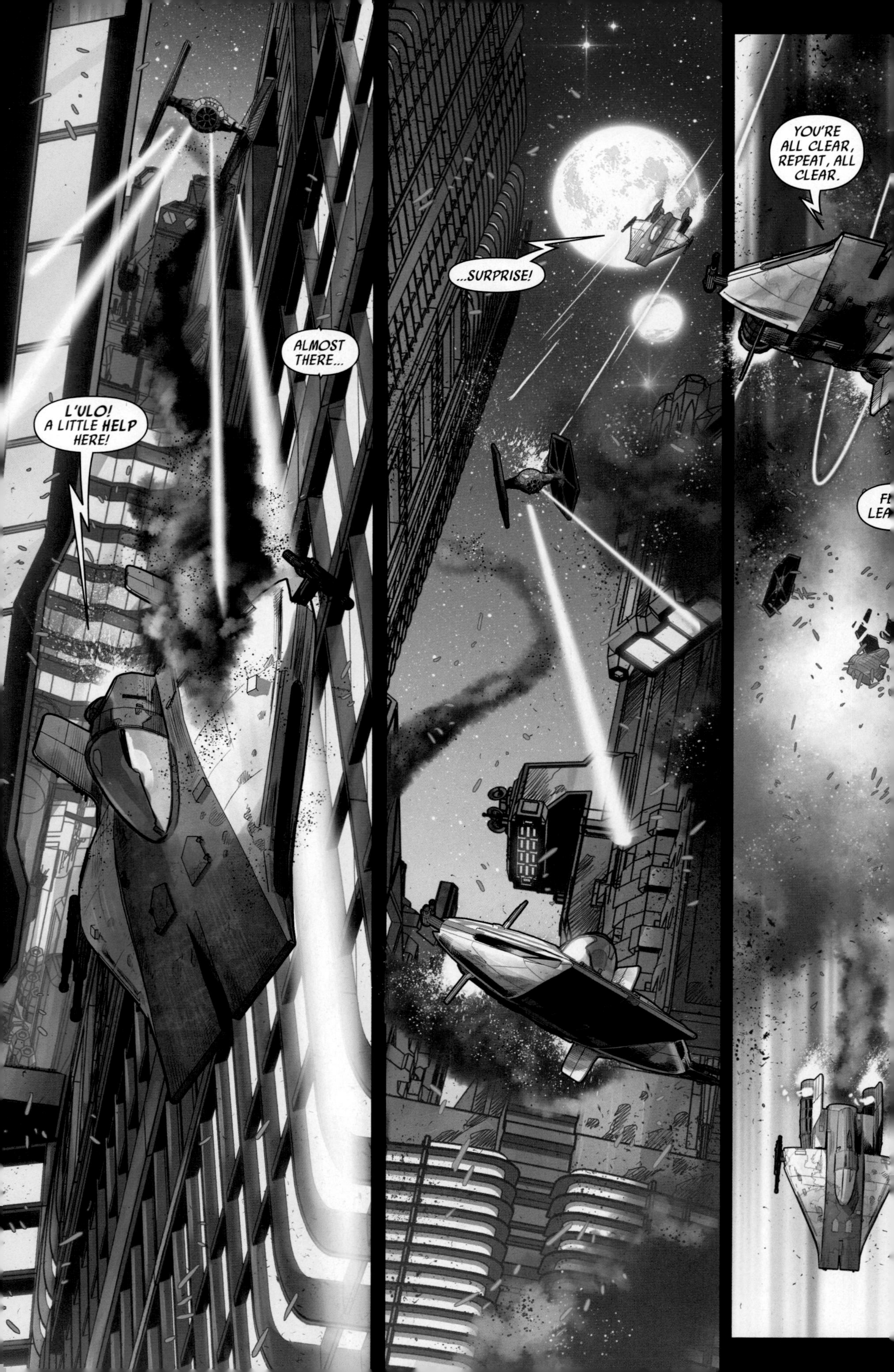
L'ULO! A LITTLE HELP HERE!
ALMOST THERE...
...SURPRISE!
YOU'RE ALL CLEAR, REPEAT, ALL CLEAR.

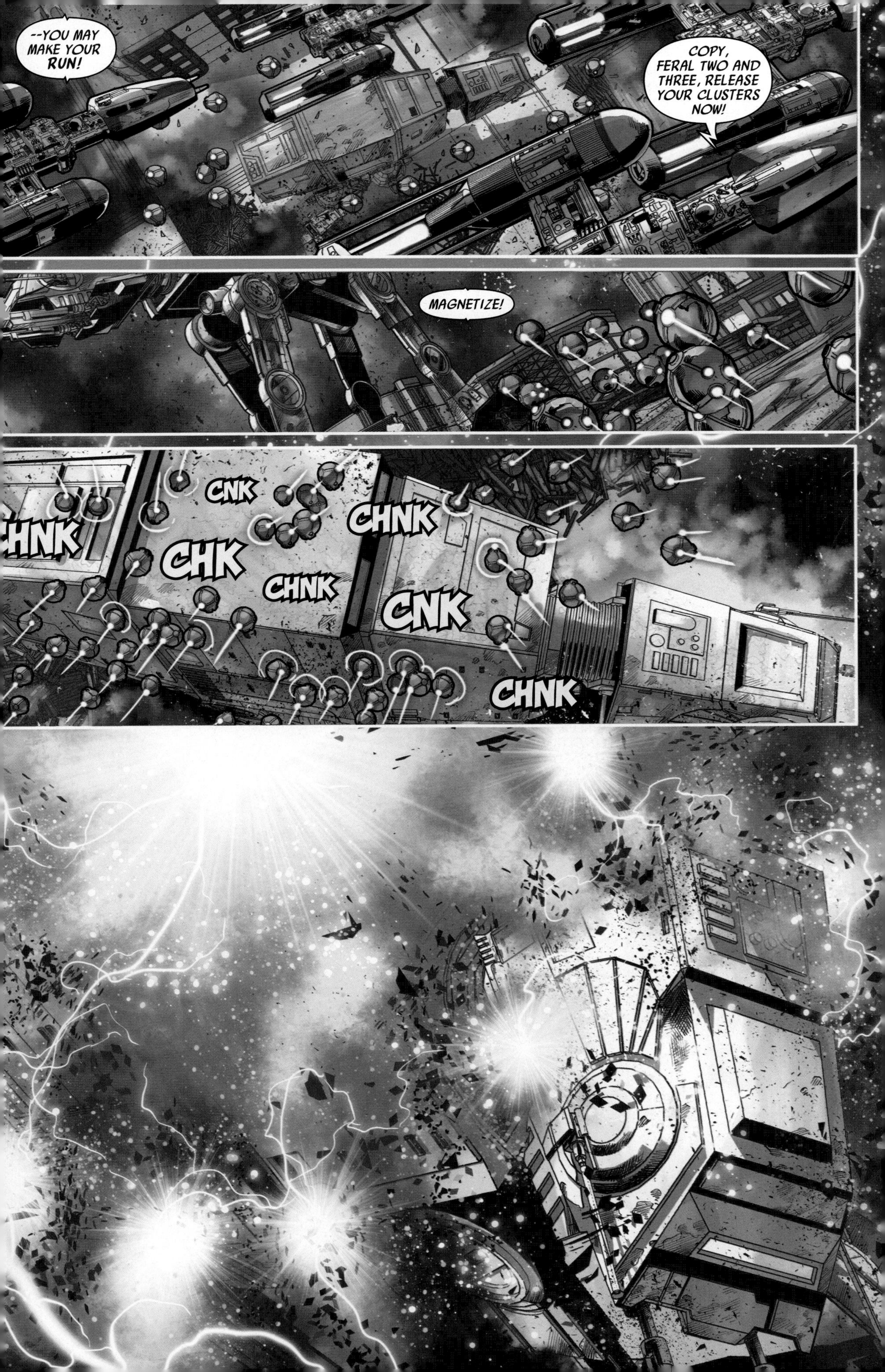
--YOU MAY MAKE YOUR RUN!
COPY, FERAL TWO AND THREE, RELEASE YOUR CLUSTERS NOW!
MAGNETIZE!
CHNK
CNK
CHK
CHNK
CHNK
CNK
CHNK

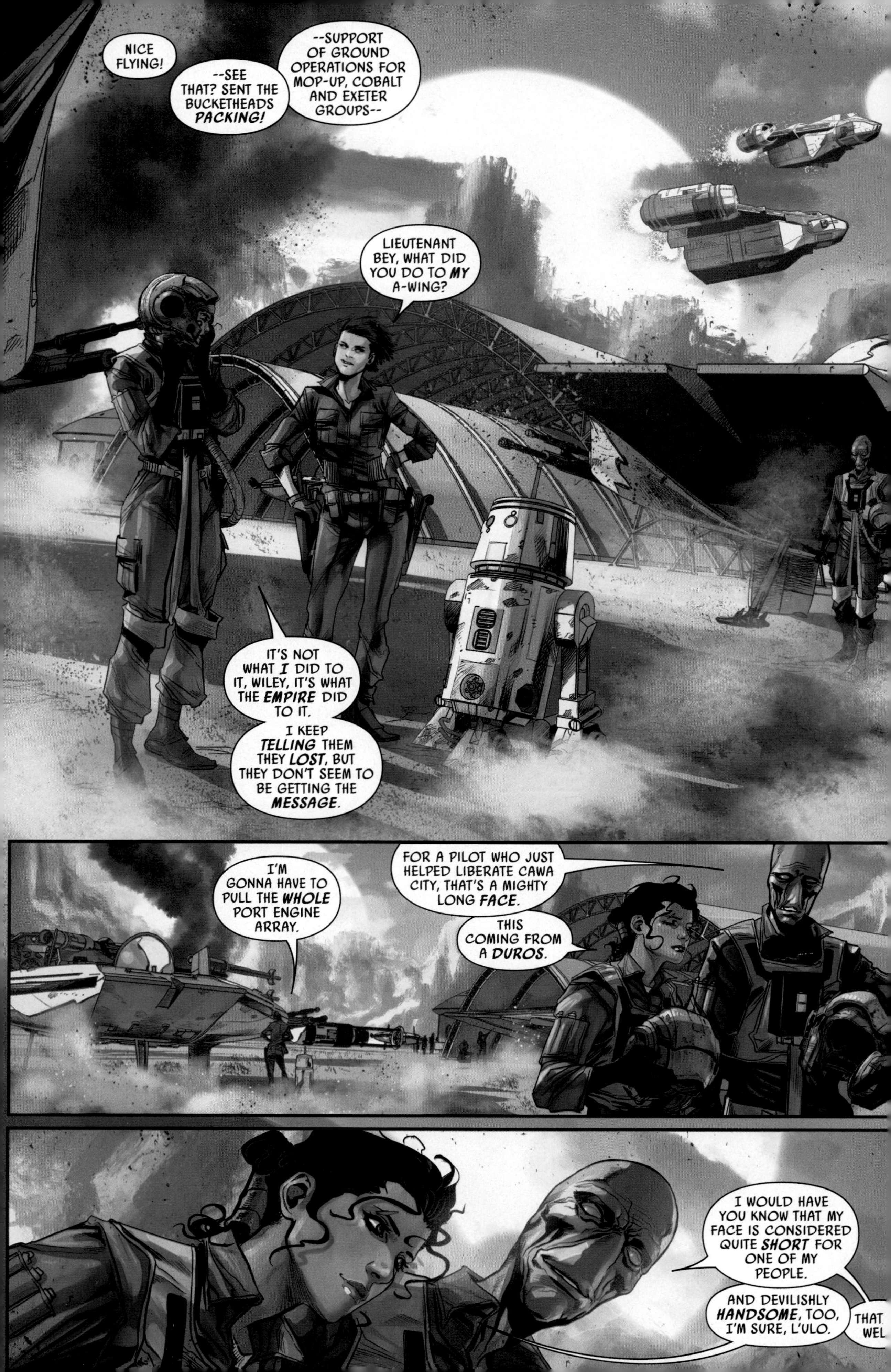
NICE FLYING!
--SEE THAT? SENT THE BUCKETHEADS PACKING!
--SUPPORT OF GROUND OPERATIONS FOR MOP-UP, COBALT AND EXETER GROUPS--
LIEUTENANT BEY, WHAT DID YOU DO TO MY A-WING?
IT'S NOT WHAT I DID TO IT, WILEY, IT'S WHAT THE EMPIRE DID TO IT.
I KEEP TELLING THEM THEY LOST, BUT THEY DON'T SEEM TO BE GETTING THE MESSAGE.
I'M GONNA HAVE TO PULL THE WHOLE PORT ENGINE ARRAY.
FOR A PILOT WHO JUST HELPED LIBERATE CAWA CITY, THAT'S A MIGHTY LONG FACE.
THIS COMING FROM A DUROS.
I WOULD HAVE YOU KNOW THAT MY FACE IS CONSIDERED QUITE SHORT FOR ONE OF MY PEOPLE.
AND DEVILISHLY HANDSOME, TOO, I'M SURE, L'ULO.
THAT WEL

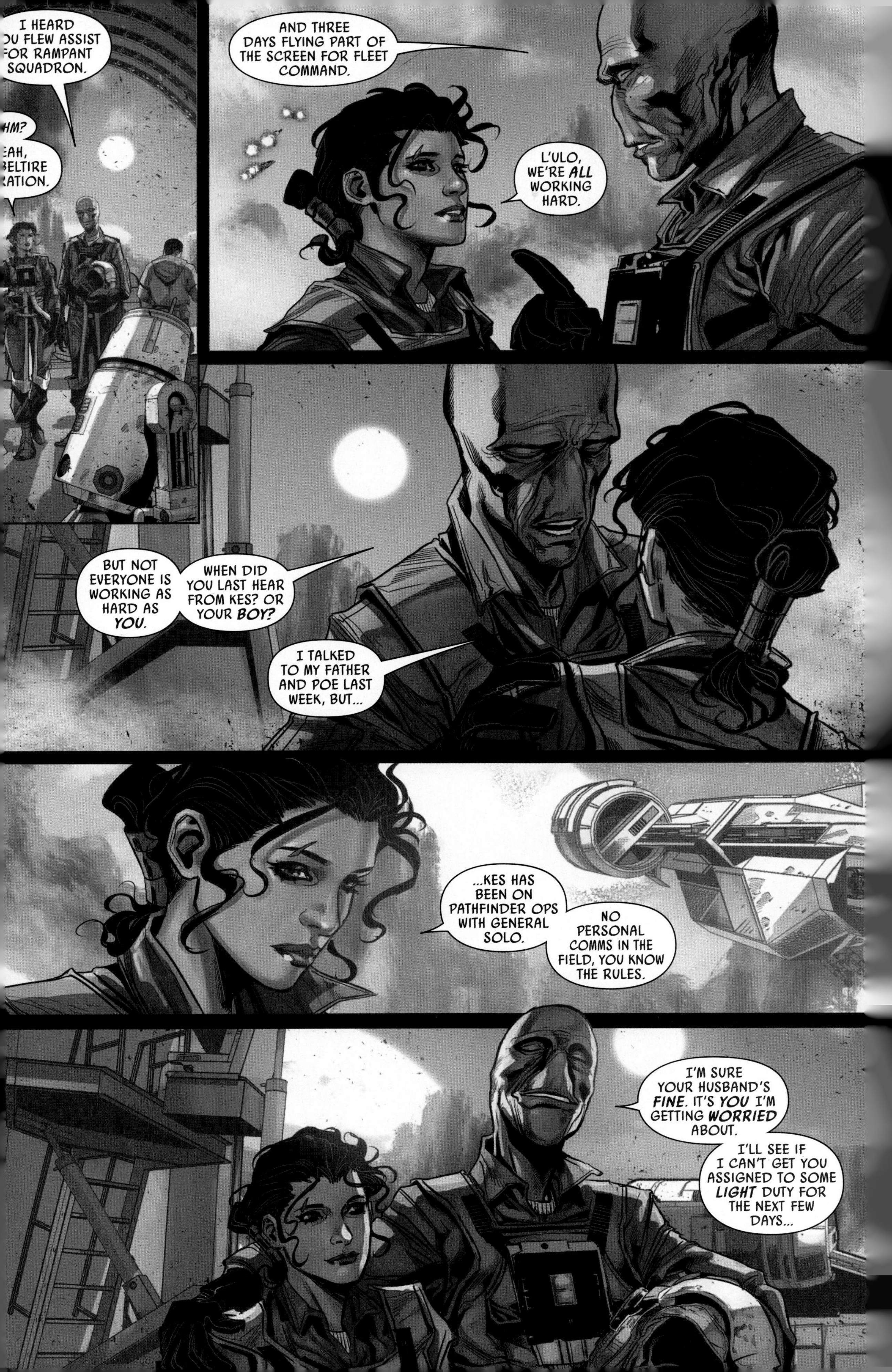
I HEARD
OU FLEW ASSIST
FOR RAMPANT
SQUADRON.
HM?
EAH,
BELTIRE
RATION.
AND THREE DAYS FLYING PART OF THE SCREEN FOR FLEET COMMAND.
L'ULO, WE'RE ALL WORKING HARD.
BUT NOT EVERYONE IS WORKING AS HARD AS YOU.
WHEN DID YOU LAST HEAR FROM KES? OR YOUR BOY?
I TALKED TO MY FATHER AND POE LAST WEEK, BUT...
...KES HAS BEEN ON PATHFINDER OPS WITH GENERAL SOLO.
NO PERSONAL COMMS IN THE FIELD, YOU KNOW THE RULES.
I'M SURE YOUR HUSBAND'S FINE. IT'S YOU I'M GETTING WORRIED ABOUT.
I'LL SEE IF I CAN'T GET YOU ASSIGNED TO SOME LIGHT DUTY FOR THE NEXT FEW DAYS...

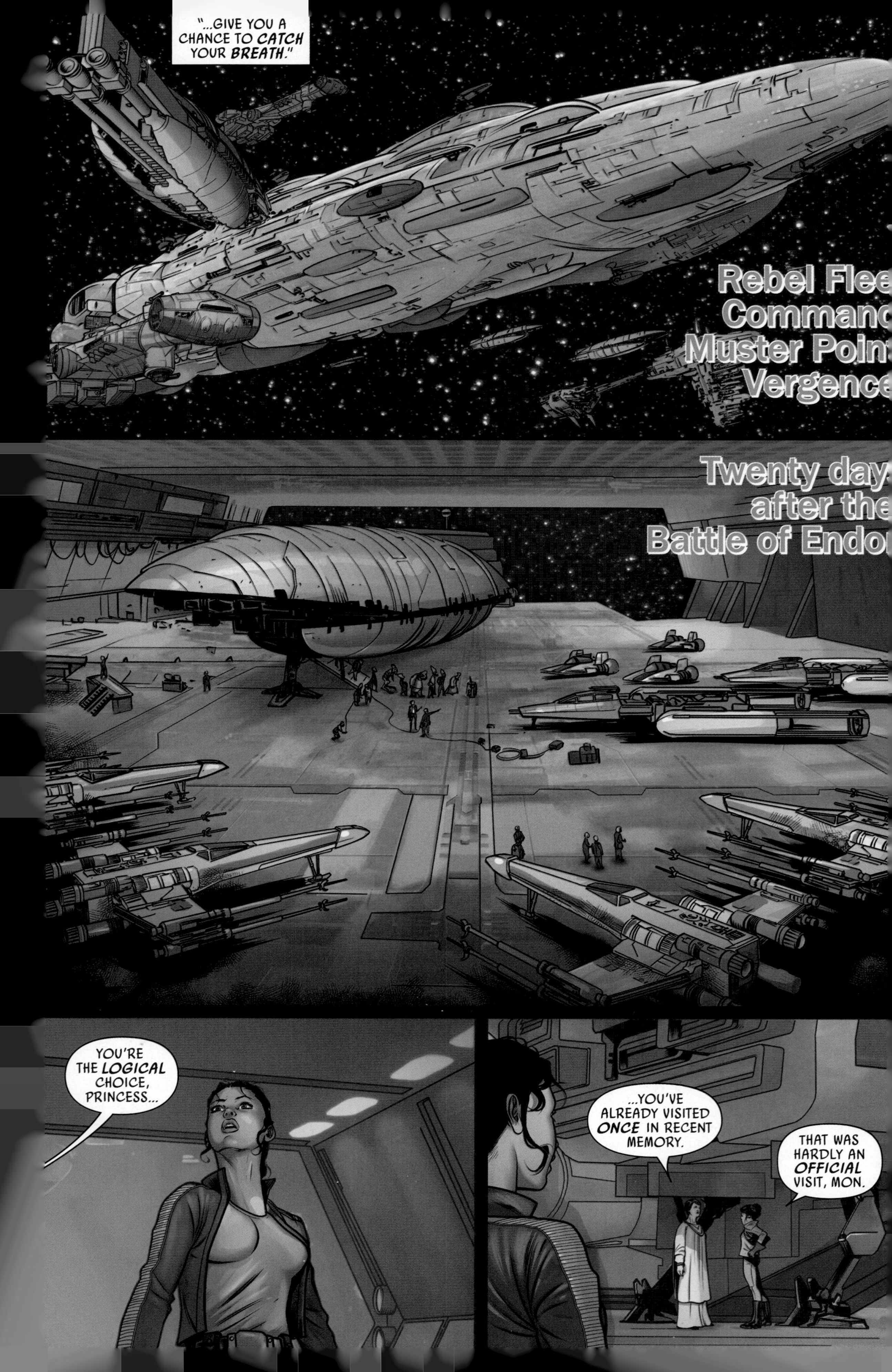
"...GIVE YOU A CHANCE TO *CATCH* YOUR *BREATH*."
Rebel Flee
Command
Muster Poin
Vergence
Twenty day
after the
Battle of Endor
YOU'RE THE *LOGICAL* CHOICE, PRINCESS...
...YOU'VE ALREADY VISITED *ONCE* IN RECENT MEMORY.
THAT WAS HARDLY AN *OFFICIAL* VISIT, MON.

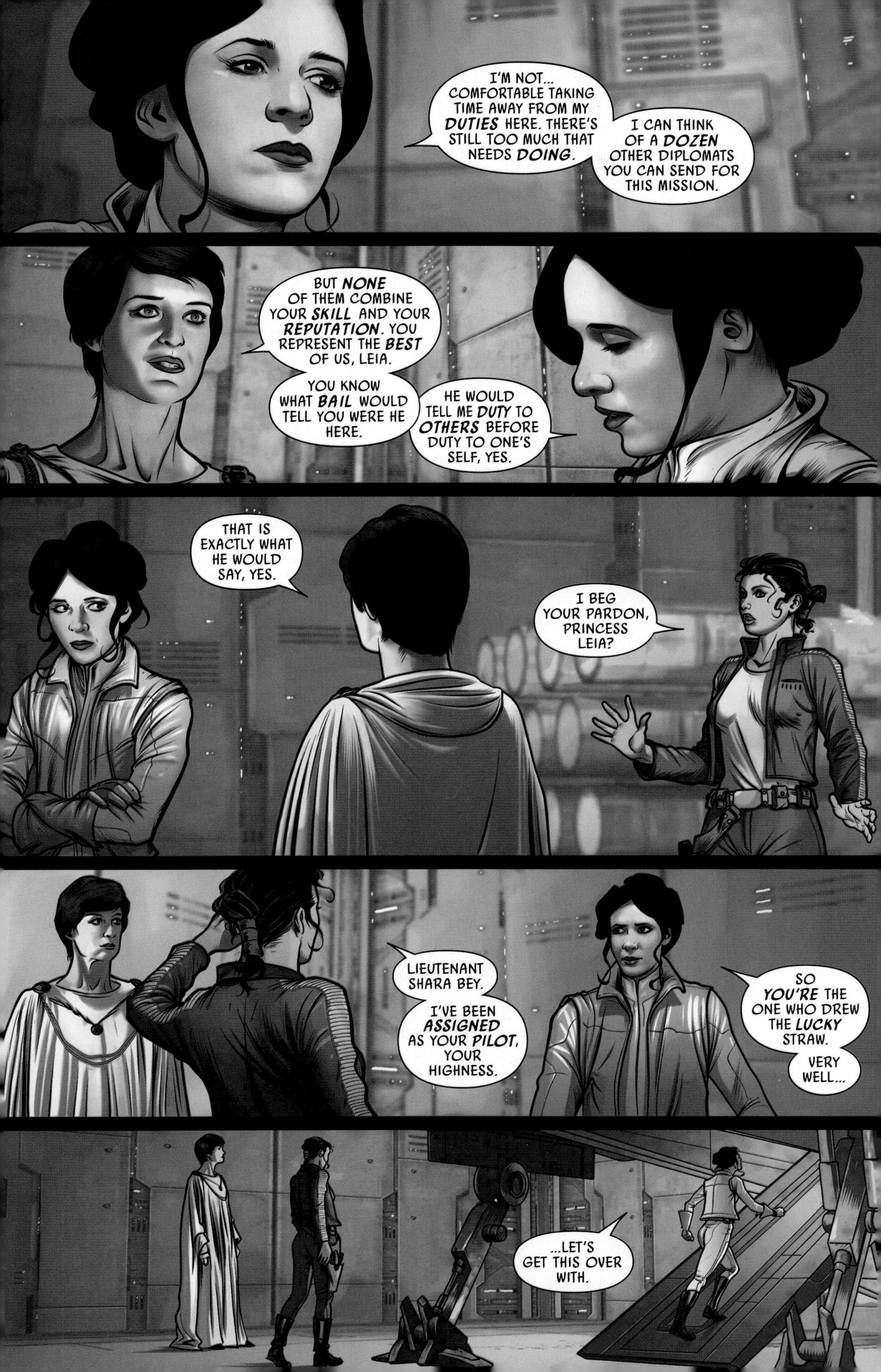
I'M NOT... COMFORTABLE TAKING TIME AWAY FROM MY DUTIES HERE. THERE'S STILL TOO MUCH THAT NEEDS DOING.
I CAN THINK OF A DOZEN OTHER DIPLOMATS YOU CAN SEND FOR THIS MISSION.
BUT NONE OF THEM COMBINE YOUR SKILL AND YOUR REPUTATION. YOU REPRESENT THE BEST OF US, LEIA.
YOU KNOW WHAT BAIL WOULD TELL YOU WERE HE HERE.
HE WOULD TELL ME DUTY TO OTHERS BEFORE DUTY TO ONE'S SELF, YES.
THAT IS EXACTLY WHAT HE WOULD SAY, YES.
I BEG YOUR PARDON, PRINCESS LEIA?
LIEUTENANT SHARA BEY.
I'VE BEEN ASSIGNED AS YOUR PILOT, YOUR HIGHNESS.
SO YOU'RE THE ONE WHO DREW THE LUCKY STRAW.
VERY WELL...
...LET'S GET THIS OVER WITH.

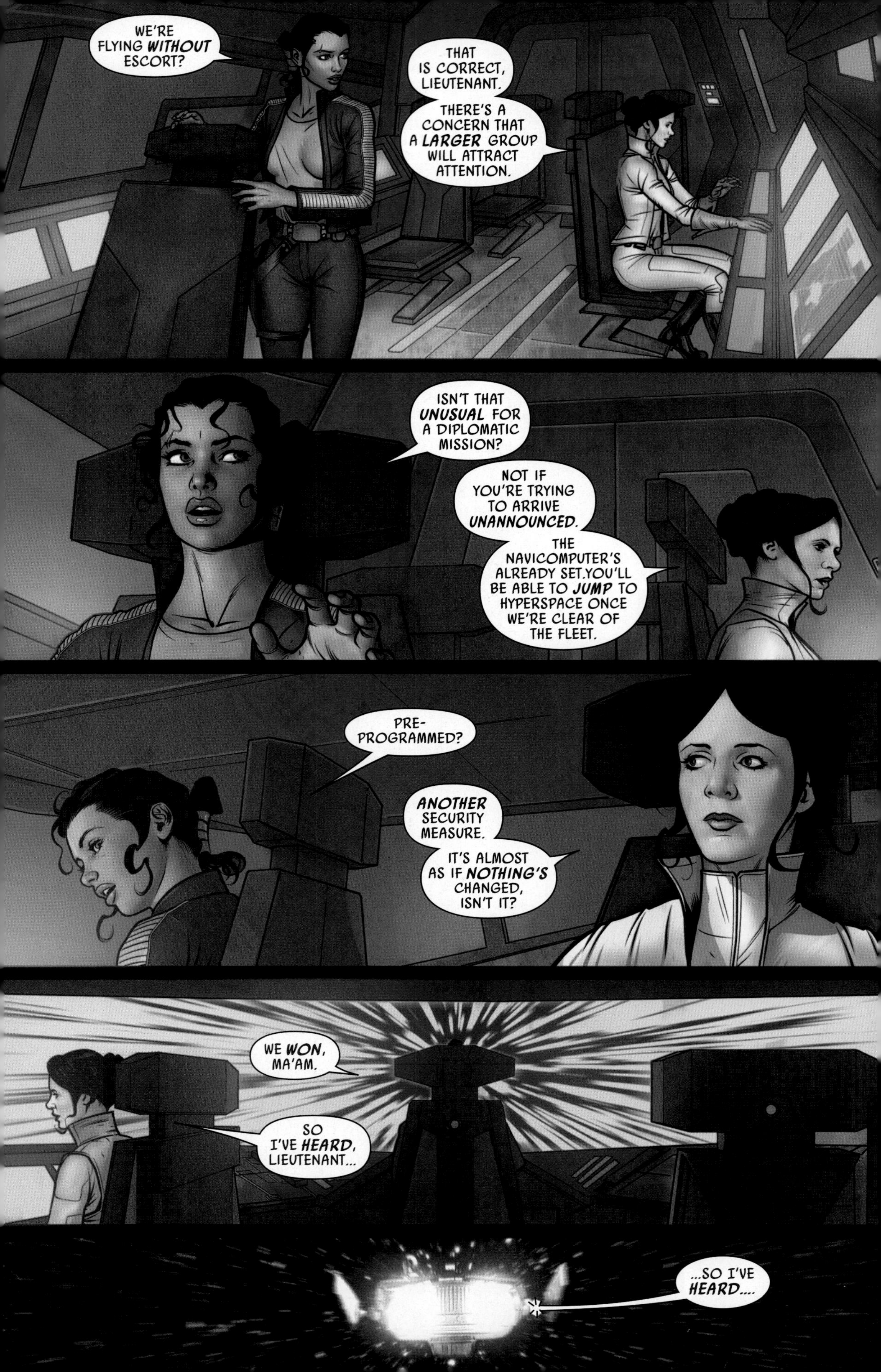
WE'RE FLYING WITHOUT ESCORT?
THAT IS CORRECT, LIEUTENANT.
THERE'S A CONCERN THAT A LARGER GROUP WILL ATTRACT ATTENTION.
ISN'T THAT UNUSUAL FOR A DIPLOMATIC MISSION?
NOT IF YOU'RE TRYING TO ARRIVE UNANNOUNCED.
THE NAVICOMPUTER'S ALREADY SET. YOU'LL BE ABLE TO JUMP TO HYPERSPACE ONCE WE'RE CLEAR OF THE FLEET.
PRE-PROGRAMMED?
ANOTHER SECURITY MEASURE.
IT'S ALMOST AS IF NOTHING'S CHANGED, ISN'T IT?
WE WON, MA'AM.
SO I'VE HEARD, LIEUTENANT...
...SO I'VE HEARD....

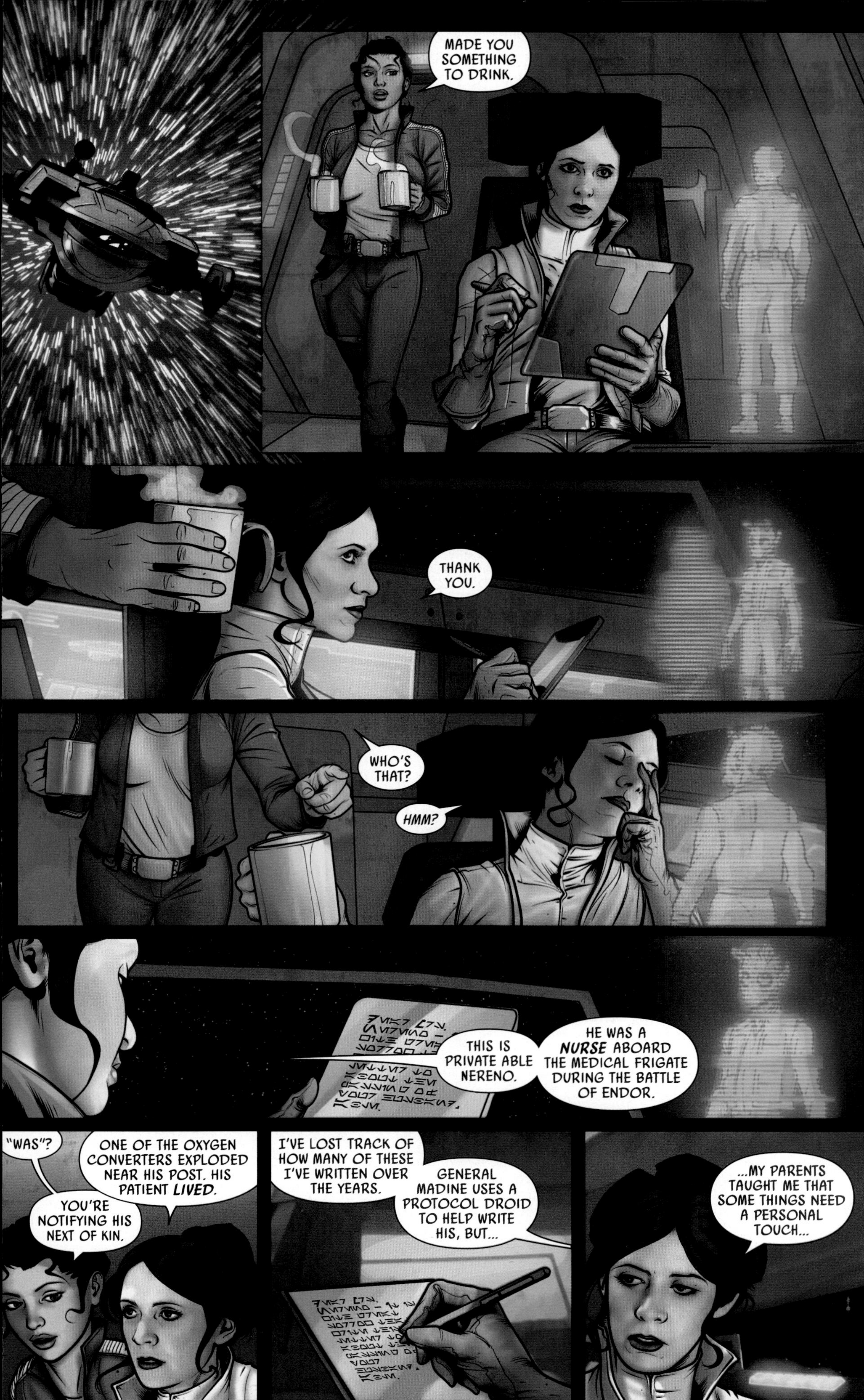
MADE YOU SOMETHING TO DRINK.
THANK YOU.
WHO'S THAT?
HMM?
THIS IS PRIVATE ABLE NERENO.
HE WAS A *NURSE* ABOARD THE MEDICAL FRIGATE DURING THE BATTLE OF ENDOR.
"WAS"?
ONE OF THE OXYGEN CONVERTERS EXPLODED NEAR HIS POST. HIS PATIENT *LIVED*.
YOU'RE NOTIFYING HIS NEXT OF KIN.
I'VE LOST TRACK OF HOW MANY OF THESE I'VE WRITTEN OVER THE YEARS.
GENERAL MADINE USES A PROTOCOL DROID TO HELP WRITE HIS, BUT...
...MY PARENTS TAUGHT ME THAT SOME THINGS NEED A PERSONAL TOUCH...

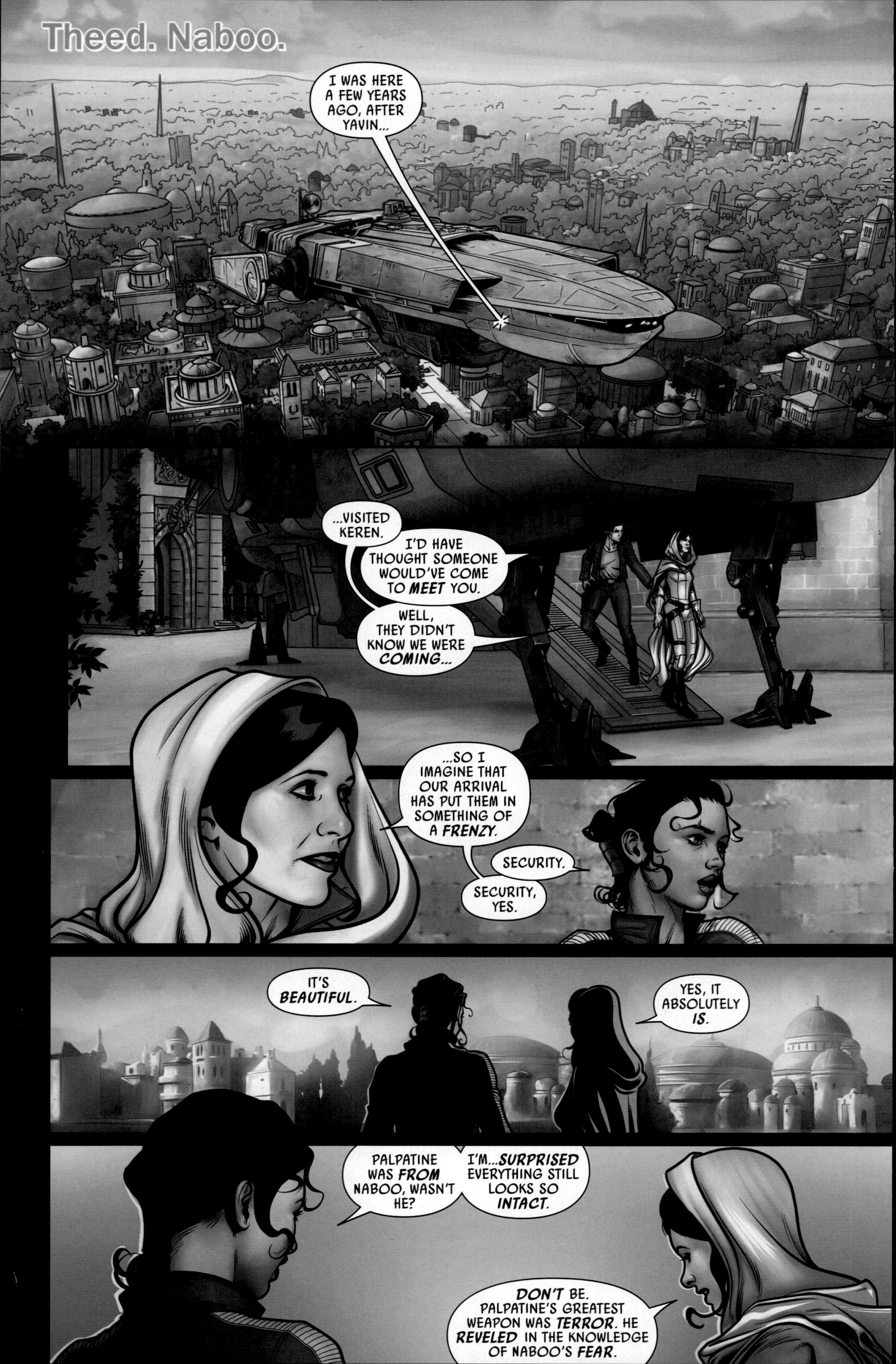
Theed. Naboo.
I WAS HERE A FEW YEARS AGO, AFTER YAVIN...
...VISITED KEREN.
I'D HAVE THOUGHT SOMEONE WOULD'VE COME TO MEET YOU.
WELL, THEY DIDN'T KNOW WE WERE COMING...
...SO I IMAGINE THAT OUR ARRIVAL HAS PUT THEM IN SOMETHING OF A FRENZY.
SECURITY.
SECURITY, YES.
IT'S BEAUTIFUL.
YES, IT ABSOLUTELY IS.
PALPATINE WAS FROM NABOO, WASN'T HE?
I'M...SURPRISED EVERYTHING STILL LOOKS SO INTACT.
DON'T BE. PALPATINE'S GREATEST WEAPON WAS TERROR. HE REVELED IN THE KNOWLEDGE OF NABOO'S FEAR.

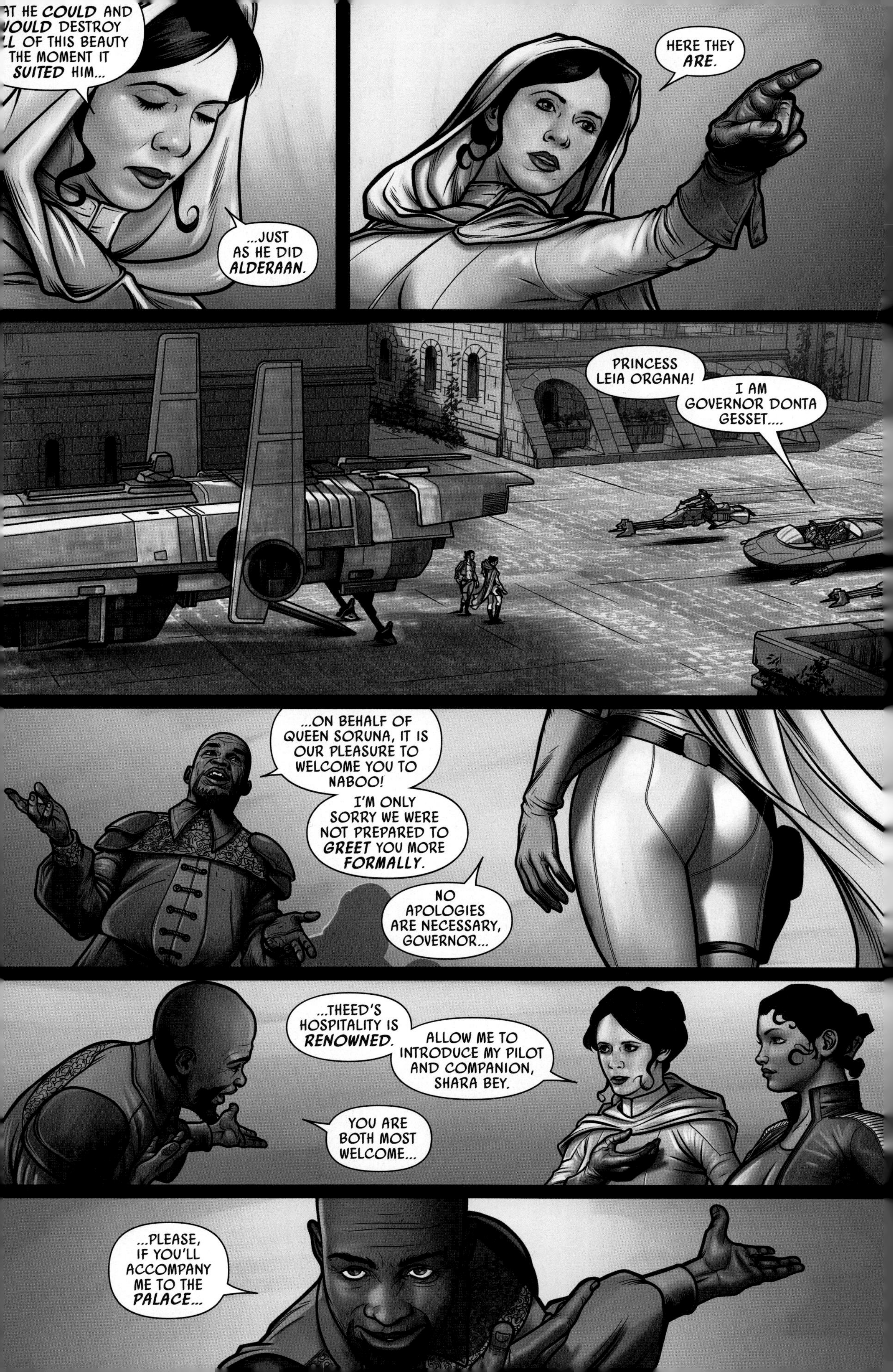
AT HE COULD AND
WOULD DESTROY
LL OF THIS BEAUTY
THE MOMENT IT
SUITED HIM...
...JUST AS HE DID ALDERAAN.
HERE THEY ARE.
PRINCESS LEIA ORGANA!
I AM GOVERNOR DONTA GESSET....
...ON BEHALF OF QUEEN SORUNA, IT IS OUR PLEASURE TO WELCOME YOU TO NABOO!
I'M ONLY SORRY WE WERE NOT PREPARED TO GREET YOU MORE FORMALLY.
NO APOLOGIES ARE NECESSARY, GOVERNOR...
...THEED'S HOSPITALITY IS RENOWNED.
ALLOW ME TO INTRODUCE MY PILOT AND COMPANION, SHARA BEY.
YOU ARE BOTH MOST WELCOME...
...PLEASE, IF YOU'LL ACCOMPANY ME TO THE PALACE...

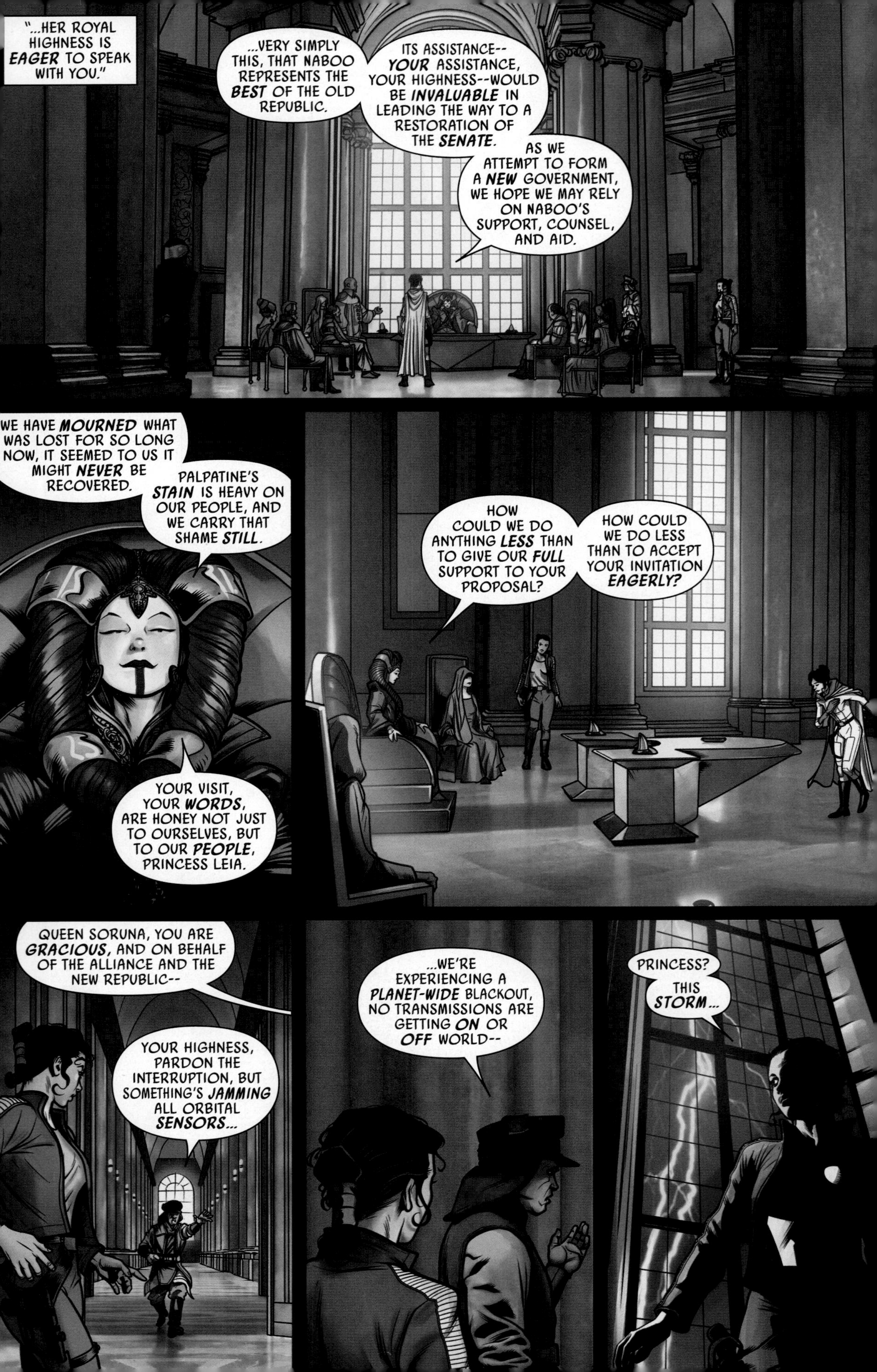
"...HER ROYAL HIGHNESS IS EAGER TO SPEAK WITH YOU."
...VERY SIMPLY THIS, THAT NABOO REPRESENTS THE BEST OF THE OLD REPUBLIC.
ITS ASSISTANCE-- YOUR ASSISTANCE, YOUR HIGHNESS--WOULD BE INVALUABLE IN LEADING THE WAY TO A RESTORATION OF THE SENATE.
AS WE ATTEMPT TO FORM A NEW GOVERNMENT, WE HOPE WE MAY RELY ON NABOO'S SUPPORT, COUNSEL, AND AID.
WE HAVE MOURNED WHAT WAS LOST FOR SO LONG NOW, IT SEEMED TO US IT MIGHT NEVER BE RECOVERED.
PALPATINE'S STAIN IS HEAVY ON OUR PEOPLE, AND WE CARRY THAT SHAME STILL.
YOUR VISIT, YOUR WORDS, ARE HONEY NOT JUST TO OURSELVES, BUT TO OUR PEOPLE, PRINCESS LEIA.
HOW COULD WE DO ANYTHING LESS THAN TO GIVE OUR FULL SUPPORT TO YOUR PROPOSAL?
HOW COULD WE DO LESS THAN TO ACCEPT YOUR INVITATION EAGERLY?
QUEEN SORUNA, YOU ARE GRACIOUS, AND ON BEHALF OF THE ALLIANCE AND THE NEW REPUBLIC--
YOUR HIGHNESS, PARDON THE INTERRUPTION, BUT SOMETHING'S JAMMING ALL ORBITAL SENSORS...
...WE'RE EXPERIENCING A PLANET-WIDE BLACKOUT, NO TRANSMISSIONS ARE GETTING ON OR OFF WORLD--
PRINCESS?
THIS STORM...

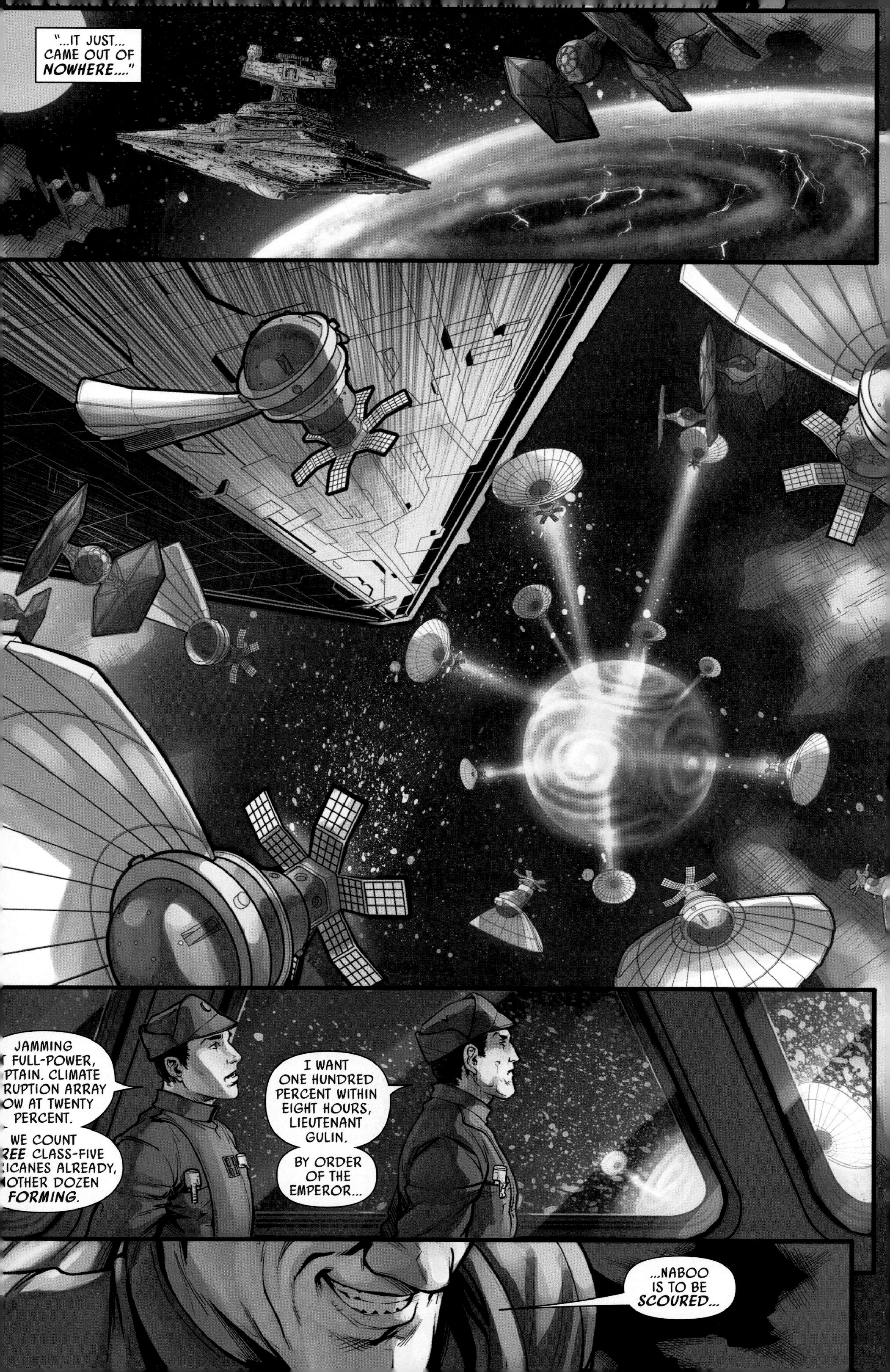
"...IT JUST... CAME OUT OF *NOWHERE*...."
JAMMING T FULL-POWER, PTAIN. CLIMATE RUPTION ARRAY OW AT TWENTY PERCENT.
WE COUNT *REE* CLASS-FIVE ICANES ALREADY, NOTHER DOZEN *FORMING*.
I WANT ONE HUNDRED PERCENT WITHIN EIGHT HOURS, LIEUTENANT GULIN.
BY ORDER OF THE EMPEROR...
...NABOO IS TO BE *SCOURED*...

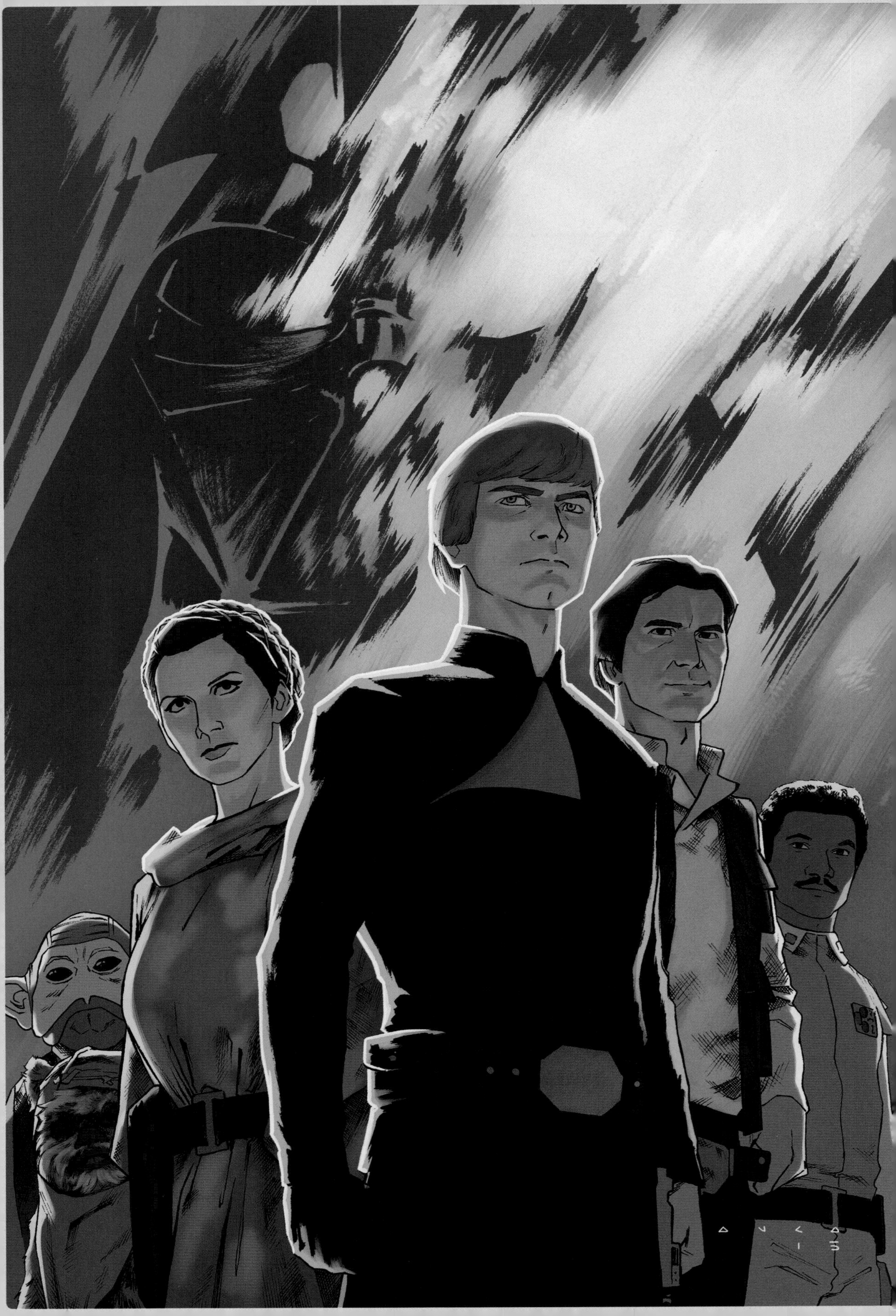

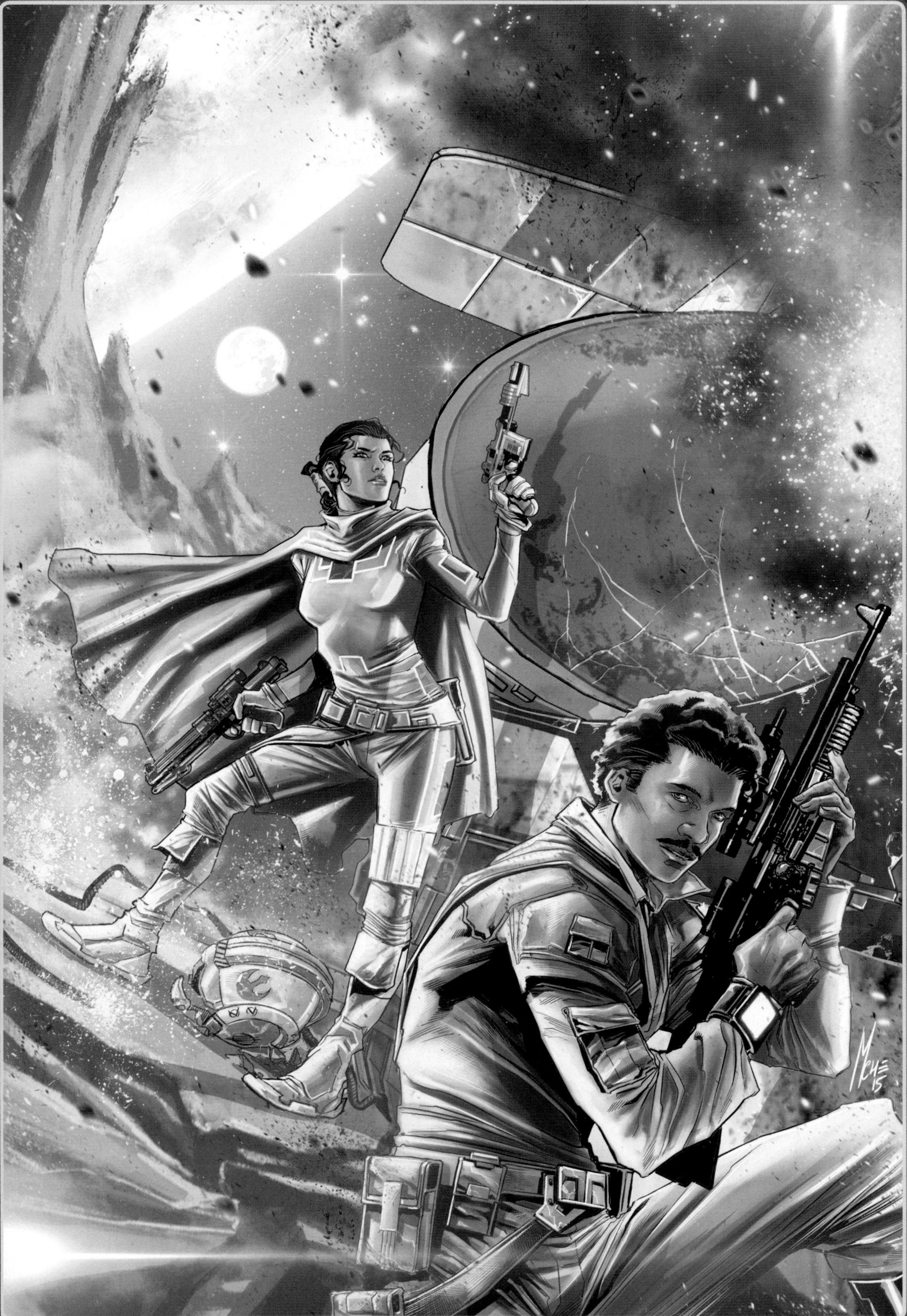

3

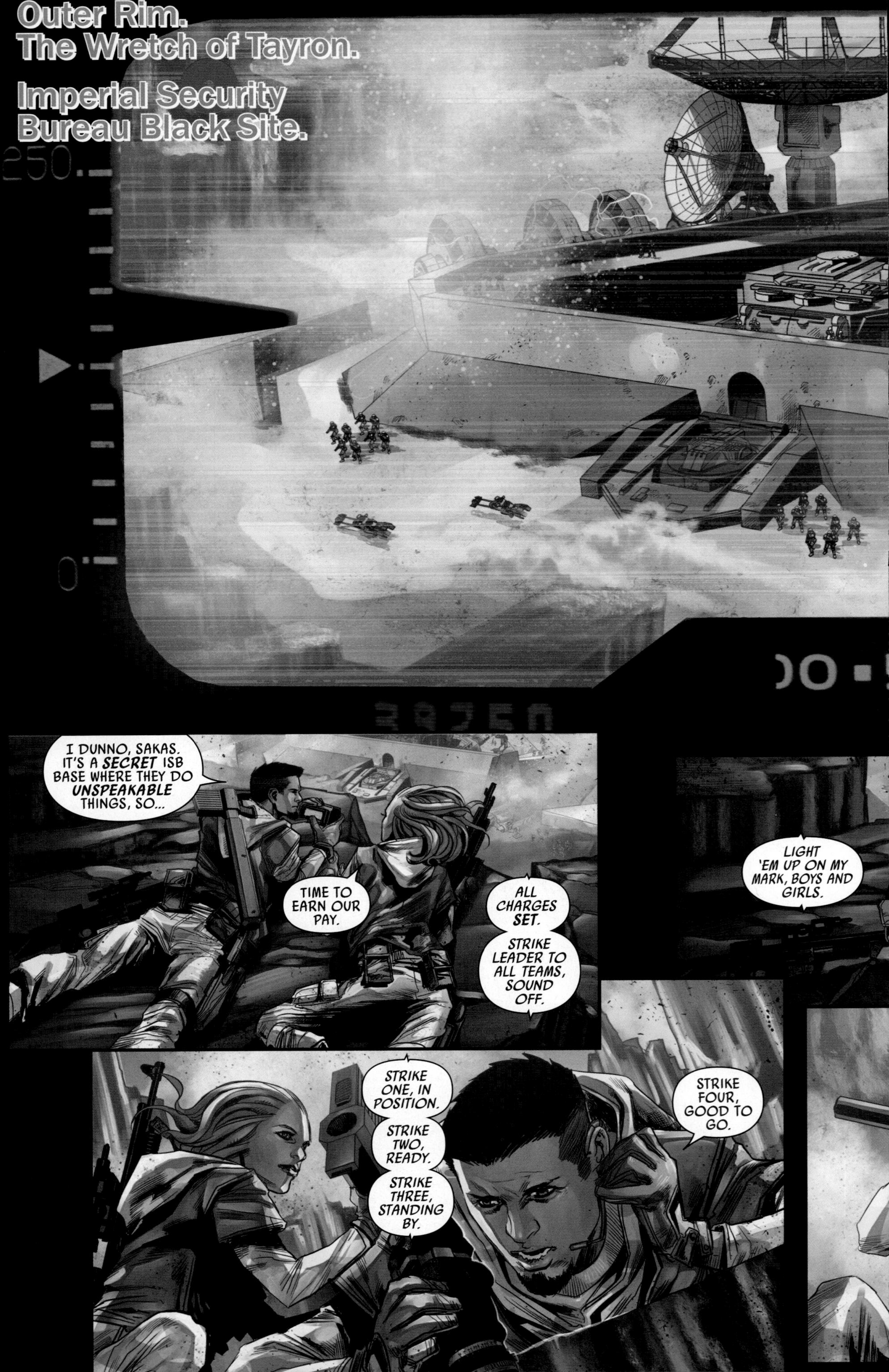
Outer Rim.
The Wretch of Tayron.
Imperial Security Bureau Black Site.
I DUNNO, SAKAS. IT'S A SECRET ISB BASE WHERE THEY DO UNSPEAKABLE THINGS, SO...
TIME TO EARN OUR PAY.
ALL CHARGES SET.
STRIKE LEADER TO ALL TEAMS, SOUND OFF.
LIGHT 'EM UP ON MY MARK, BOYS AND GIRLS.
STRIKE ONE, IN POSITION.
STRIKE TWO, READY.
STRIKE THREE, STANDING BY.
STRIKE FOUR, GOOD TO GO.

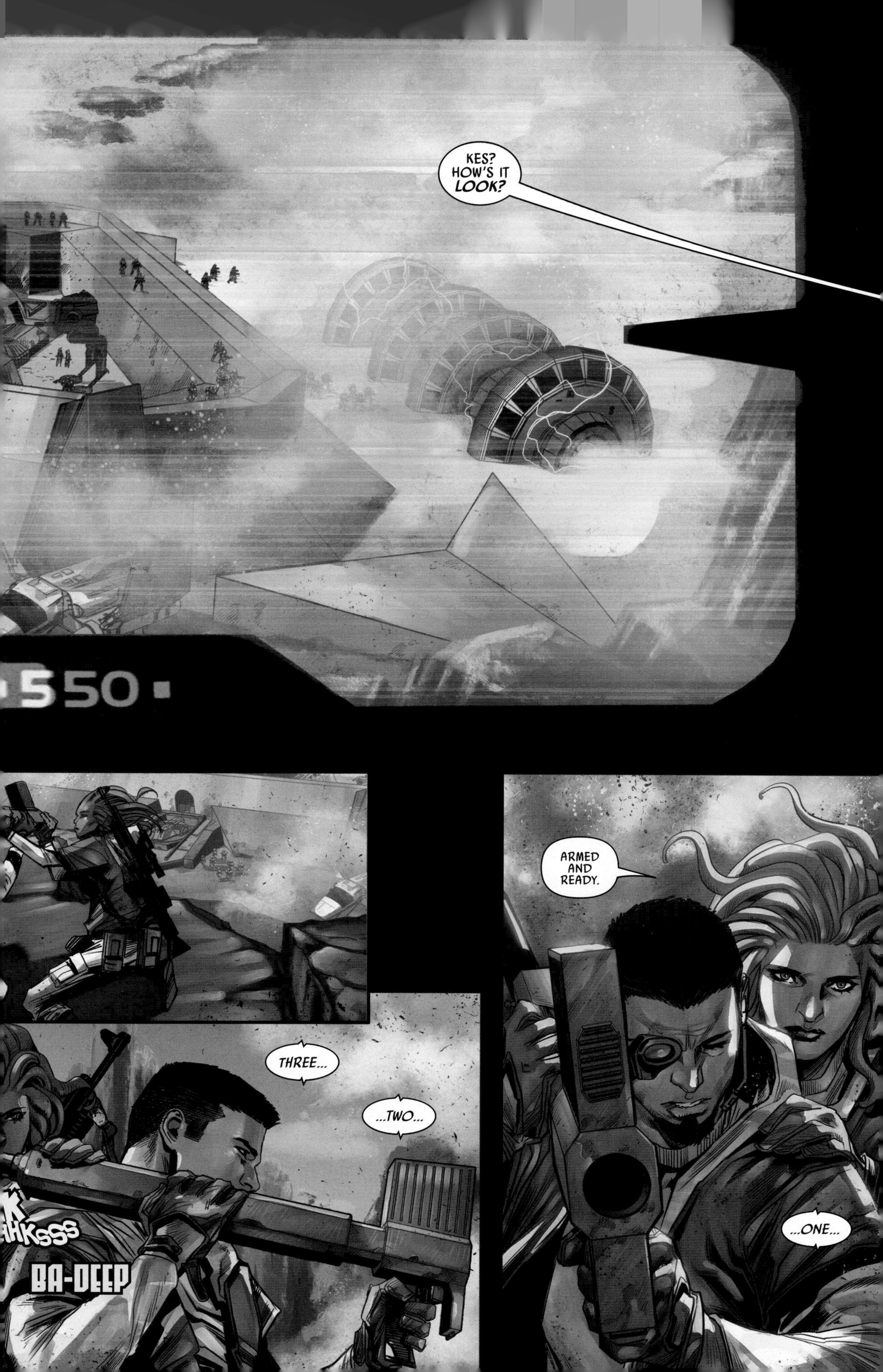
KES? HOW'S IT LOOK?
550
ARMED AND READY.
THREE...
...TWO...
...ONE...
HKSSS
BA-DEEP

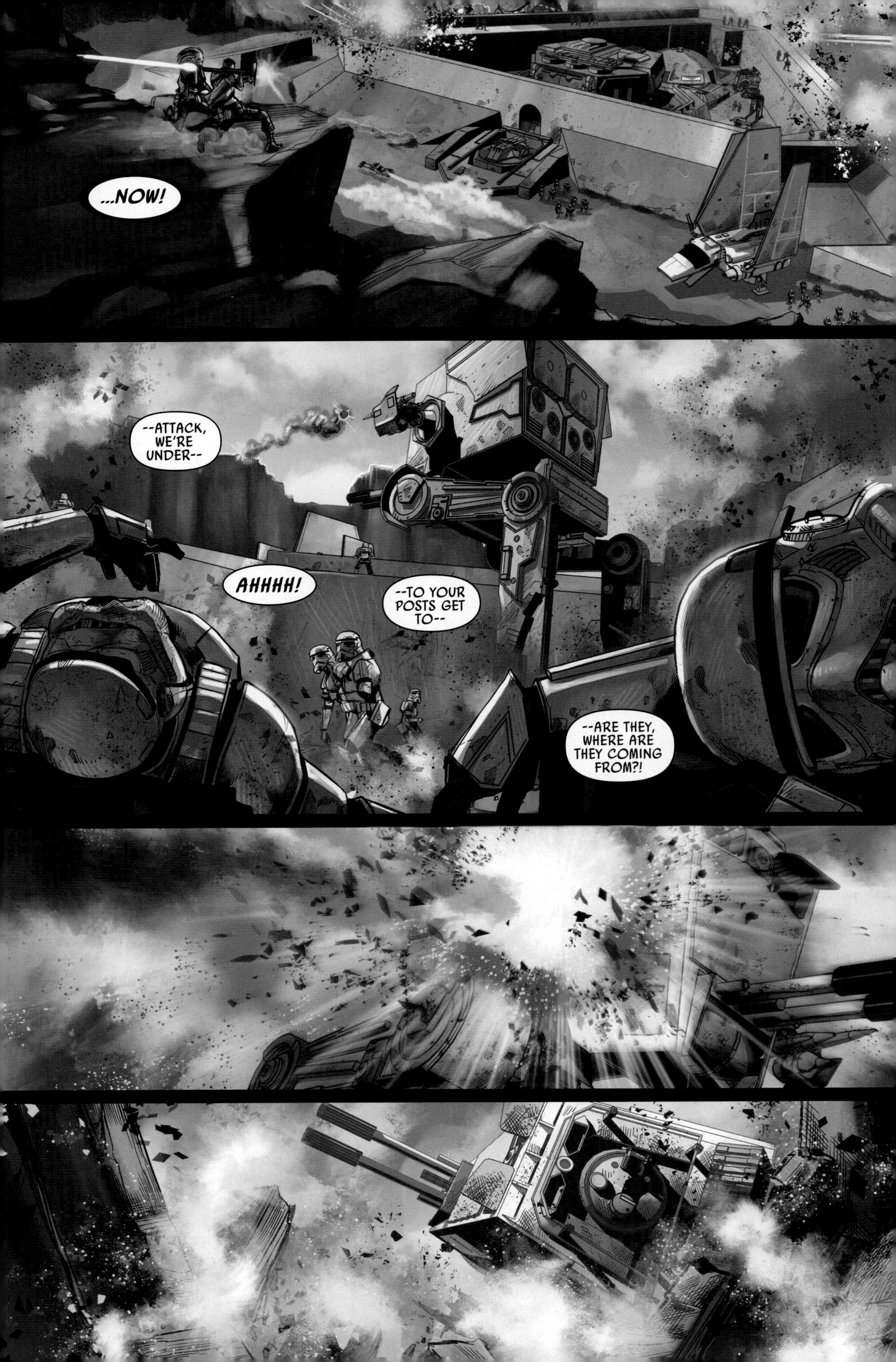
...NOW!
--ATTACK, WE'RE UNDER--
AHHHH!
--TO YOUR POSTS GET TO--
--ARE THEY, WHERE ARE THEY COMING FROM?!

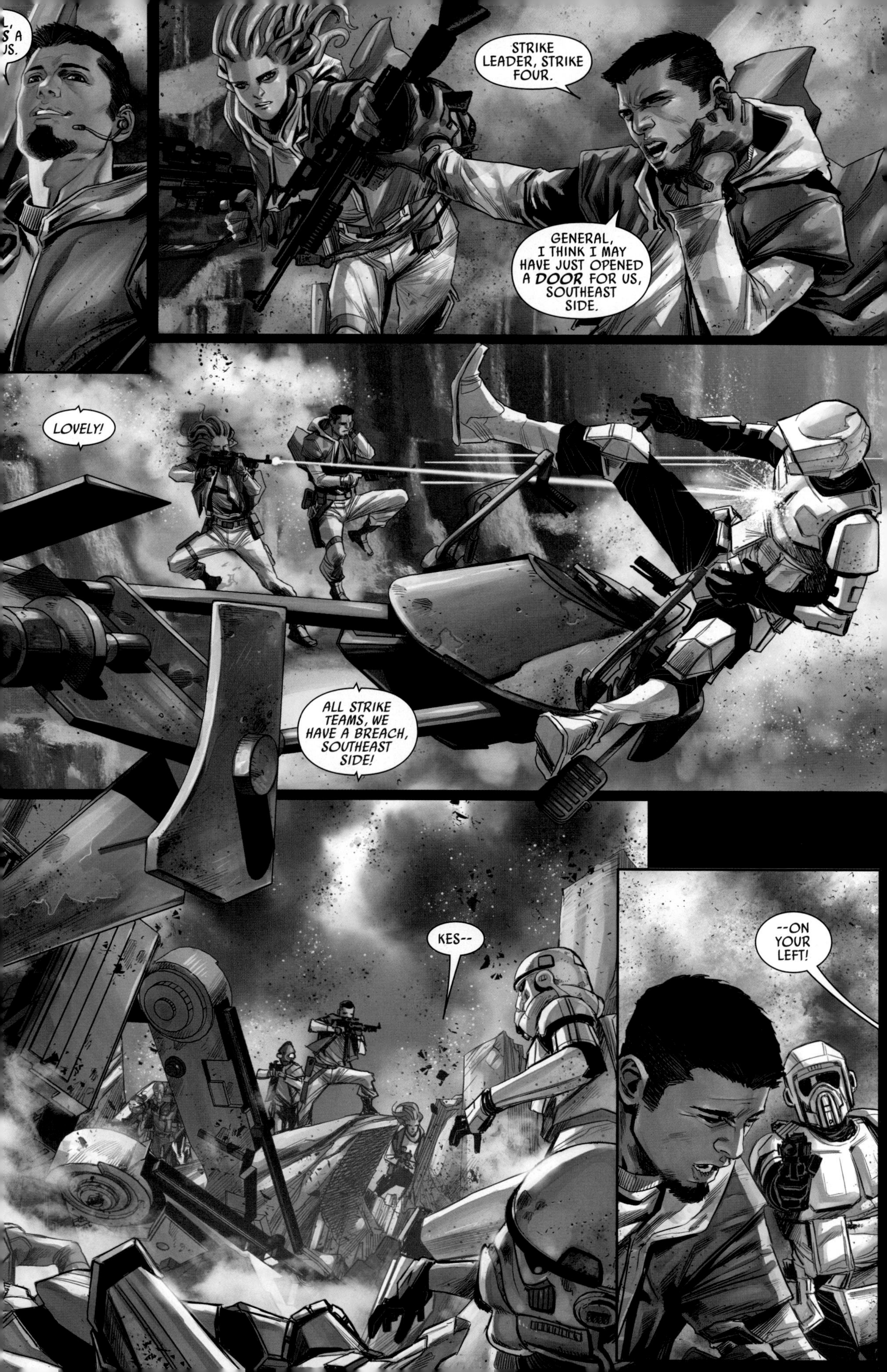
STRIKE LEADER, STRIKE FOUR.
GENERAL, I THINK I MAY HAVE JUST OPENED A DOOR FOR US, SOUTHEAST SIDE.
LOVELY!
ALL STRIKE TEAMS, WE HAVE A BREACH, SOUTHEAST SIDE!
KES--
--ON YOUR LEFT!

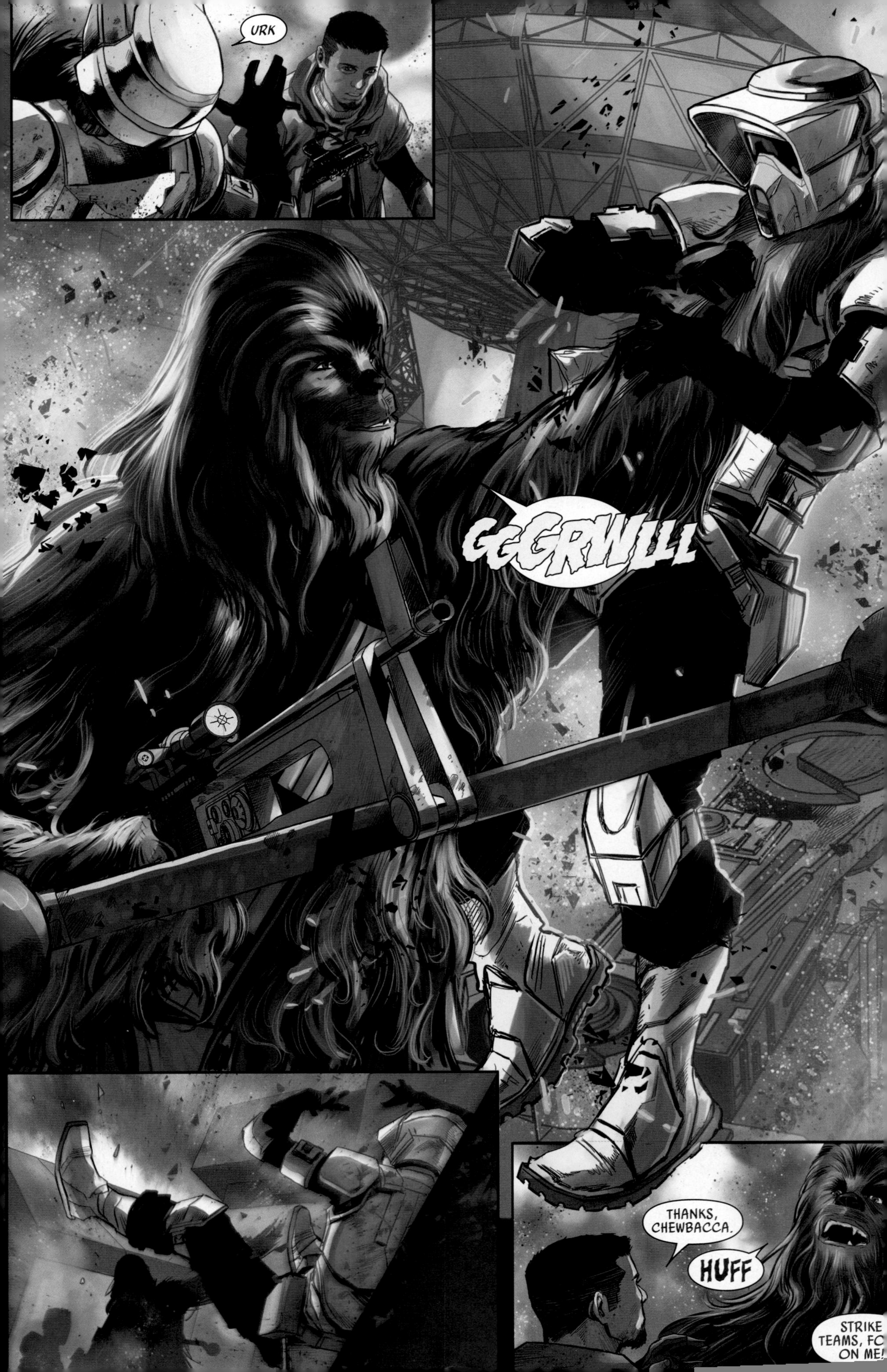
URK
GGGRWLLL
THANKS, CHEWBACCA.
HUFF
STRIKE TEAMS, FO
ON ME!

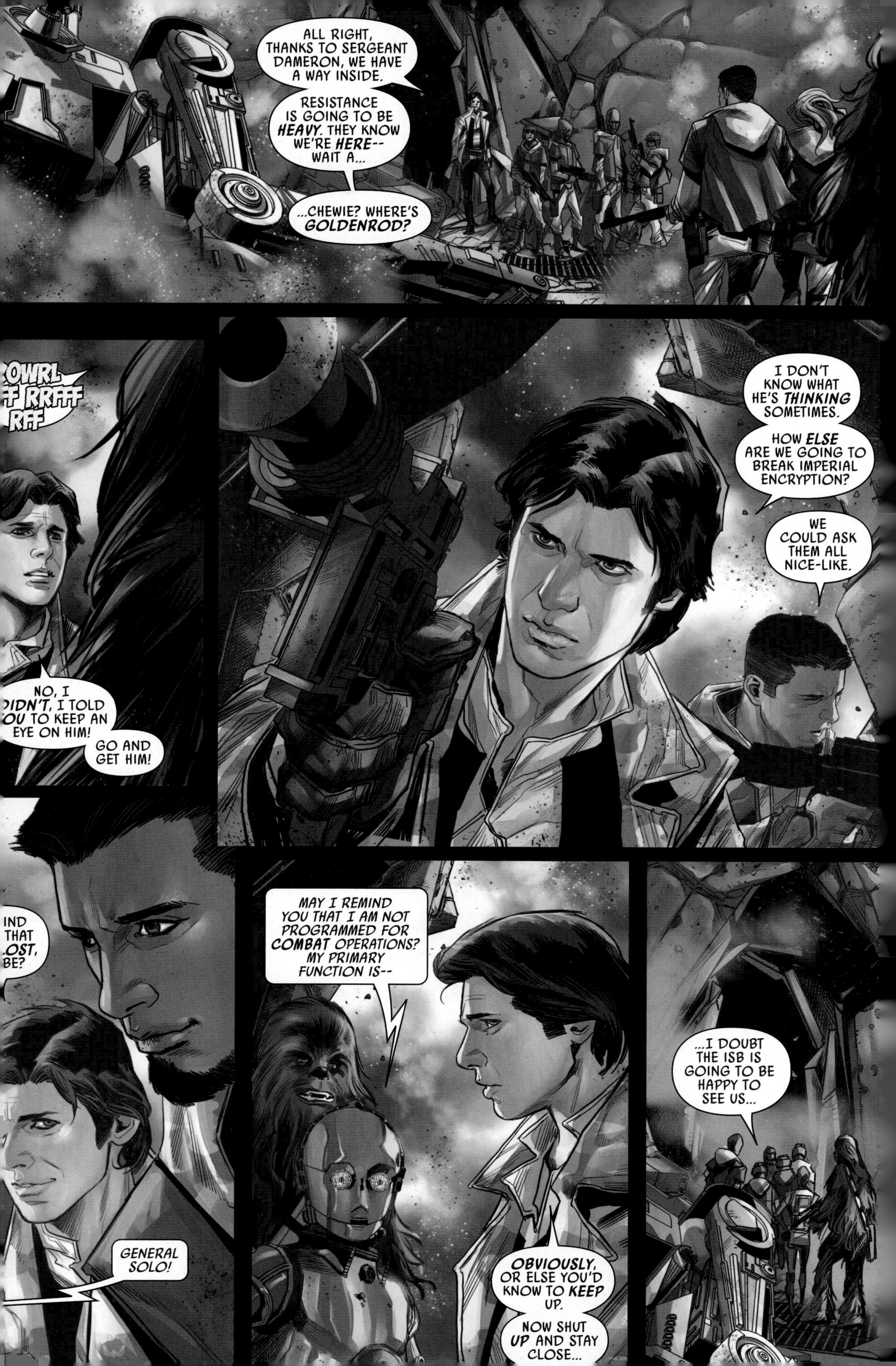
ALL RIGHT, THANKS TO SERGEANT DAMERON, WE HAVE A WAY INSIDE.
RESISTANCE IS GOING TO BE HEAVY. THEY KNOW WE'RE HERE-- WAIT A...
...CHEWIE? WHERE'S GOLDENROD?
GO AND GET HIM!
I DON'T KNOW WHAT HE'S THINKING SOMETIMES.
HOW ELSE ARE WE GOING TO BREAK IMPERIAL ENCRYPTION?
WE COULD ASK THEM ALL NICE-LIKE.
GENERAL SOLO!
MAY I REMIND YOU THAT I AM NOT PROGRAMMED FOR COMBAT OPERATIONS? MY PRIMARY FUNCTION IS--
OBVIOUSLY, OR ELSE YOU'D KNOW TO KEEP UP.
NOW SHUT UP AND STAY CLOSE...
...I DOUBT THE ISB IS GOING TO BE HAPPY TO SEE US...

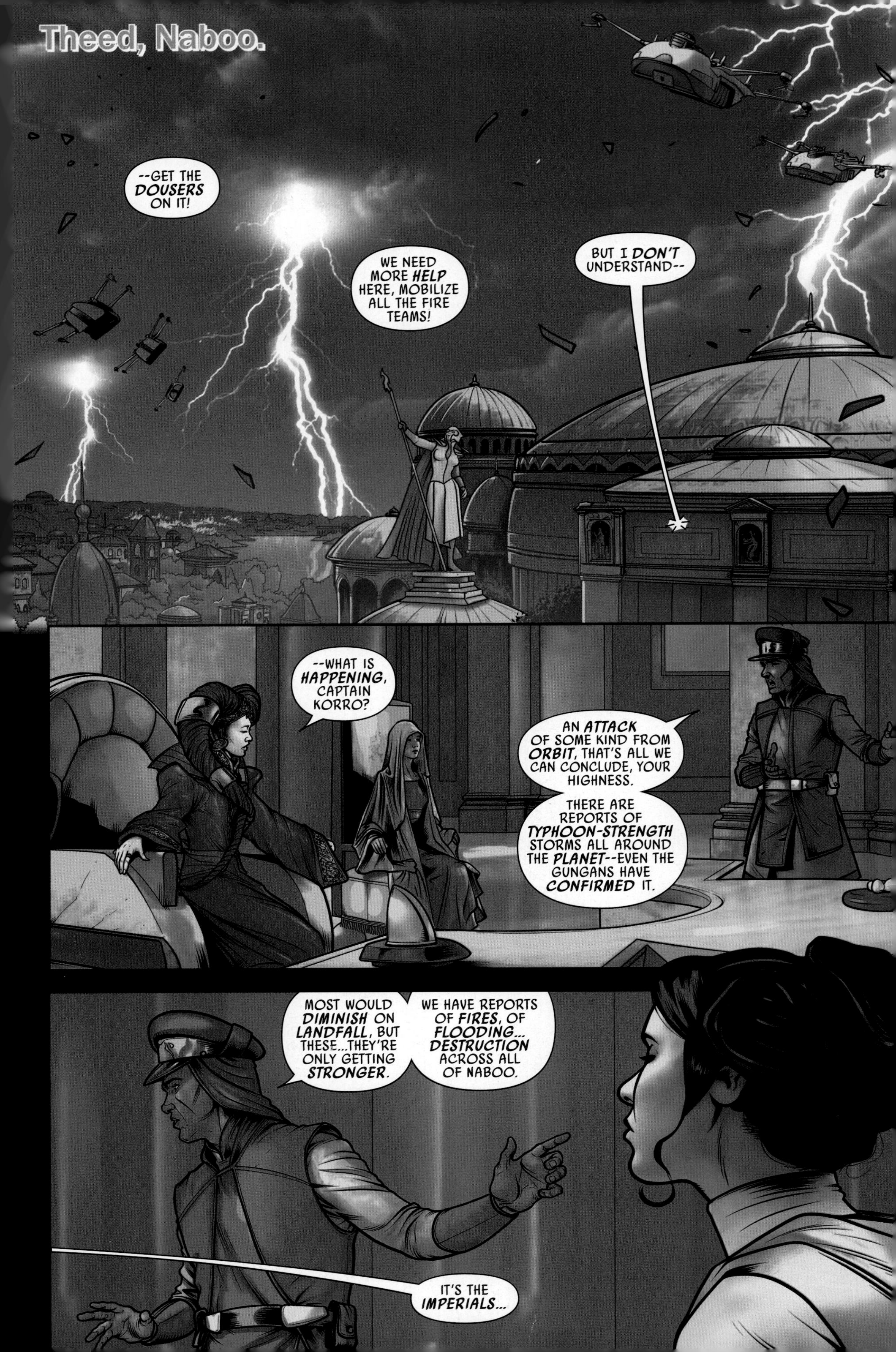
Theed, Naboo.
--GET THE DOUSERS ON IT!
WE NEED MORE HELP HERE, MOBILIZE ALL THE FIRE TEAMS!
BUT I DON'T UNDERSTAND--
--WHAT IS HAPPENING, CAPTAIN KORRO?
AN ATTACK OF SOME KIND FROM ORBIT, THAT'S ALL WE CAN CONCLUDE, YOUR HIGHNESS.
THERE ARE REPORTS OF TYPHOON-STRENGTH STORMS ALL AROUND THE PLANET--EVEN THE GUNGANS HAVE CONFIRMED IT.
MOST WOULD DIMINISH ON LANDFALL, BUT THESE...THEY'RE ONLY GETTING STRONGER.
WE HAVE REPORTS OF FIRES, OF FLOODING... DESTRUCTION ACROSS ALL OF NABOO.
IT'S THE IMPERIALS...

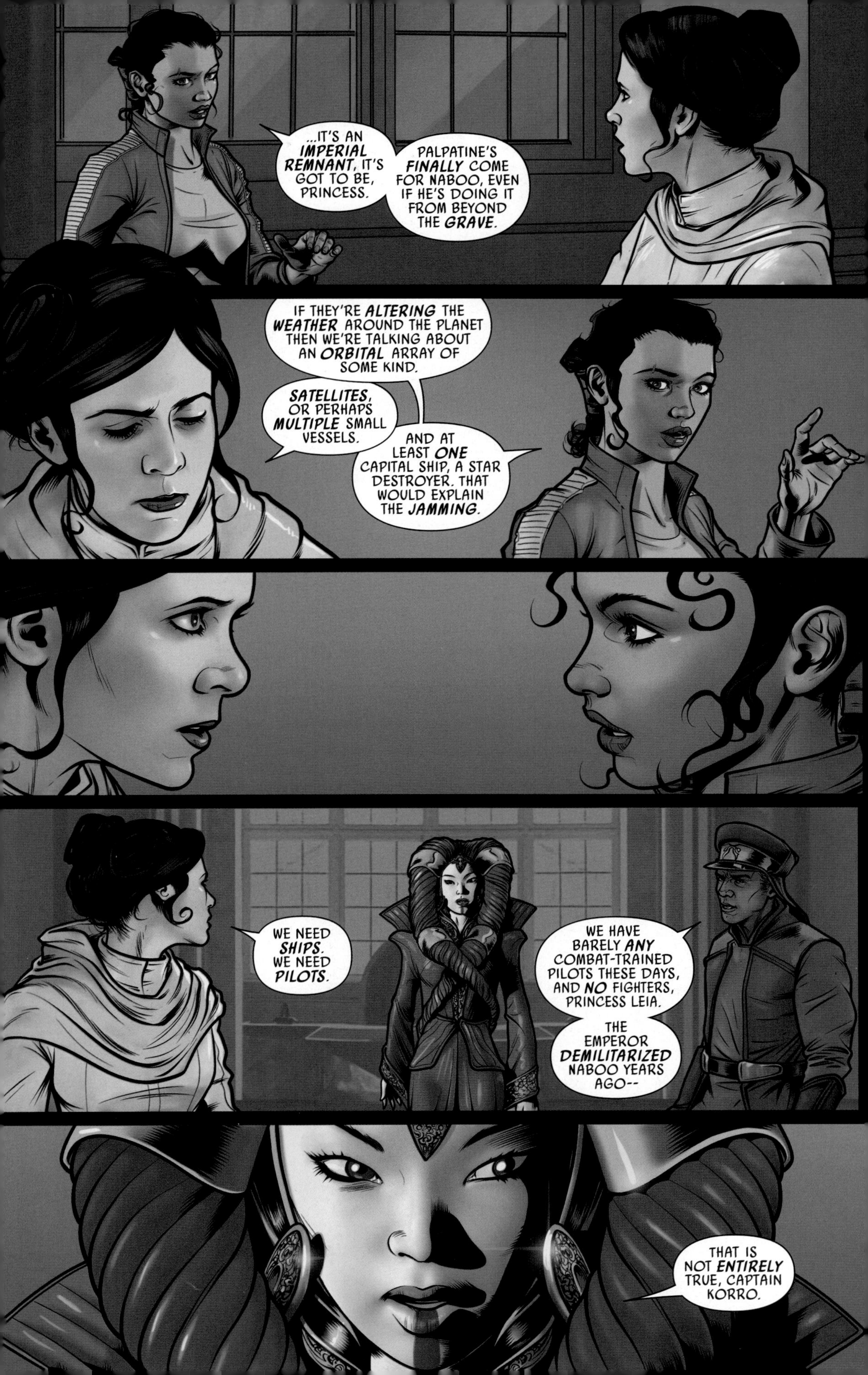
...IT'S AN IMPERIAL REMNANT, IT'S GOT TO BE, PRINCESS.
PALPATINE'S FINALLY COME FOR NABOO, EVEN IF HE'S DOING IT FROM BEYOND THE GRAVE.
IF THEY'RE ALTERING THE WEATHER AROUND THE PLANET THEN WE'RE TALKING ABOUT AN ORBITAL ARRAY OF SOME KIND.
SATELLITES, OR PERHAPS MULTIPLE SMALL VESSELS.
AND AT LEAST ONE CAPITAL SHIP, A STAR DESTROYER. THAT WOULD EXPLAIN THE JAMMING.
WE NEED SHIPS. WE NEED PILOTS.
WE HAVE BARELY ANY COMBAT-TRAINED PILOTS THESE DAYS, AND NO FIGHTERS, PRINCESS LEIA.
THE EMPEROR DEMILITARIZED NABOO YEARS AGO--
THAT IS NOT ENTIRELY TRUE, CAPTAIN KORRO.

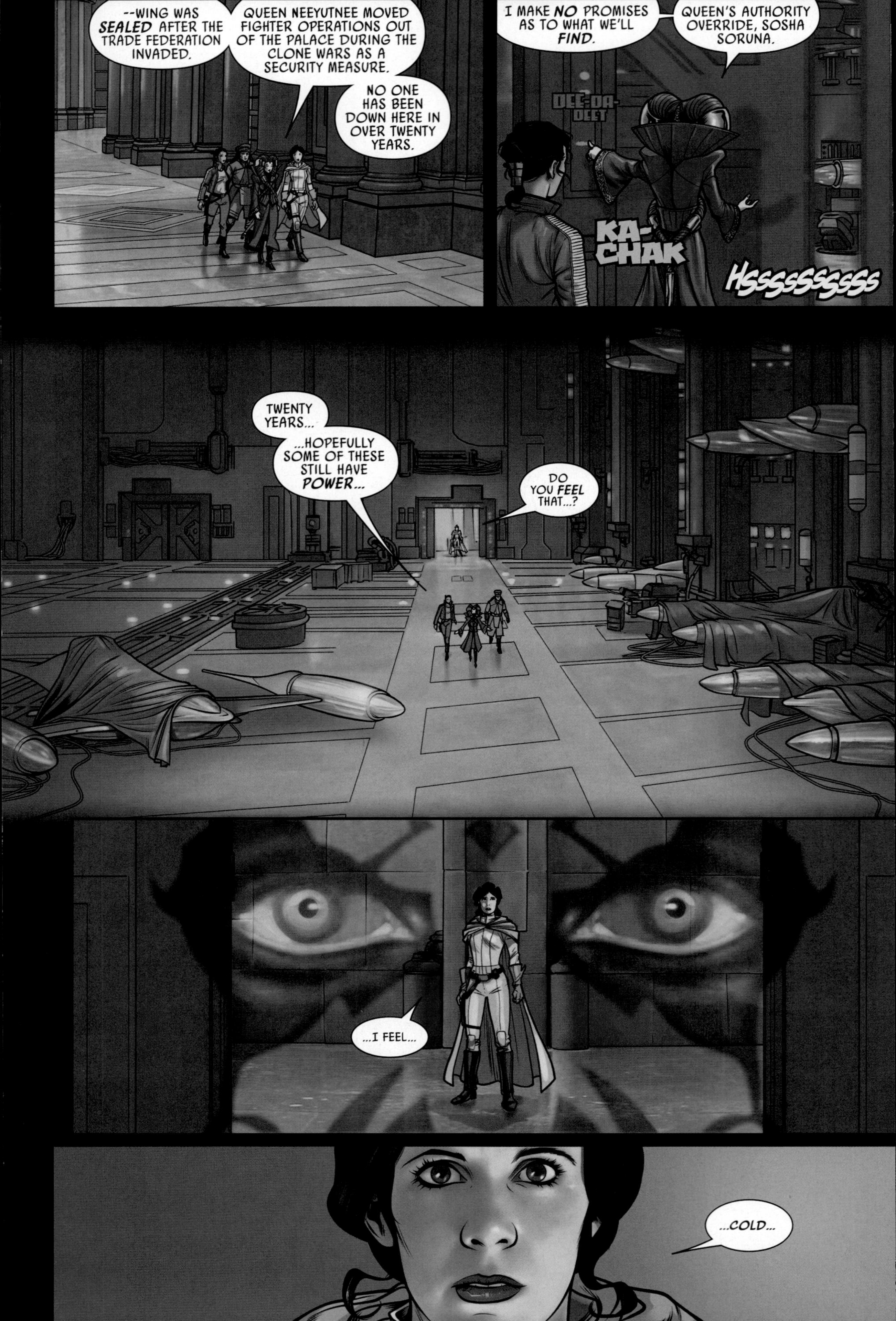
--WING WAS SEALED AFTER THE TRADE FEDERATION INVADED.
QUEEN NEEYUTNEE MOVED FIGHTER OPERATIONS OUT OF THE PALACE DURING THE CLONE WARS AS A SECURITY MEASURE.
NO ONE HAS BEEN DOWN HERE IN OVER TWENTY YEARS.
I MAKE NO PROMISES AS TO WHAT WE'LL FIND.
QUEEN'S AUTHORITY OVERRIDE, SOSHA SORUNA.
DEE-DA-DEET
KA-CHAK
Hssssssssss
TWENTY YEARS...
...HOPEFULLY SOME OF THESE STILL HAVE POWER...
DO YOU FEEL THAT...?
...I FEEL...
...COLD...

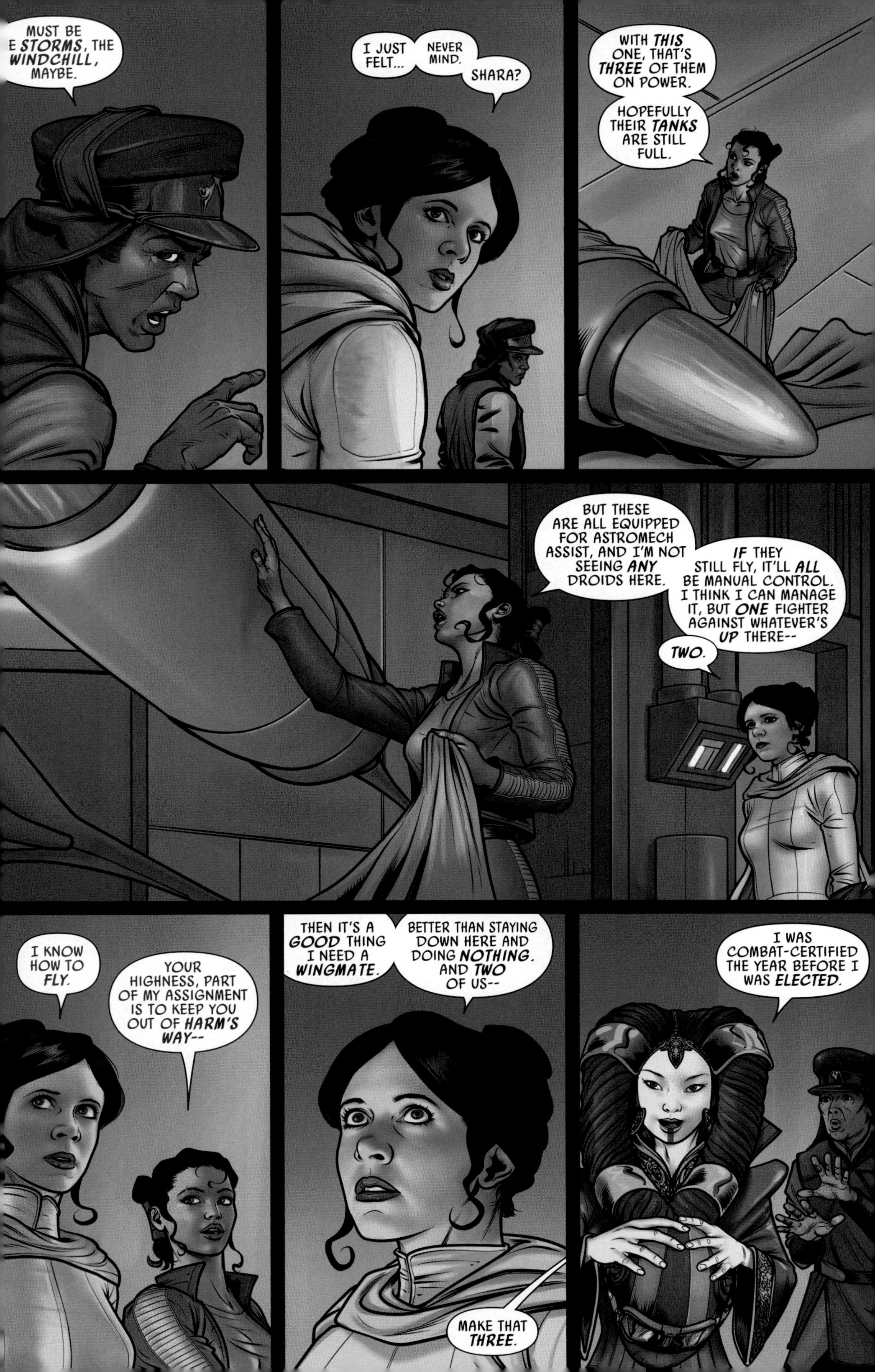
MUST BE E STORMS, THE WINDCHILL, MAYBE.
I JUST FELT...
NEVER MIND.
SHARA?
WITH THIS ONE, THAT'S THREE OF THEM ON POWER.
HOPEFULLY THEIR TANKS ARE STILL FULL.
BUT THESE ARE ALL EQUIPPED FOR ASTROMECH ASSIST, AND I'M NOT SEEING ANY DROIDS HERE.
IF THEY STILL FLY, IT'LL ALL BE MANUAL CONTROL. I THINK I CAN MANAGE IT, BUT ONE FIGHTER AGAINST WHATEVER'S UP THERE--
TWO.
I KNOW HOW TO FLY.
YOUR HIGHNESS, PART OF MY ASSIGNMENT IS TO KEEP YOU OUT OF HARM'S WAY--
THEN IT'S A GOOD THING I NEED A WINGMATE.
BETTER THAN STAYING DOWN HERE AND DOING NOTHING. AND TWO OF US--
MAKE THAT THREE.
I WAS COMBAT-CERTIFIED THE YEAR BEFORE I WAS ELECTED.

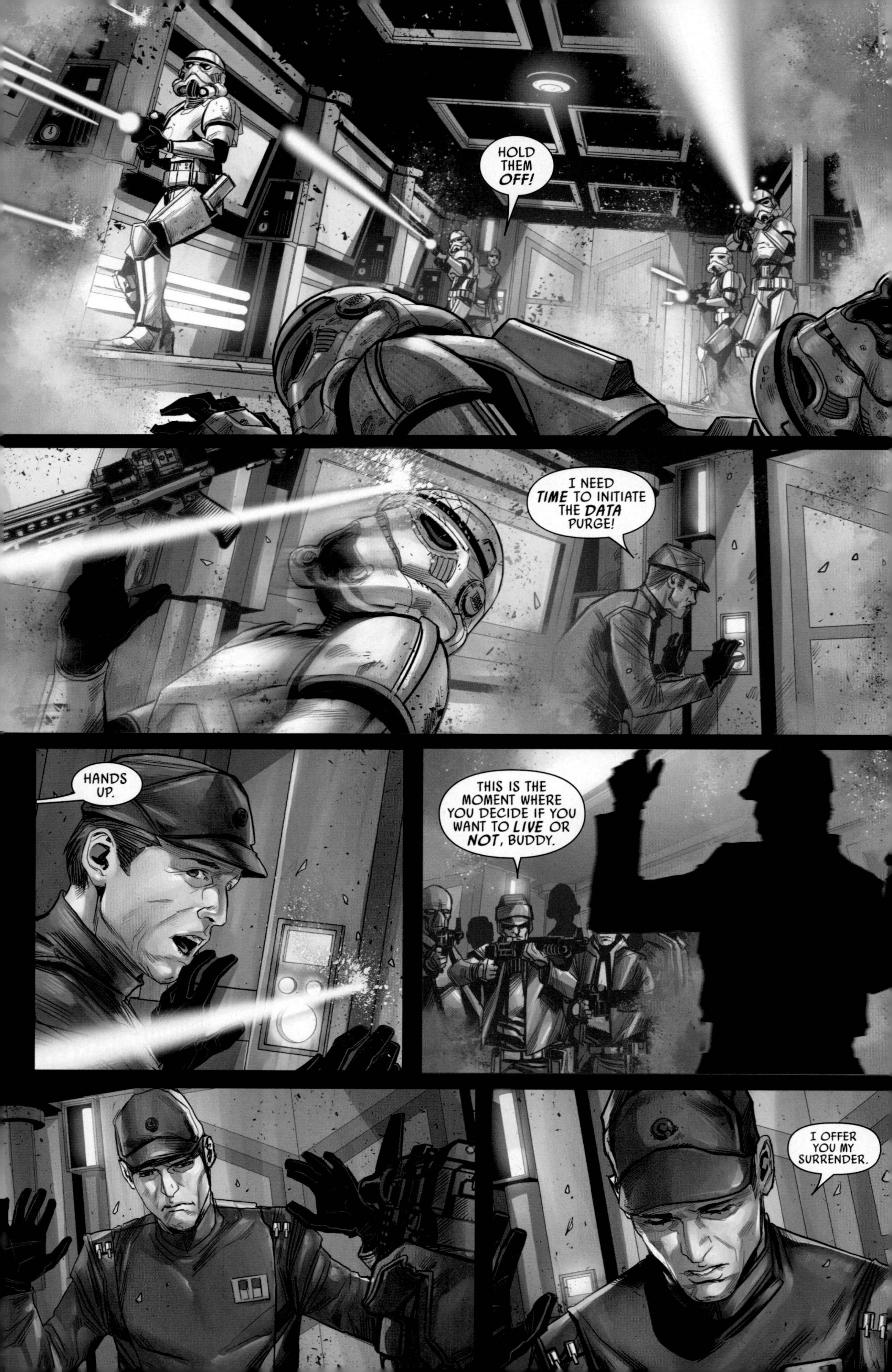

HOLD THEM OFF!
I NEED TIME TO INITIATE THE DATA PURGE!
HANDS UP.
THIS IS THE MOMENT WHERE YOU DECIDE IF YOU WANT TO LIVE OR NOT, BUDDY.
I OFFER YOU MY SURRENDER.

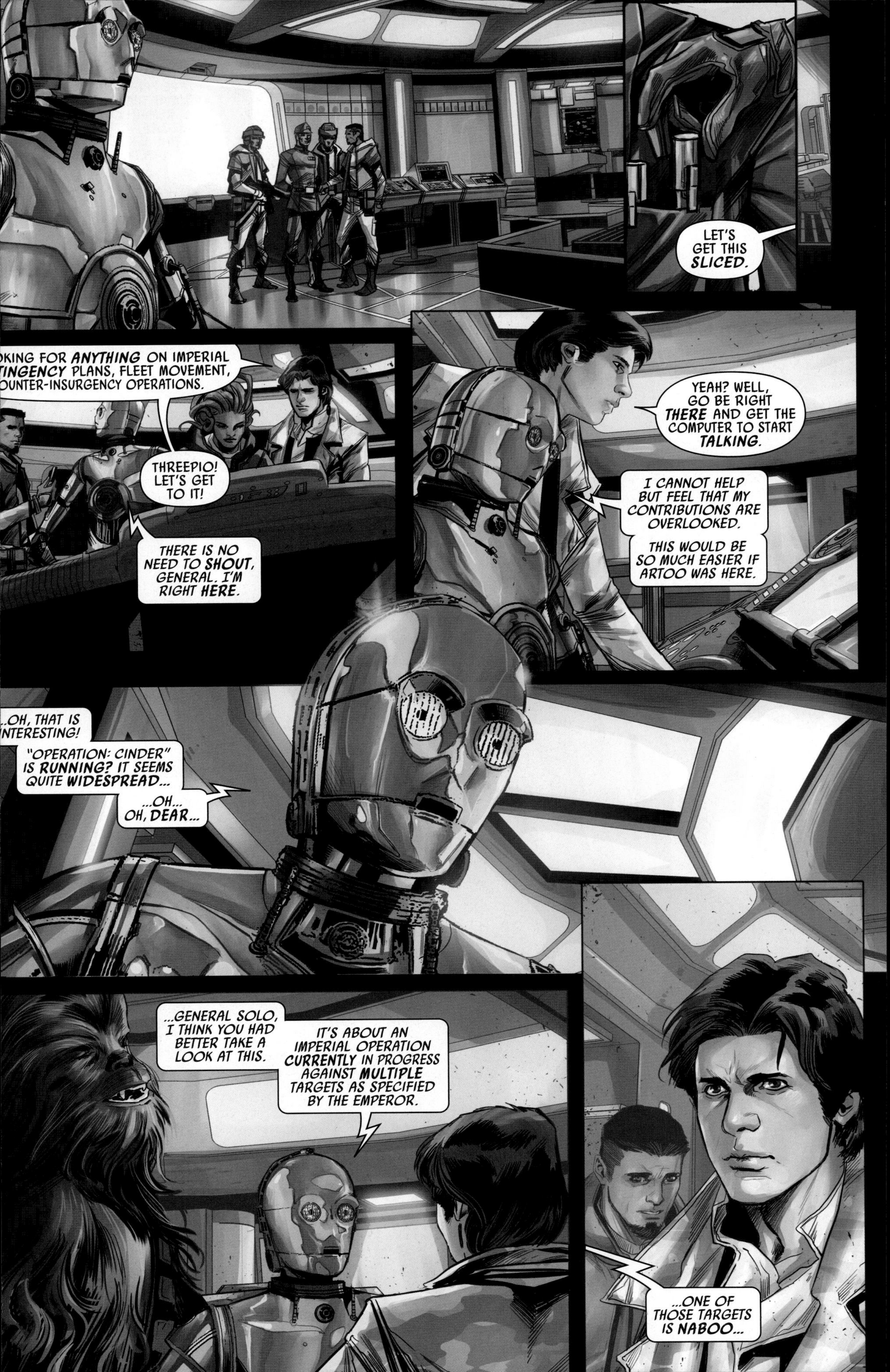
LET'S GET THIS SLICED.
OKING FOR ANYTHING ON IMPERIAL TINGENCY PLANS, FLEET MOVEMENT, OUNTER-INSURGENCY OPERATIONS.
THREEPIO! LET'S GET TO IT!
THERE IS NO NEED TO SHOUT, GENERAL. I'M RIGHT HERE.
YEAH? WELL, GO BE RIGHT THERE AND GET THE COMPUTER TO START TALKING.
I CANNOT HELP BUT FEEL THAT MY CONTRIBUTIONS ARE OVERLOOKED.
THIS WOULD BE SO MUCH EASIER IF ARTOO WAS HERE.
...OH, THAT IS INTERESTING!
"OPERATION: CINDER" IS RUNNING? IT SEEMS QUITE WIDESPREAD...
...OH... OH, DEAR...
...GENERAL SOLO, I THINK YOU HAD BETTER TAKE A LOOK AT THIS.
IT'S ABOUT AN IMPERIAL OPERATION CURRENTLY IN PROGRESS AGAINST MULTIPLE TARGETS AS SPECIFIED BY THE EMPEROR.
...ONE OF THOSE TARGETS IS NABOO...

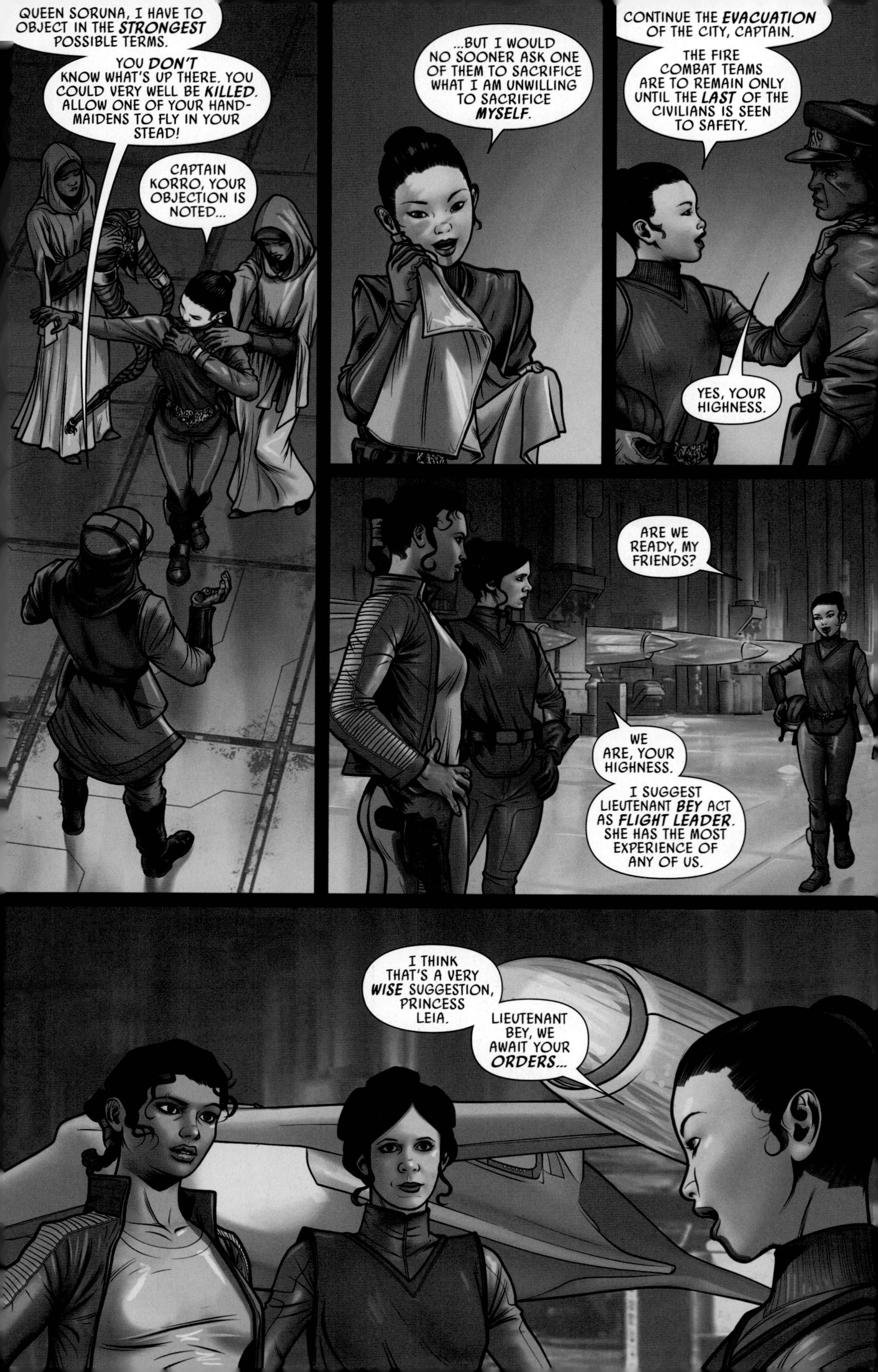
QUEEN SORUNA, I HAVE TO OBJECT IN THE STRONGEST POSSIBLE TERMS.
YOU DON'T KNOW WHAT'S UP THERE. YOU COULD VERY WELL BE KILLED. ALLOW ONE OF YOUR HAND-MAIDENS TO FLY IN YOUR STEAD!
CAPTAIN KORRO, YOUR OBJECTION IS NOTED...
...BUT I WOULD NO SOONER ASK ONE OF THEM TO SACRIFICE WHAT I AM UNWILLING TO SACRIFICE MYSELF.
CONTINUE THE EVACUATION OF THE CITY, CAPTAIN.
THE FIRE COMBAT TEAMS ARE TO REMAIN ONLY UNTIL THE LAST OF THE CIVILIANS IS SEEN TO SAFETY.
YES, YOUR HIGHNESS.
ARE WE READY, MY FRIENDS?
WE ARE, YOUR HIGHNESS.
I SUGGEST LIEUTENANT BEY ACT AS FLIGHT LEADER. SHE HAS THE MOST EXPERIENCE OF ANY OF US.
I THINK THAT'S A VERY WISE SUGGESTION, PRINCESS LEIA.
LIEUTENANT BEY, WE AWAIT YOUR ORDERS...

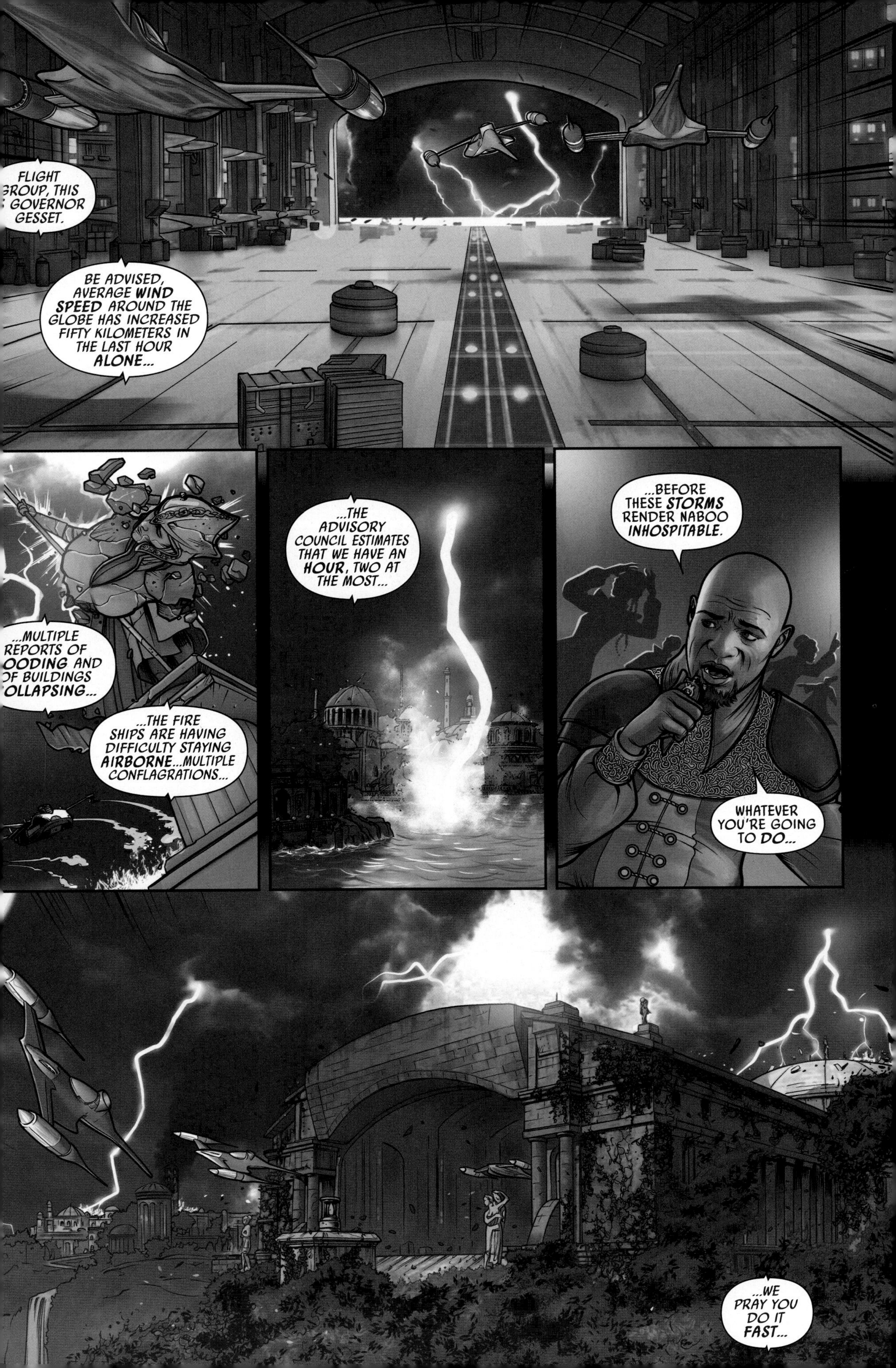
FLIGHT GROUP, THIS S GOVERNOR GESSET.
BE ADVISED, AVERAGE WIND SPEED AROUND THE GLOBE HAS INCREASED FIFTY KILOMETERS IN THE LAST HOUR ALONE...
...MULTIPLE REPORTS OF OODING AND OF BUILDINGS OLLAPSING...
...THE FIRE SHIPS ARE HAVING DIFFICULTY STAYING AIRBORNE...MULTIPLE CONFLAGRATIONS...
...THE ADVISORY COUNCIL ESTIMATES THAT WE HAVE AN HOUR, TWO AT THE MOST...
...BEFORE THESE STORMS RENDER NABOO INHOSPITABLE.
WHATEVER YOU'RE GOING TO DO...
...WE PRAY YOU DO IT FAST...

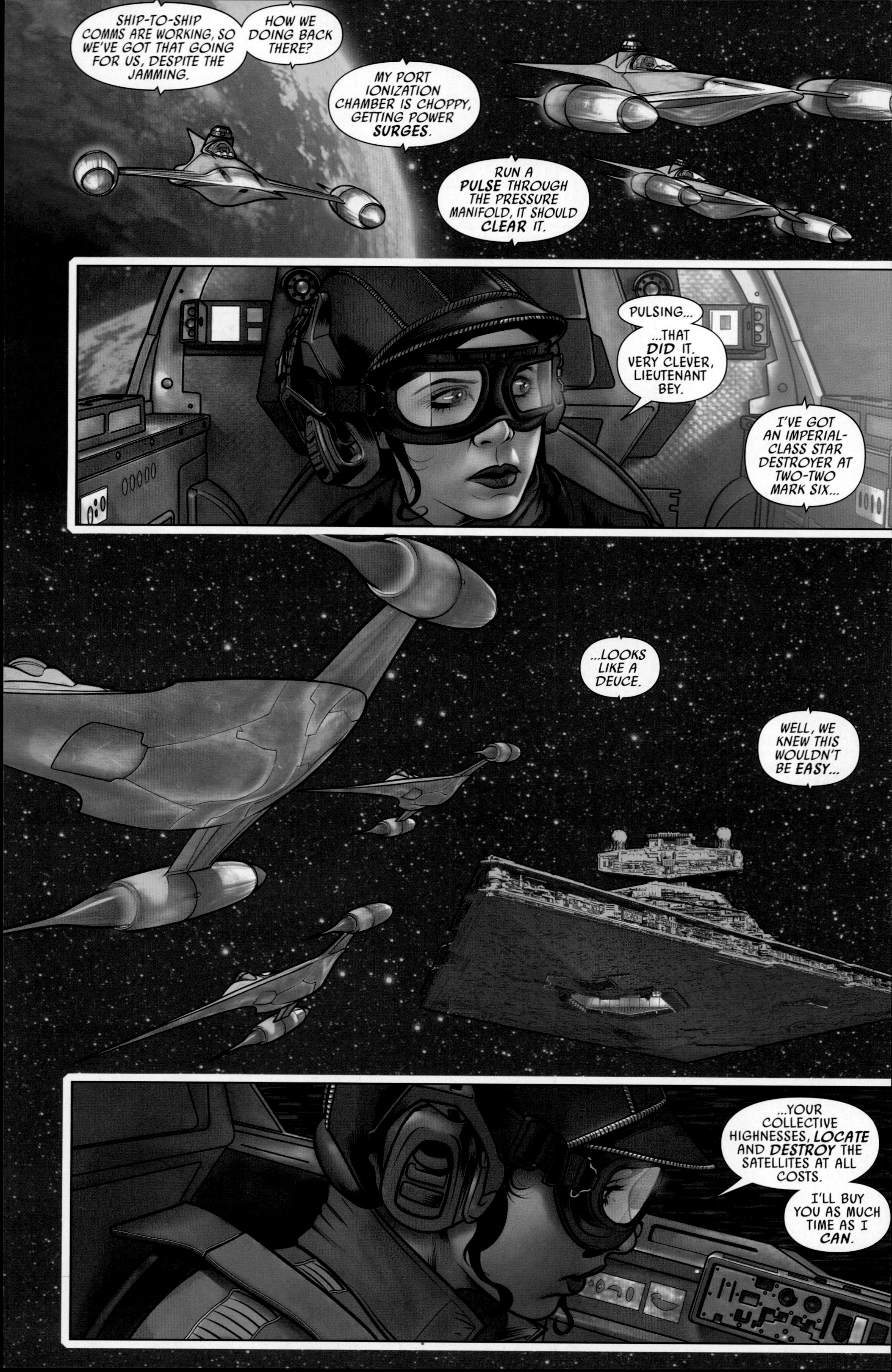
SHIP-TO-SHIP COMMS ARE WORKING, SO WE'VE GOT THAT GOING FOR US, DESPITE THE JAMMING.
HOW WE DOING BACK THERE?
MY PORT IONIZATION CHAMBER IS CHOPPY, GETTING POWER SURGES.
RUN A PULSE THROUGH THE PRESSURE MANIFOLD, IT SHOULD CLEAR IT.
PULSING...
...THAT DID IT. VERY CLEVER, LIEUTENANT BEY.
I'VE GOT AN IMPERIAL-CLASS STAR DESTROYER AT TWO-TWO MARK SIX...
...LOOKS LIKE A DEUCE.
WELL, WE KNEW THIS WOULDN'T BE EASY...
...YOUR COLLECTIVE HIGHNESSES, LOCATE AND DESTROY THE SATELLITES AT ALL COSTS.
I'LL BUY YOU AS MUCH TIME AS I CAN.

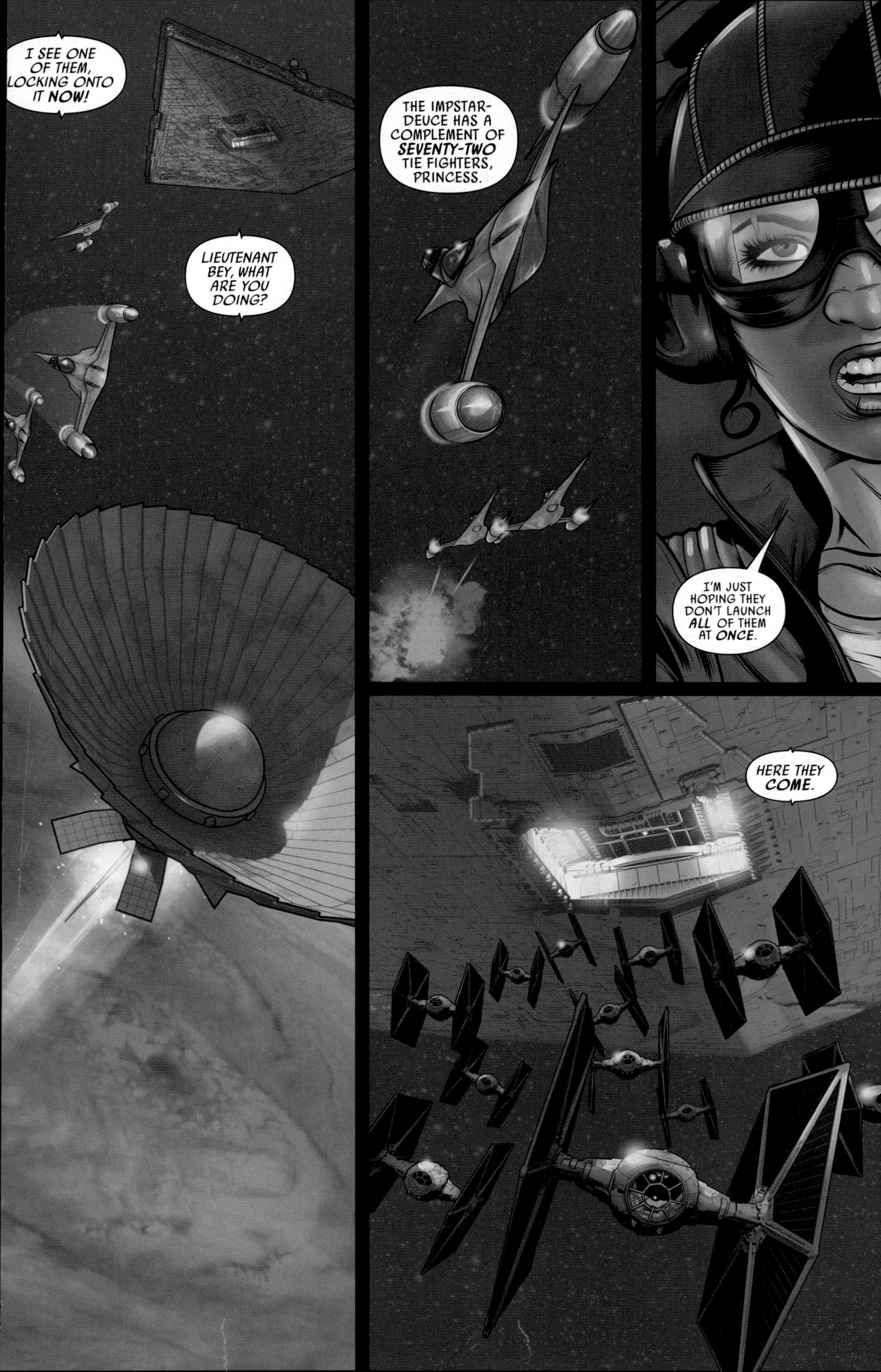
I SEE ONE OF THEM, LOCKING ONTO IT NOW!
LIEUTENANT BEY, WHAT ARE YOU DOING?
THE IMPSTAR-DEUCE HAS A COMPLEMENT OF SEVENTY-TWO TIE FIGHTERS, PRINCESS.
I'M JUST HOPING THEY DON'T LAUNCH ALL OF THEM AT ONCE.
HERE THEY COME.

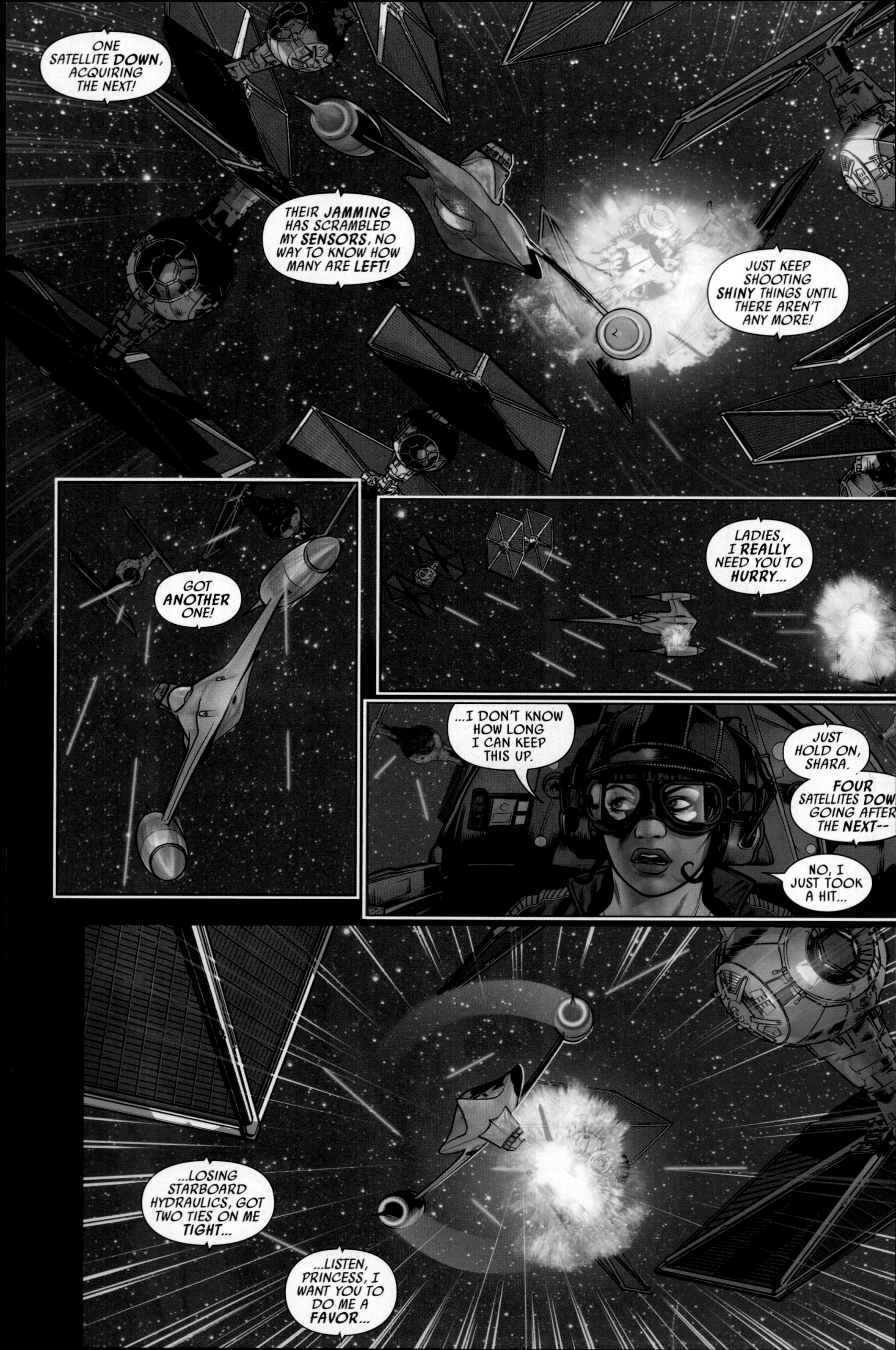
ONE SATELLITE DOWN, ACQUIRING THE NEXT!
THEIR JAMMING HAS SCRAMBLED MY SENSORS, NO WAY TO KNOW HOW MANY ARE LEFT!
JUST KEEP SHOOTING SHINY THINGS UNTIL THERE AREN'T ANY MORE!
GOT ANOTHER ONE!
LADIES, I REALLY NEED YOU TO HURRY...
...I DON'T KNOW HOW LONG I CAN KEEP THIS UP.
JUST HOLD ON, SHARA.
FOUR SATELLITES DOWN GOING AFTER THE NEXT--
NO, I JUST TOOK A HIT...
...LOSING STARBOARD HYDRAULICS, GOT TWO TIES ON ME TIGHT...
...LISTEN, PRINCESS, I WANT YOU TO DO ME A FAVOR...

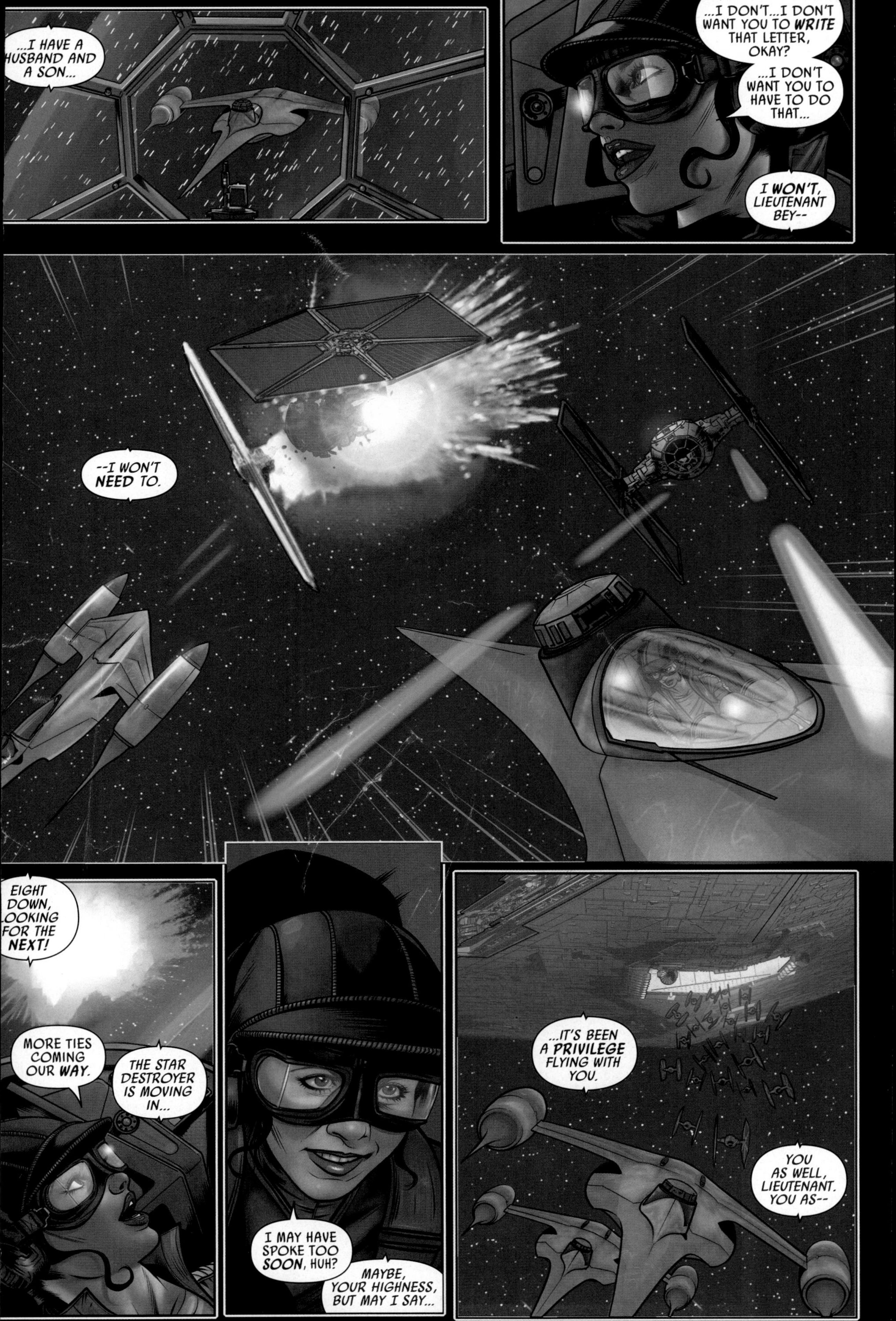
...I HAVE A HUSBAND AND A SON...
...I DON'T...I DON'T WANT YOU TO WRITE THAT LETTER, OKAY?
...I DON'T WANT YOU TO HAVE TO DO THAT...
I WON'T, LIEUTENANT BEY--
--I WON'T NEED TO.
EIGHT DOWN, LOOKING FOR THE NEXT!
MORE TIES COMING OUR WAY.
THE STAR DESTROYER IS MOVING IN...
I MAY HAVE SPOKE TOO SOON, HUH?
MAYBE, YOUR HIGHNESS, BUT MAY I SAY...
...IT'S BEEN A PRIVILEGE FLYING WITH YOU.
YOU AS WELL, LIEUTENANT. YOU AS--

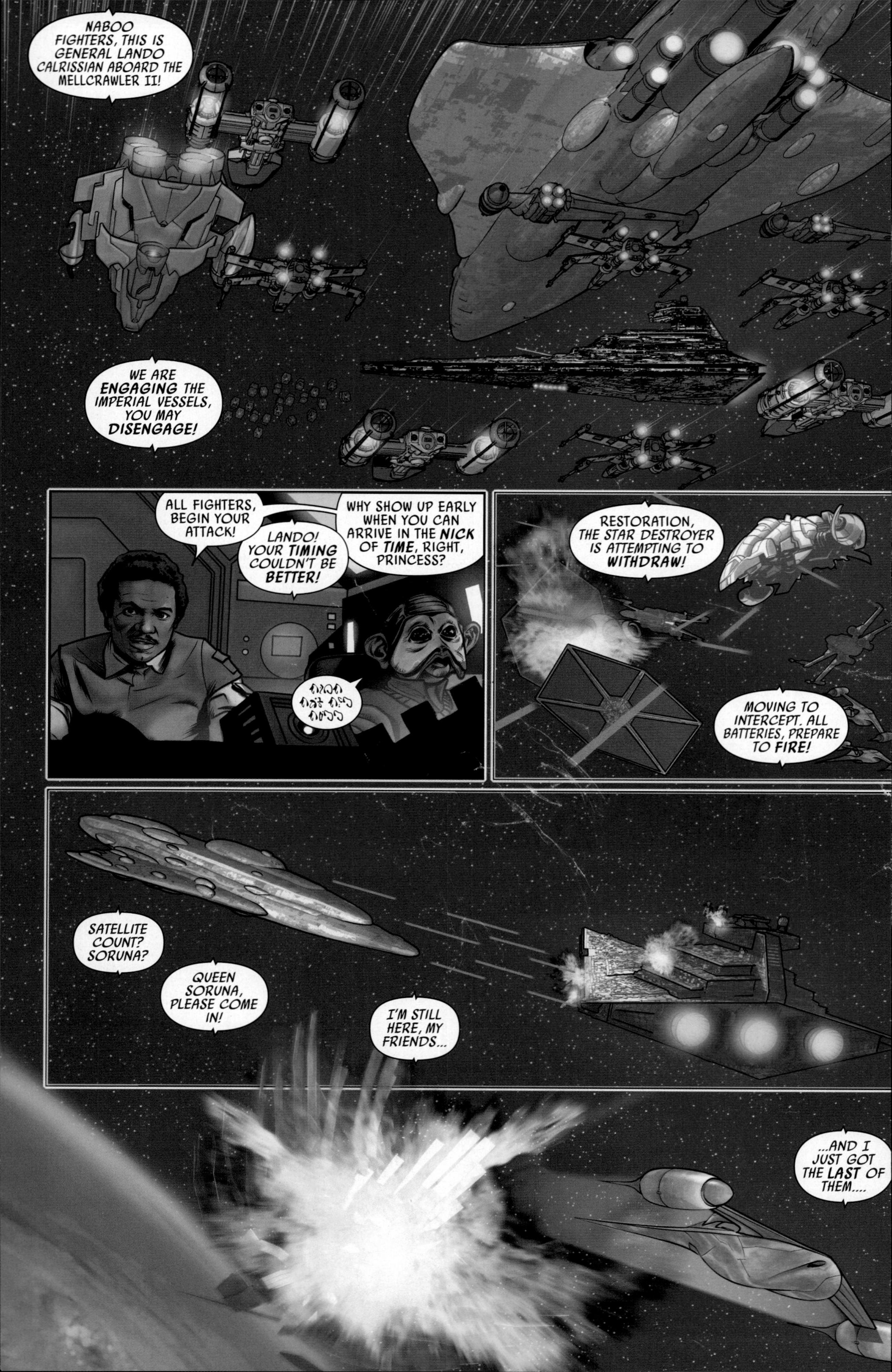
NABOO FIGHTERS, THIS IS GENERAL LANDO CALRISSIAN ABOARD THE MELLCRAWLER II!
WE ARE ENGAGING THE IMPERIAL VESSELS, YOU MAY DISENGAGE!
ALL FIGHTERS, BEGIN YOUR ATTACK!
LANDO! YOUR TIMING COULDN'T BE BETTER!
WHY SHOW UP EARLY WHEN YOU CAN ARRIVE IN THE NICK OF TIME, RIGHT, PRINCESS?
RESTORATION, THE STAR DESTROYER IS ATTEMPTING TO WITHDRAW!
MOVING TO INTERCEPT. ALL BATTERIES, PREPARE TO FIRE!
SATELLITE COUNT? SORUNA?
QUEEN SORUNA, PLEASE COME IN!
I'M STILL HERE, MY FRIENDS...
...AND I JUST GOT THE LAST OF THEM....

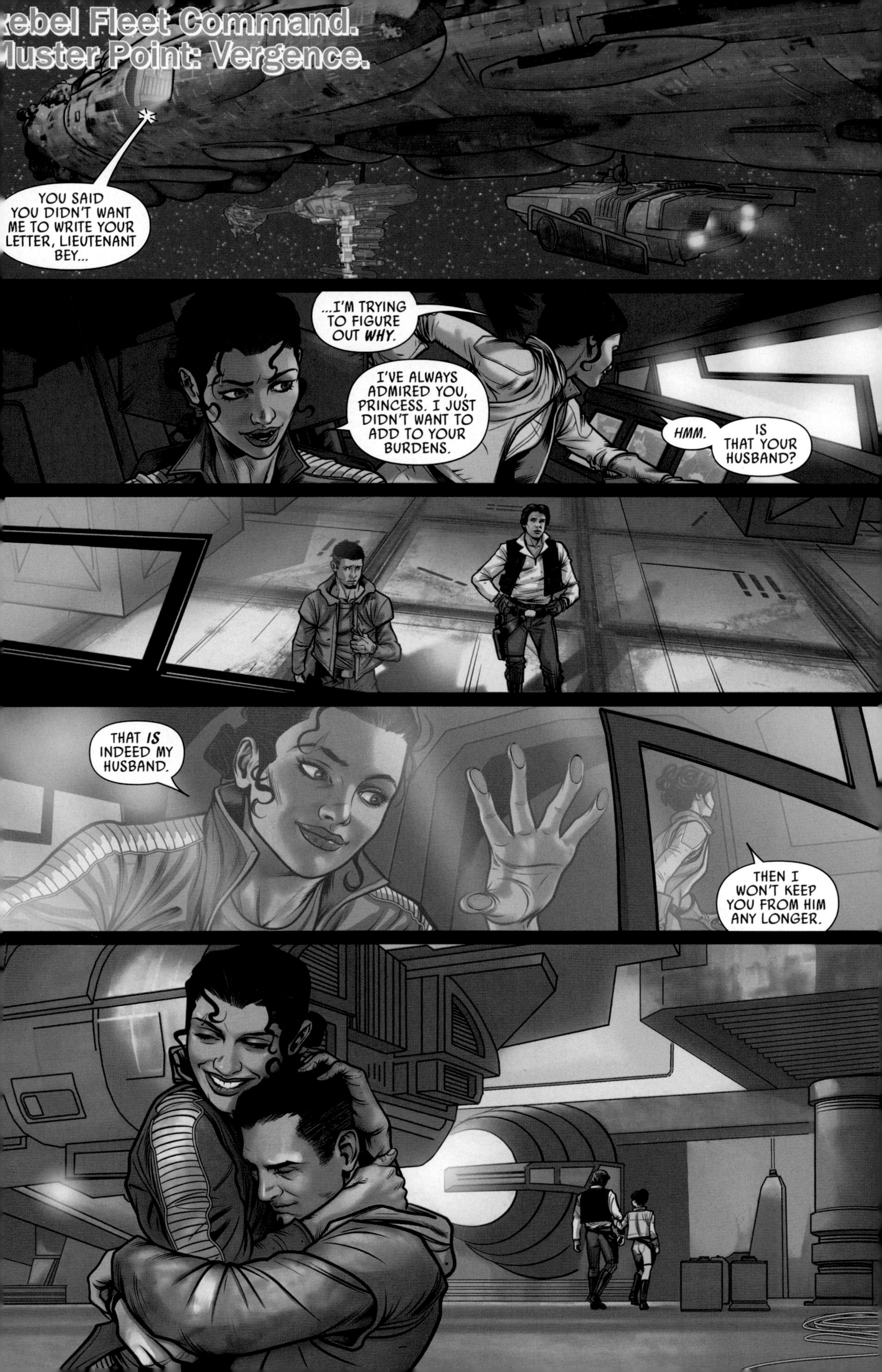
Rebel Fleet Command.
Muster Point: Vergence.
YOU SAID YOU DIDN'T WANT ME TO WRITE YOUR LETTER, LIEUTENANT BEY...
...I'M TRYING TO FIGURE OUT WHY.
I'VE ALWAYS ADMIRED YOU, PRINCESS. I JUST DIDN'T WANT TO ADD TO YOUR BURDENS.
HMM.
IS THAT YOUR HUSBAND?
THAT IS INDEED MY HUSBAND.
THEN I WON'T KEEP YOU FROM HIM ANY LONGER.

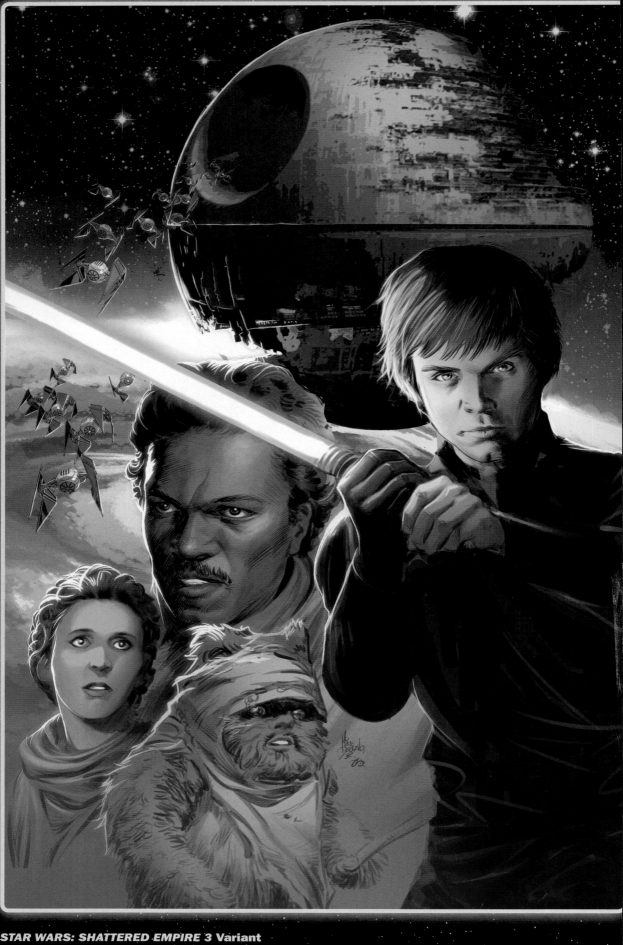

STAR WARS: SHATTERED EMPIRE 3 Variant
by MIKE DEODATO

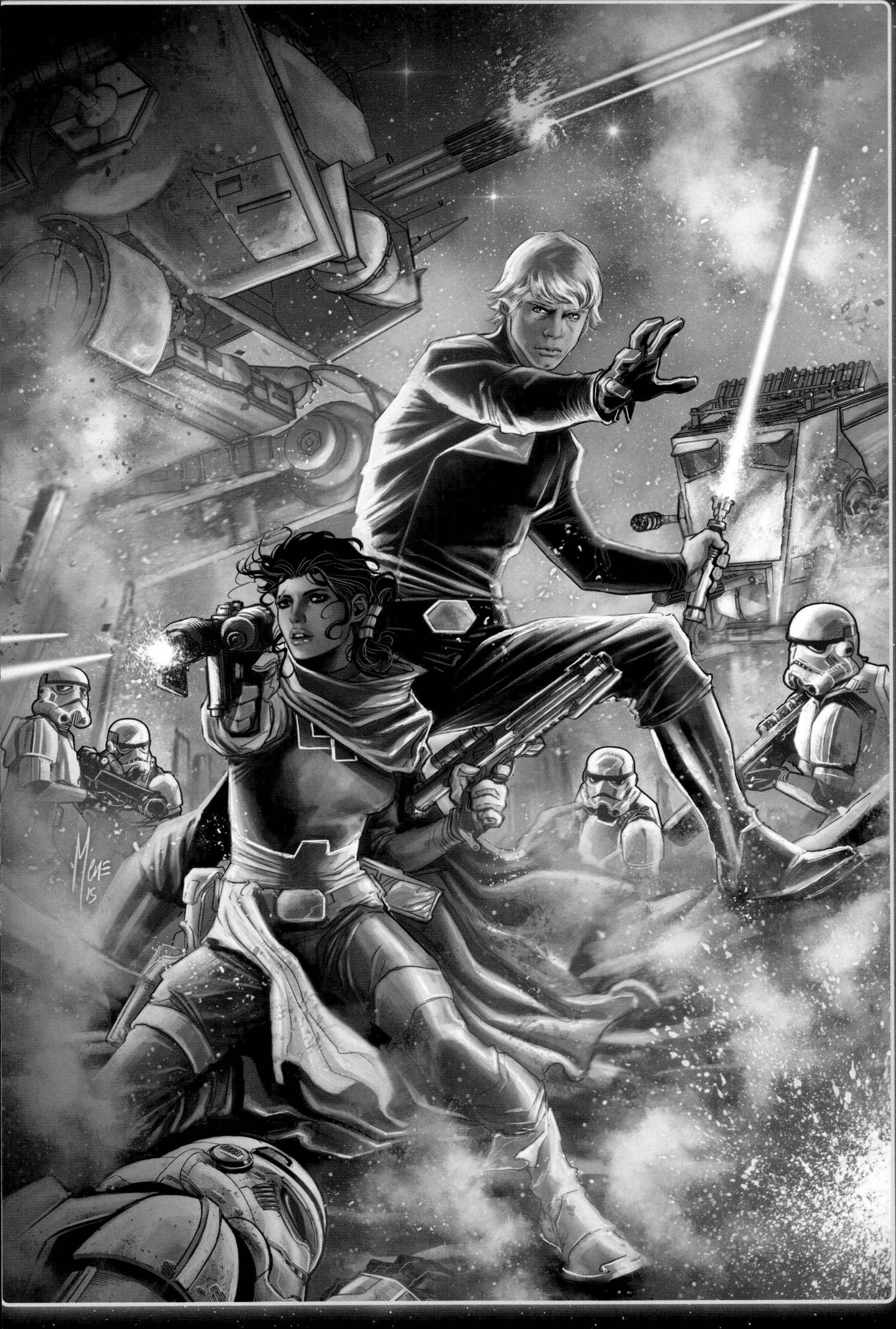

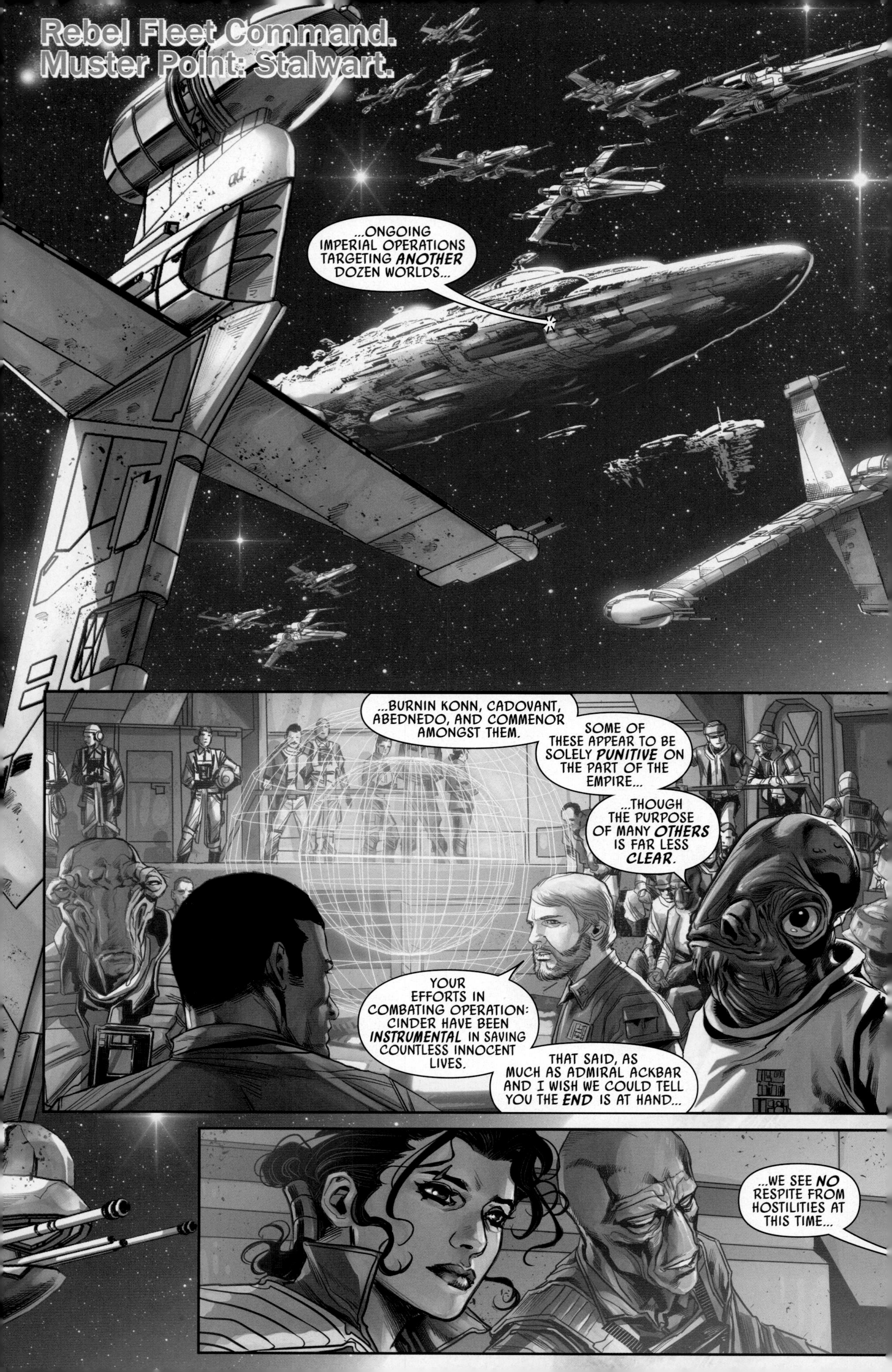
Rebel Fleet Command.
Muster Point: Stalwart.
...ONGOING IMPERIAL OPERATIONS TARGETING ANOTHER DOZEN WORLDS...
...BURNIN KONN, CADOVANT, ABEDNEDO, AND COMMENOR AMONGST THEM.
SOME OF THESE APPEAR TO BE SOLELY PUNITIVE ON THE PART OF THE EMPIRE...
...THOUGH THE PURPOSE OF MANY OTHERS IS FAR LESS CLEAR.
YOUR EFFORTS IN COMBATING OPERATION: CINDER HAVE BEEN INSTRUMENTAL IN SAVING COUNTLESS INNOCENT LIVES.
THAT SAID, AS MUCH AS ADMIRAL ACKBAR AND I WISH WE COULD TELL YOU THE END IS AT HAND...
...WE SEE NO RESPITE FROM HOSTILITIES AT THIS TIME...

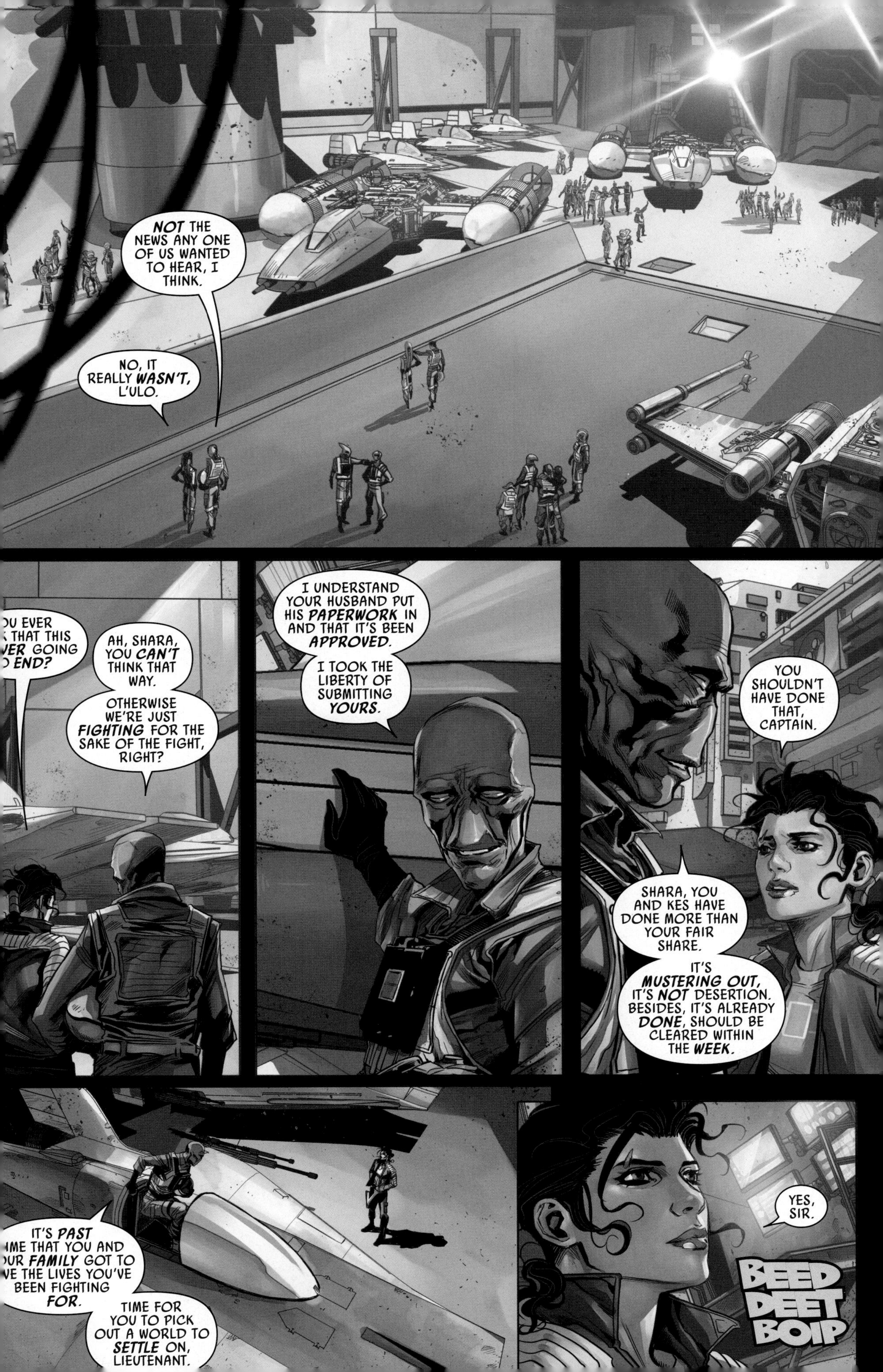
NOT THE NEWS ANY ONE OF US WANTED TO HEAR, I THINK.
NO, IT REALLY WASN'T, L'ULO.
OU EVER THAT THIS VER GOING END?
AH, SHARA, YOU CAN'T THINK THAT WAY.
OTHERWISE WE'RE JUST FIGHTING FOR THE SAKE OF THE FIGHT, RIGHT?
I UNDERSTAND YOUR HUSBAND PUT HIS PAPERWORK IN AND THAT IT'S BEEN APPROVED.
I TOOK THE LIBERTY OF SUBMITTING YOURS.
YOU SHOULDN'T HAVE DONE THAT, CAPTAIN.
SHARA, YOU AND KES HAVE DONE MORE THAN YOUR FAIR SHARE.
IT'S MUSTERING OUT, IT'S NOT DESERTION. BESIDES, IT'S ALREADY DONE, SHOULD BE CLEARED WITHIN THE WEEK.
IT'S PAST IME THAT YOU AND UR FAMILY GOT TO VE THE LIVES YOU'VE BEEN FIGHTING FOR.
TIME FOR YOU TO PICK OUT A WORLD TO SETTLE ON, LIEUTENANT.
YES, SIR.
BEED DEET BOIP

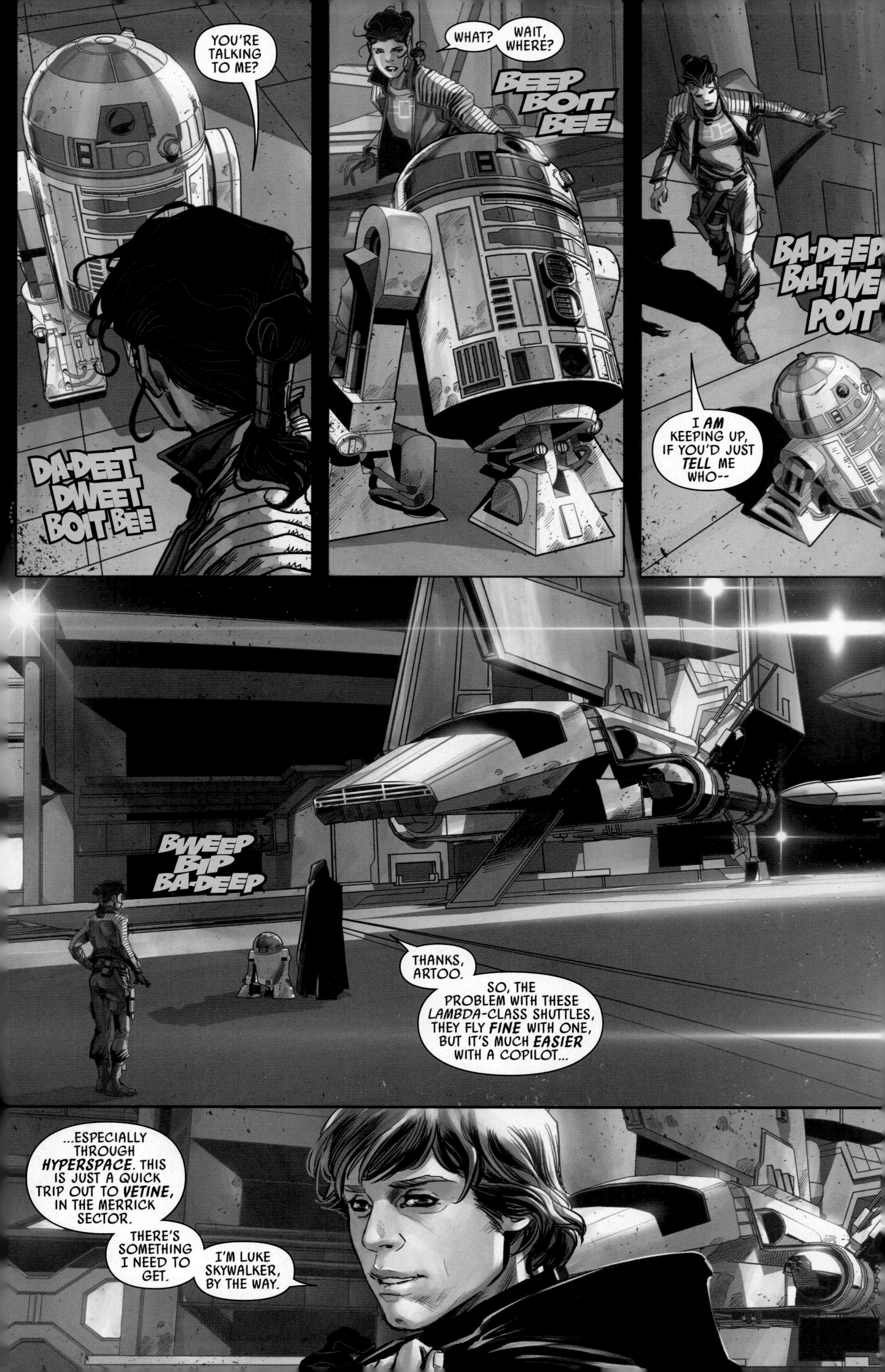
YOU'RE TALKING TO ME?
DA-DEET DWEET BOIT BEE
WHAT?
WAIT, WHERE?
BEEP BOIT BEE
BA-DEEP BA-TWE POIT
I AM KEEPING UP, IF YOU'D JUST TELL ME WHO--
BWEEP BIP BA-DEEP
THANKS, ARTOO.
SO, THE PROBLEM WITH THESE LAMBDA-CLASS SHUTTLES, THEY FLY FINE WITH ONE, BUT IT'S MUCH EASIER WITH A COPILOT...
...ESPECIALLY THROUGH HYPERSPACE. THIS IS JUST A QUICK TRIP OUT TO VETINE, IN THE MERRICK SECTOR.
THERE'S SOMETHING I NEED TO GET.
I'M LUKE SKYWALKER, BY THE WAY.

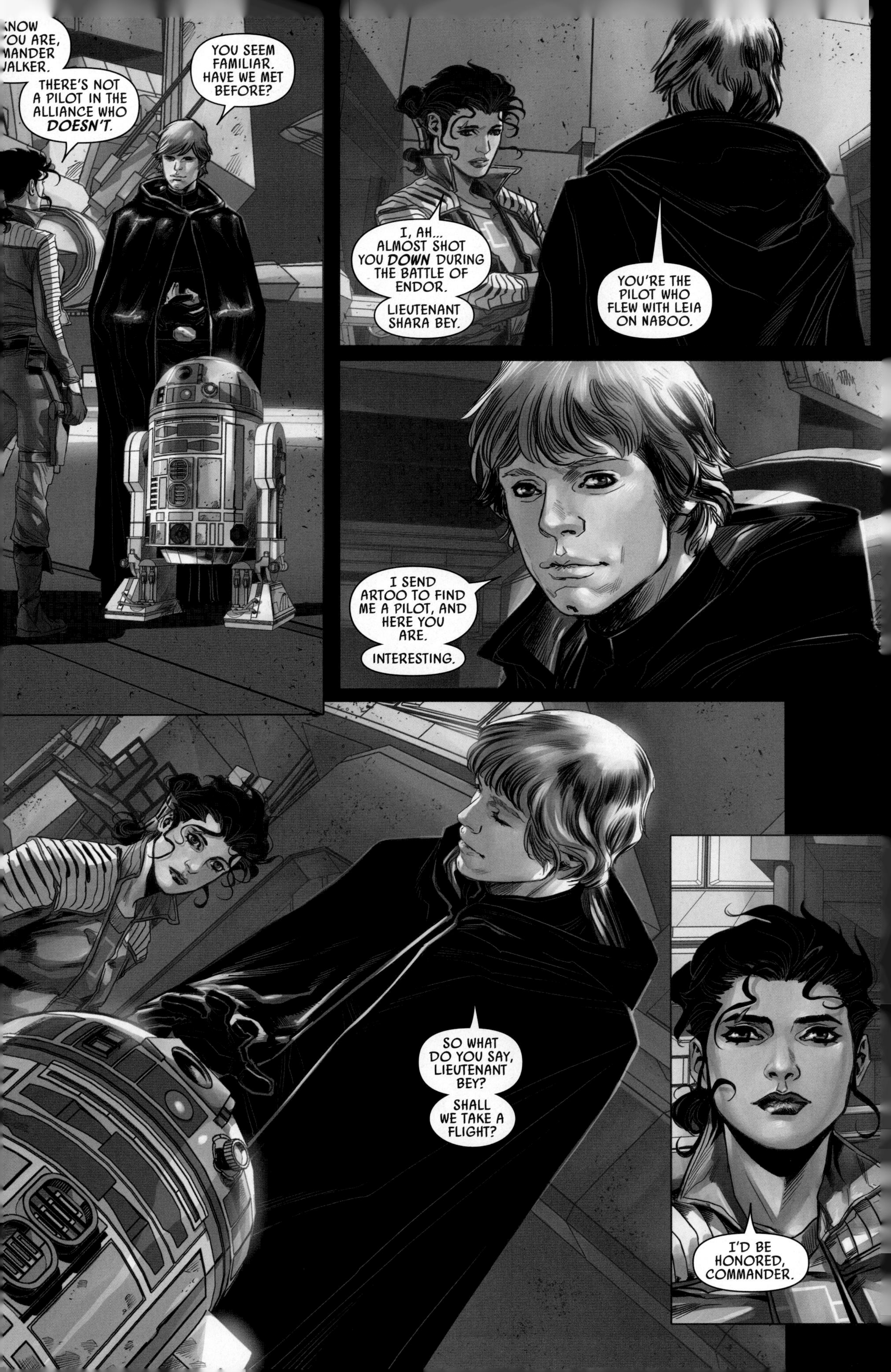
KNOW YOU ARE, MANDER WALKER.
THERE'S NOT A PILOT IN THE ALLIANCE WHO DOESN'T.
YOU SEEM FAMILIAR. HAVE WE MET BEFORE?
I, AH... ALMOST SHOT YOU DOWN DURING THE BATTLE OF ENDOR.
LIEUTENANT SHARA BEY.
YOU'RE THE PILOT WHO FLEW WITH LEIA ON NABOO.
I SEND ARTOO TO FIND ME A PILOT, AND HERE YOU ARE.
INTERESTING.
SO WHAT DO YOU SAY, LIEUTENANT BEY?
SHALL WE TAKE A FLIGHT?
I'D BE HONORED, COMMANDER.

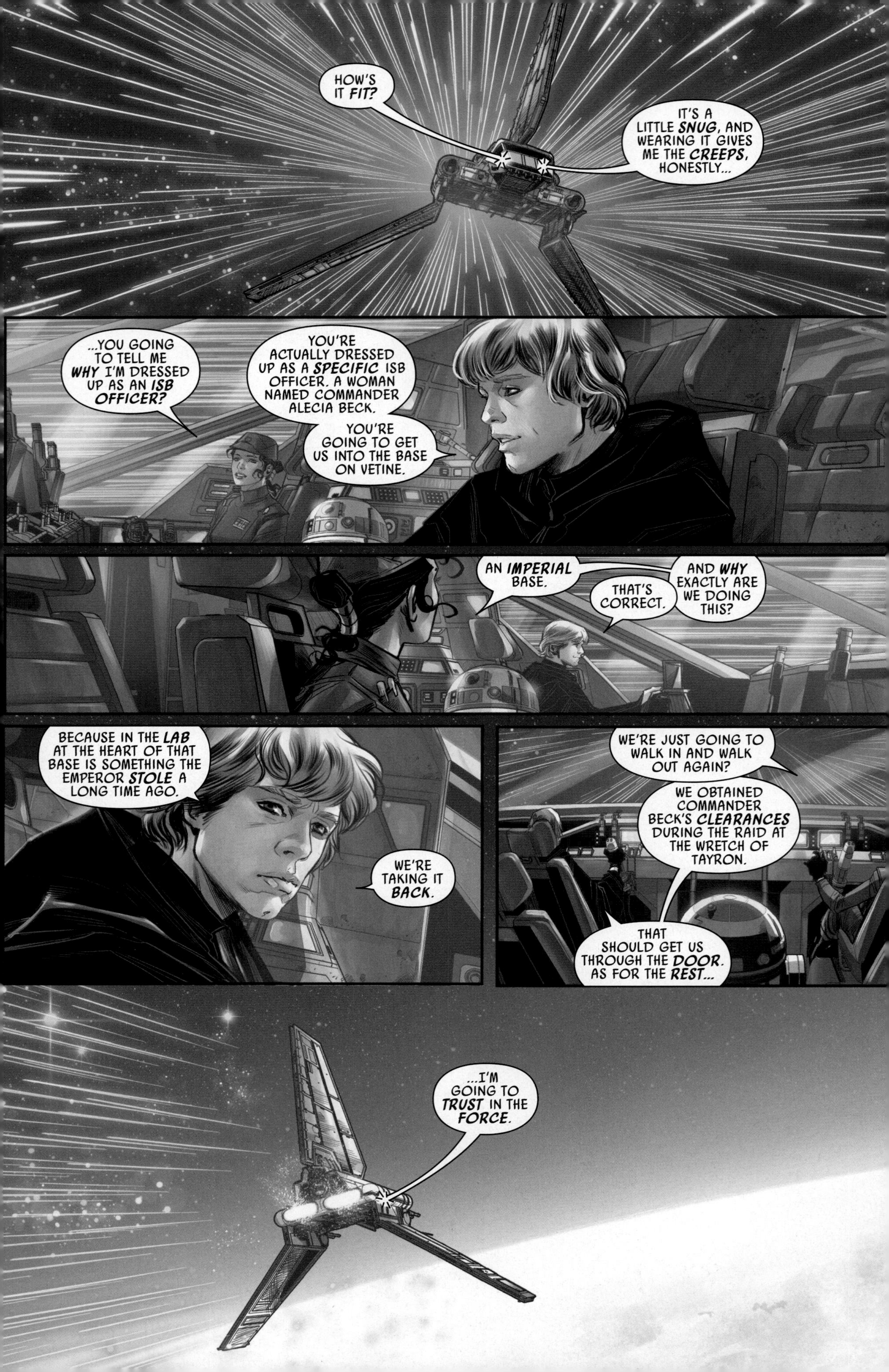
HOW'S IT *FIT?*
IT'S A LITTLE *SNUG*, AND WEARING IT GIVES ME THE *CREEPS*, HONESTLY...
...YOU GOING TO TELL ME *WHY* I'M DRESSED UP AS AN *ISB OFFICER?*
YOU'RE ACTUALLY DRESSED UP AS A *SPECIFIC* ISB OFFICER. A WOMAN NAMED COMMANDER ALECIA BECK.
YOU'RE GOING TO GET US INTO THE BASE ON VETINE.
AN *IMPERIAL* BASE.
THAT'S CORRECT.
AND *WHY* EXACTLY ARE WE DOING THIS?
BECAUSE IN THE *LAB* AT THE HEART OF THAT BASE IS SOMETHING THE EMPEROR *STOLE* A LONG TIME AGO.
WE'RE TAKING IT *BACK*.
WE'RE JUST GOING TO WALK IN AND WALK OUT AGAIN?
WE OBTAINED COMMANDER BECK'S *CLEARANCES* DURING THE RAID AT THE WRETCH OF TAYRON.
THAT SHOULD GET US THROUGH THE *DOOR*. AS FOR THE *REST*...
...I'M GOING TO *TRUST* IN THE *FORCE*.

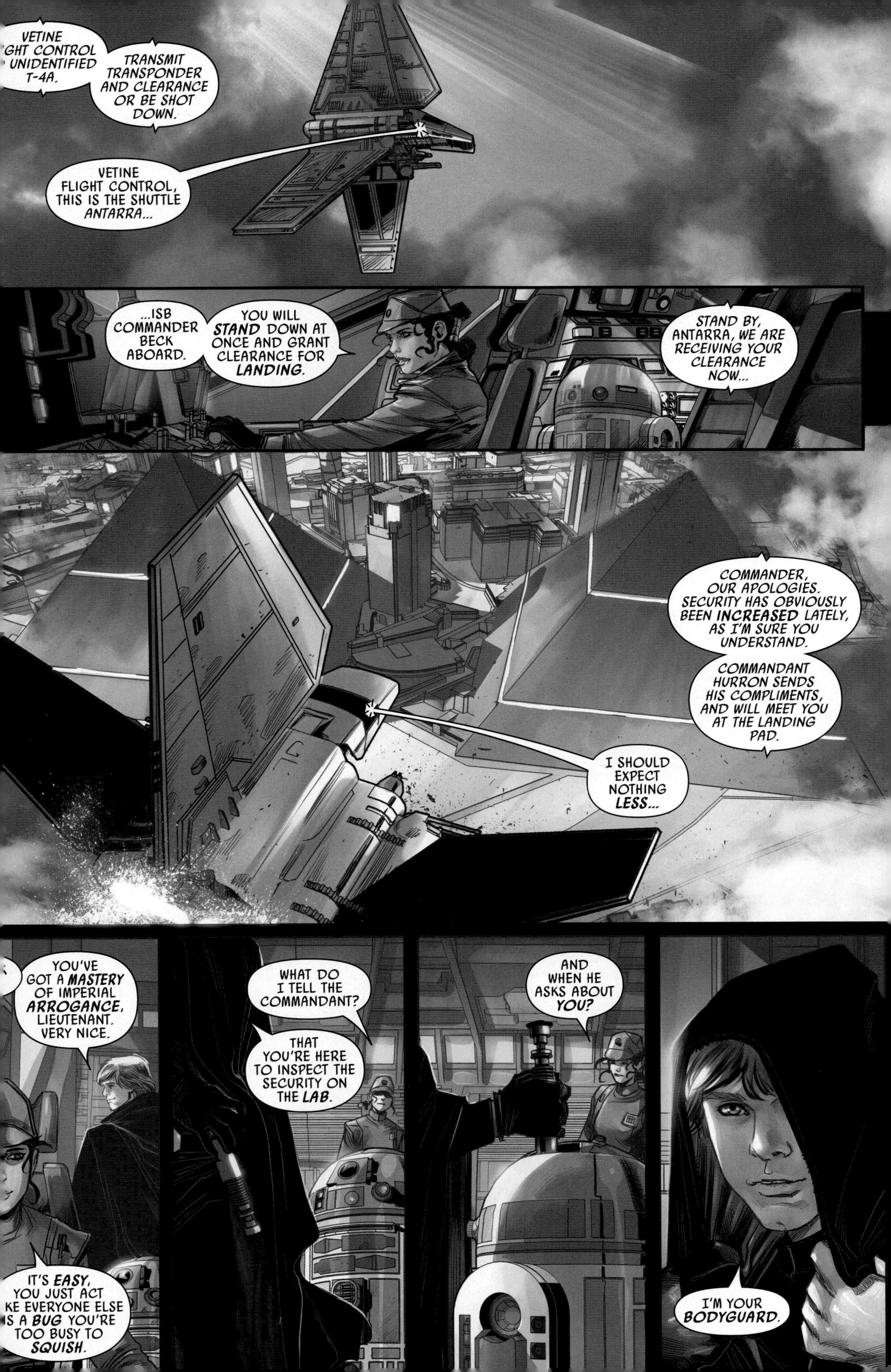
VETINE
GHT CONTROL
UNIDENTIFIED
T-4A.
TRANSMIT TRANSPONDER AND CLEARANCE OR BE SHOT DOWN.
VETINE FLIGHT CONTROL, THIS IS THE SHUTTLE ANTARRA...
...ISB COMMANDER BECK ABOARD.
YOU WILL STAND DOWN AT ONCE AND GRANT CLEARANCE FOR LANDING.
STAND BY, ANTARRA, WE ARE RECEIVING YOUR CLEARANCE NOW...
COMMANDER, OUR APOLOGIES. SECURITY HAS OBVIOUSLY BEEN INCREASED LATELY, AS I'M SURE YOU UNDERSTAND.
COMMANDANT HURRON SENDS HIS COMPLIMENTS, AND WILL MEET YOU AT THE LANDING PAD.
I SHOULD EXPECT NOTHING LESS...
YOU'VE GOT A MASTERY OF IMPERIAL ARROGANCE, LIEUTENANT. VERY NICE.
IT'S EASY, YOU JUST ACT
KE EVERYONE ELSE
S A BUG YOU'RE TOO BUSY TO SQUISH.
WHAT DO I TELL THE COMMANDANT?
THAT YOU'RE HERE TO INSPECT THE SECURITY ON THE LAB.
AND WHEN HE ASKS ABOUT YOU?
I'M YOUR BODYGUARD.

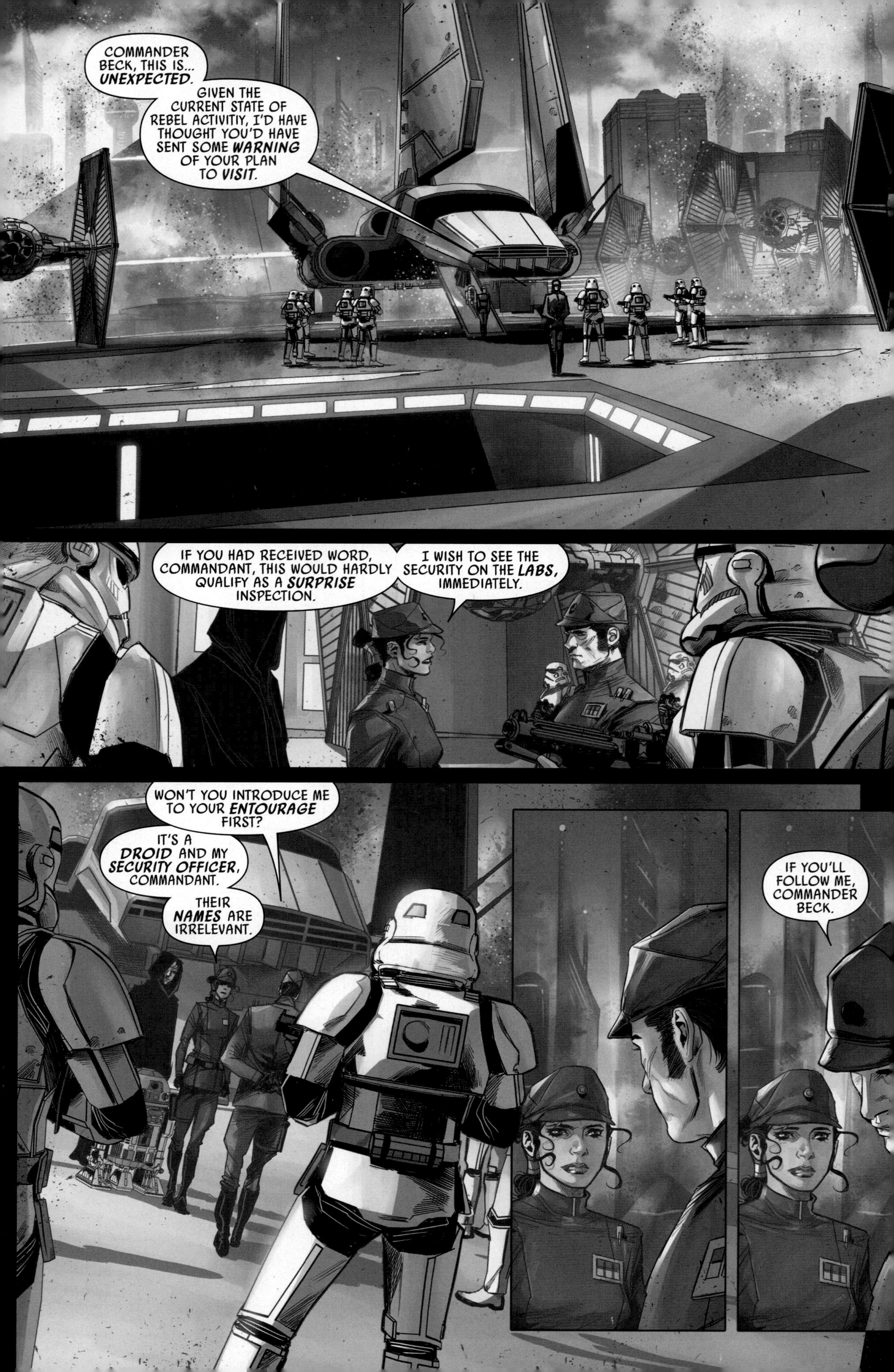
COMMANDER BECK, THIS IS... UNEXPECTED.
GIVEN THE CURRENT STATE OF REBEL ACTIVITIY, I'D HAVE THOUGHT YOU'D HAVE SENT SOME WARNING OF YOUR PLAN TO VISIT.
IF YOU HAD RECEIVED WORD, COMMANDANT, THIS WOULD HARDLY QUALIFY AS A SURPRISE INSPECTION.
I WISH TO SEE THE SECURITY ON THE LABS, IMMEDIATELY.
WON'T YOU INTRODUCE ME TO YOUR ENTOURAGE FIRST?
IT'S A DROID AND MY SECURITY OFFICER, COMMANDANT.
THEIR NAMES ARE IRRELEVANT.
IF YOU'LL FOLLOW ME, COMMANDER BECK.

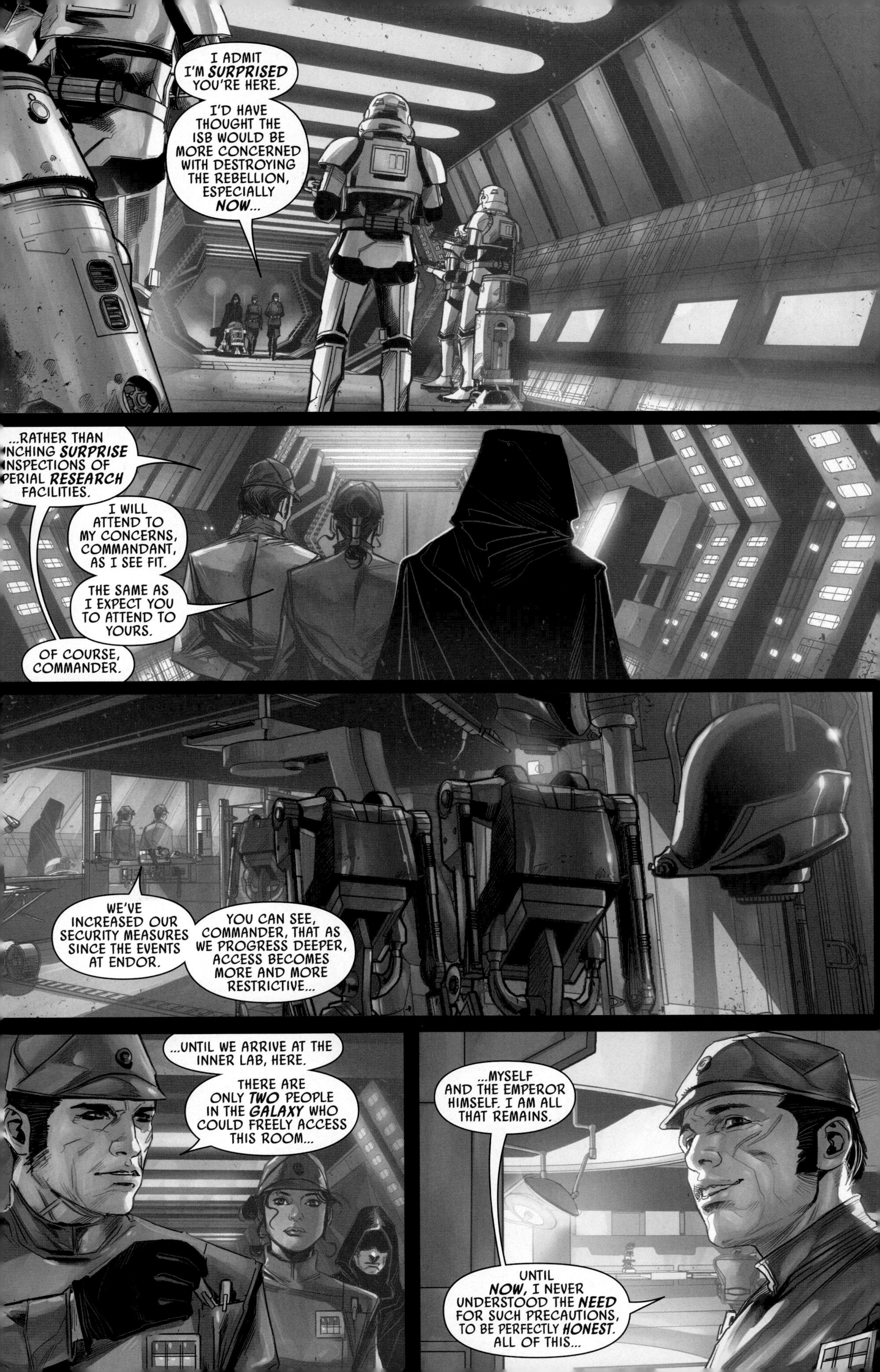
I ADMIT I'M SURPRISED YOU'RE HERE.
I'D HAVE THOUGHT THE ISB WOULD BE MORE CONCERNED WITH DESTROYING THE REBELLION, ESPECIALLY NOW...
...RATHER THAN ...NCHING SURPRISE INSPECTIONS OF ...PERIAL RESEARCH FACILITIES.
I WILL ATTEND TO MY CONCERNS, COMMANDANT, AS I SEE FIT.
THE SAME AS I EXPECT YOU TO ATTEND TO YOURS.
OF COURSE, COMMANDER.
WE'VE INCREASED OUR SECURITY MEASURES SINCE THE EVENTS AT ENDOR.
YOU CAN SEE, COMMANDER, THAT AS WE PROGRESS DEEPER, ACCESS BECOMES MORE AND MORE RESTRICTIVE...
...UNTIL WE ARRIVE AT THE INNER LAB, HERE.
THERE ARE ONLY TWO PEOPLE IN THE GALAXY WHO COULD FREELY ACCESS THIS ROOM...
...MYSELF AND THE EMPEROR HIMSELF. I AM ALL THAT REMAINS.
UNTIL NOW, I NEVER UNDERSTOOD THE NEED FOR SUCH PRECAUTIONS, TO BE PERFECTLY HONEST. ALL OF THIS...

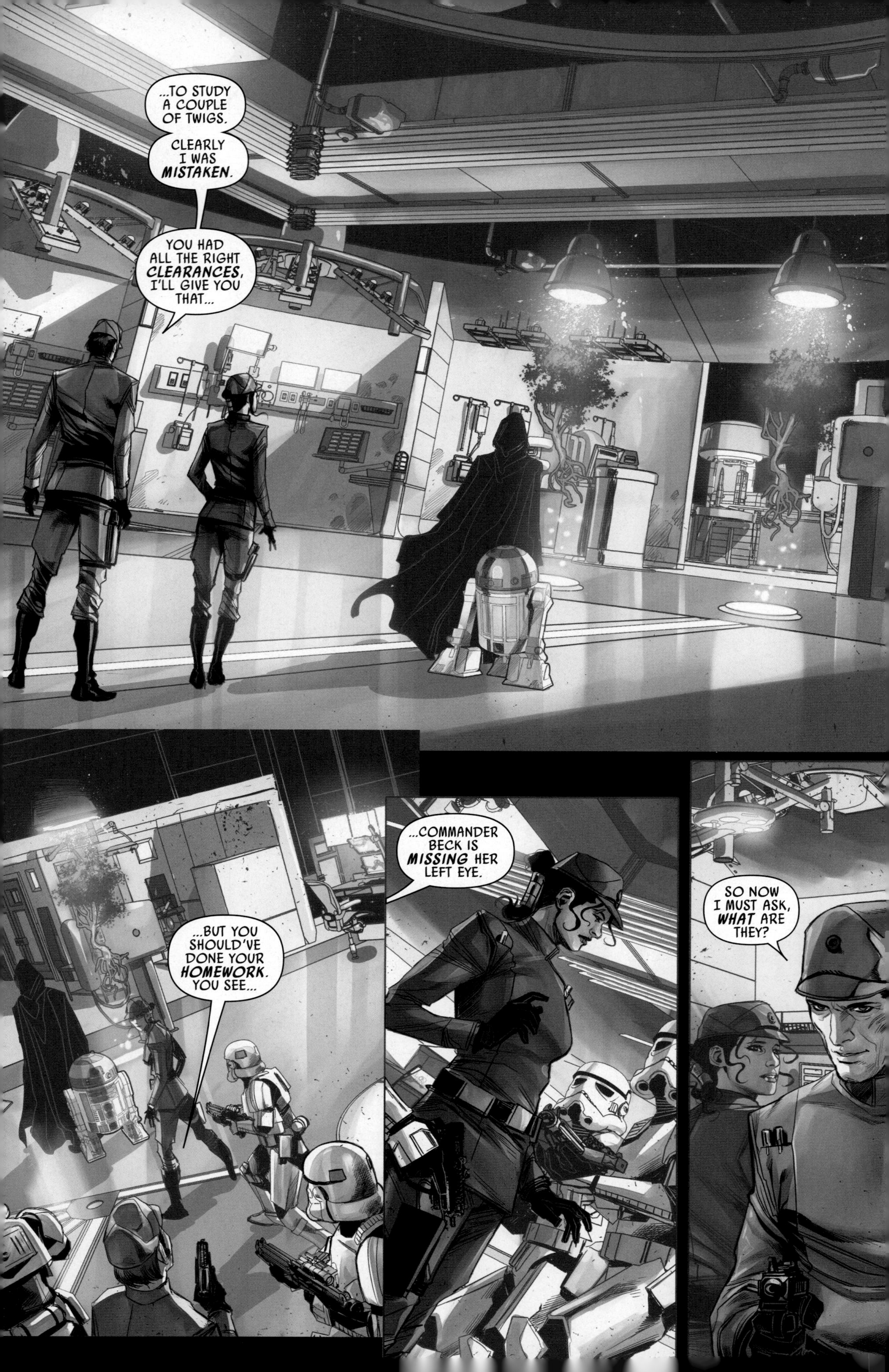
...TO STUDY A COUPLE OF TWIGS.
CLEARLY I WAS MISTAKEN.
YOU HAD ALL THE RIGHT CLEARANCES, I'LL GIVE YOU THAT...
...BUT YOU SHOULD'VE DONE YOUR HOMEWORK. YOU SEE...
...COMMANDER BECK IS MISSING HER LEFT EYE.
SO NOW I MUST ASK, WHAT ARE THEY?

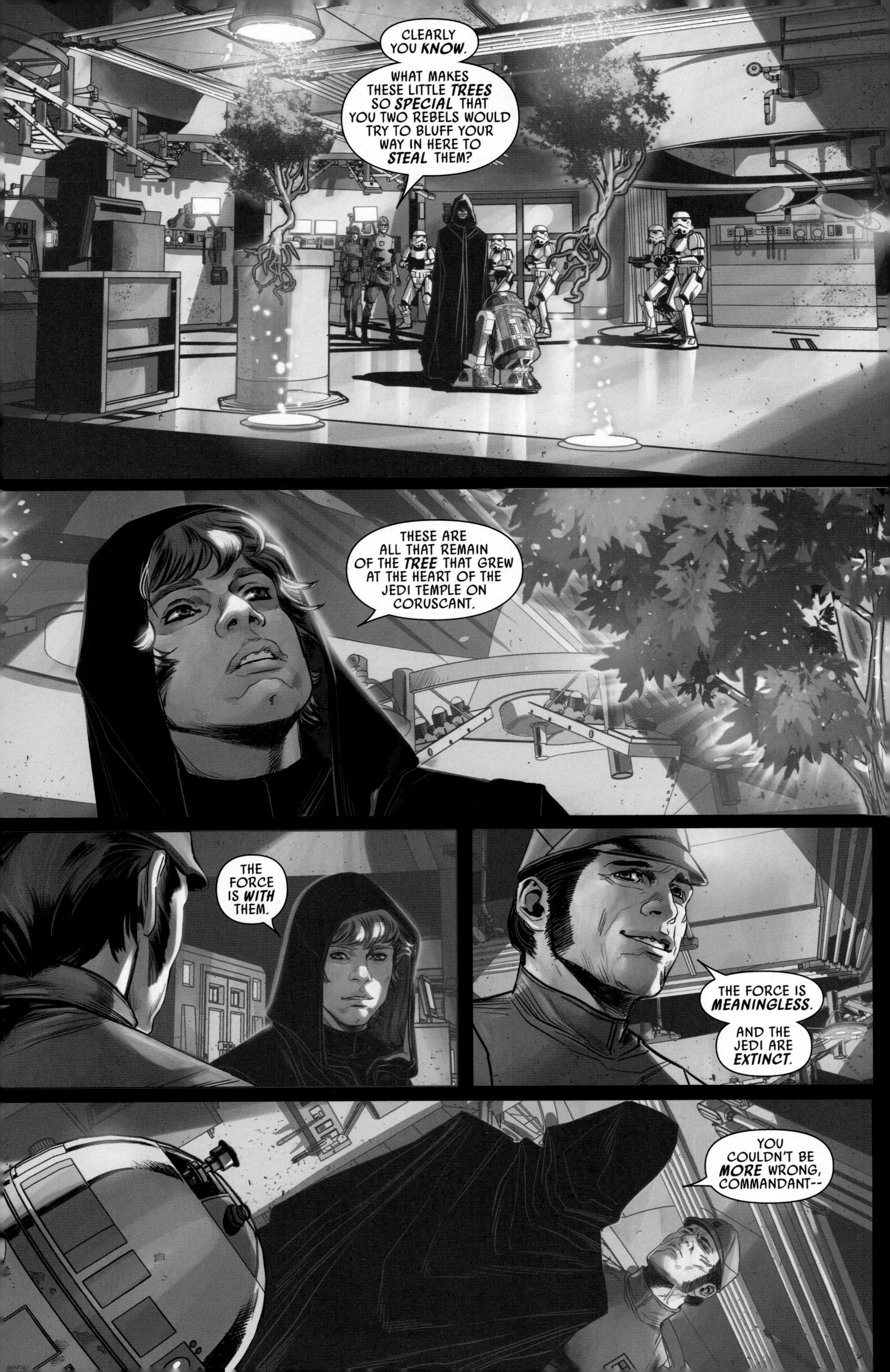
CLEARLY YOU KNOW.
WHAT MAKES THESE LITTLE TREES SO SPECIAL THAT YOU TWO REBELS WOULD TRY TO BLUFF YOUR WAY IN HERE TO STEAL THEM?
THESE ARE ALL THAT REMAIN OF THE TREE THAT GREW AT THE HEART OF THE JEDI TEMPLE ON CORUSCANT.
THE FORCE IS WITH THEM.
THE FORCE IS MEANINGLESS.
AND THE JEDI ARE EXTINCT.
YOU COULDN'T BE MORE WRONG, COMMANDANT--

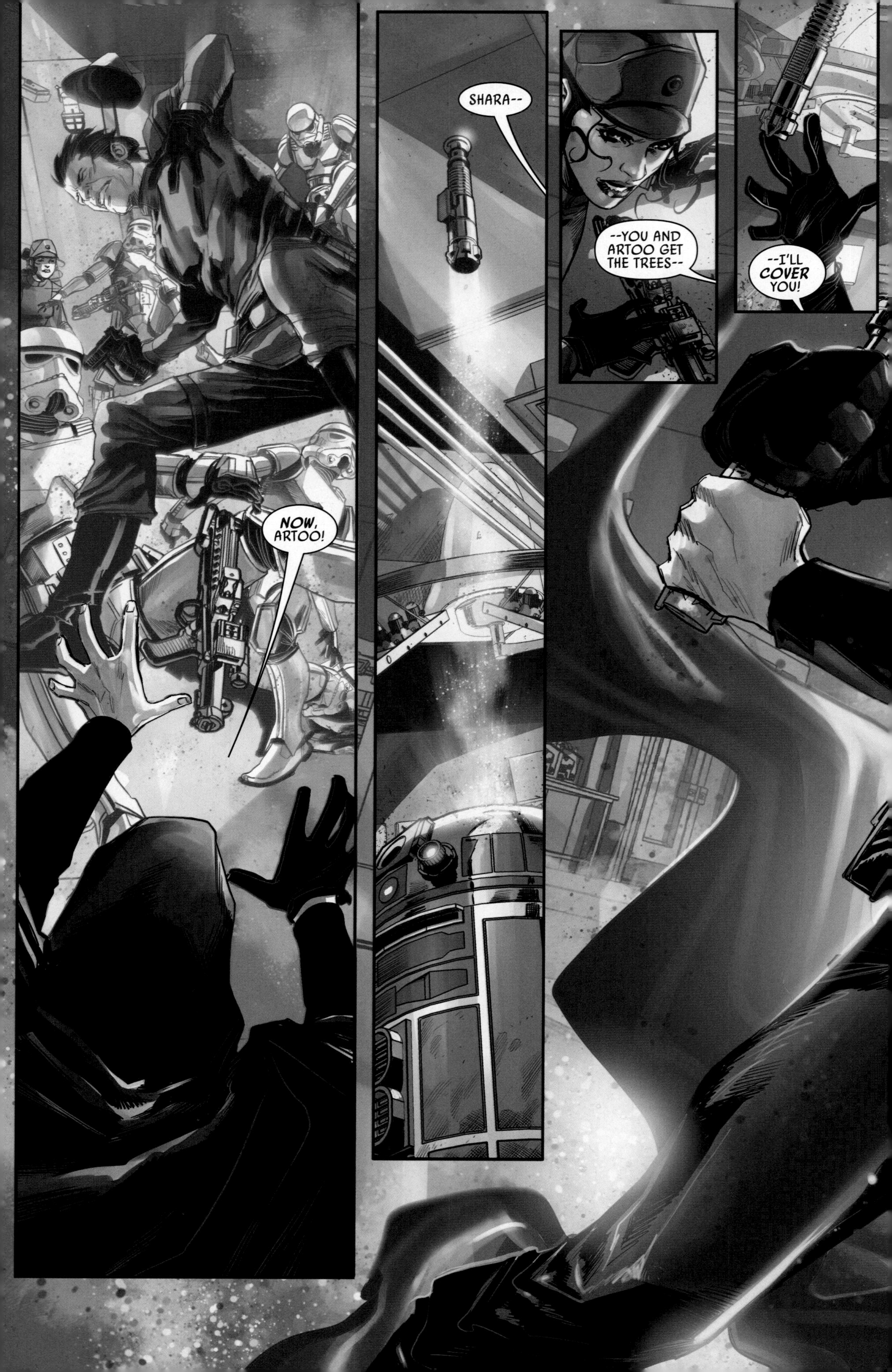
NOW, ARTOO!
SHARA--
--YOU AND ARTOO GET THE TREES--
--I'LL COVER YOU!

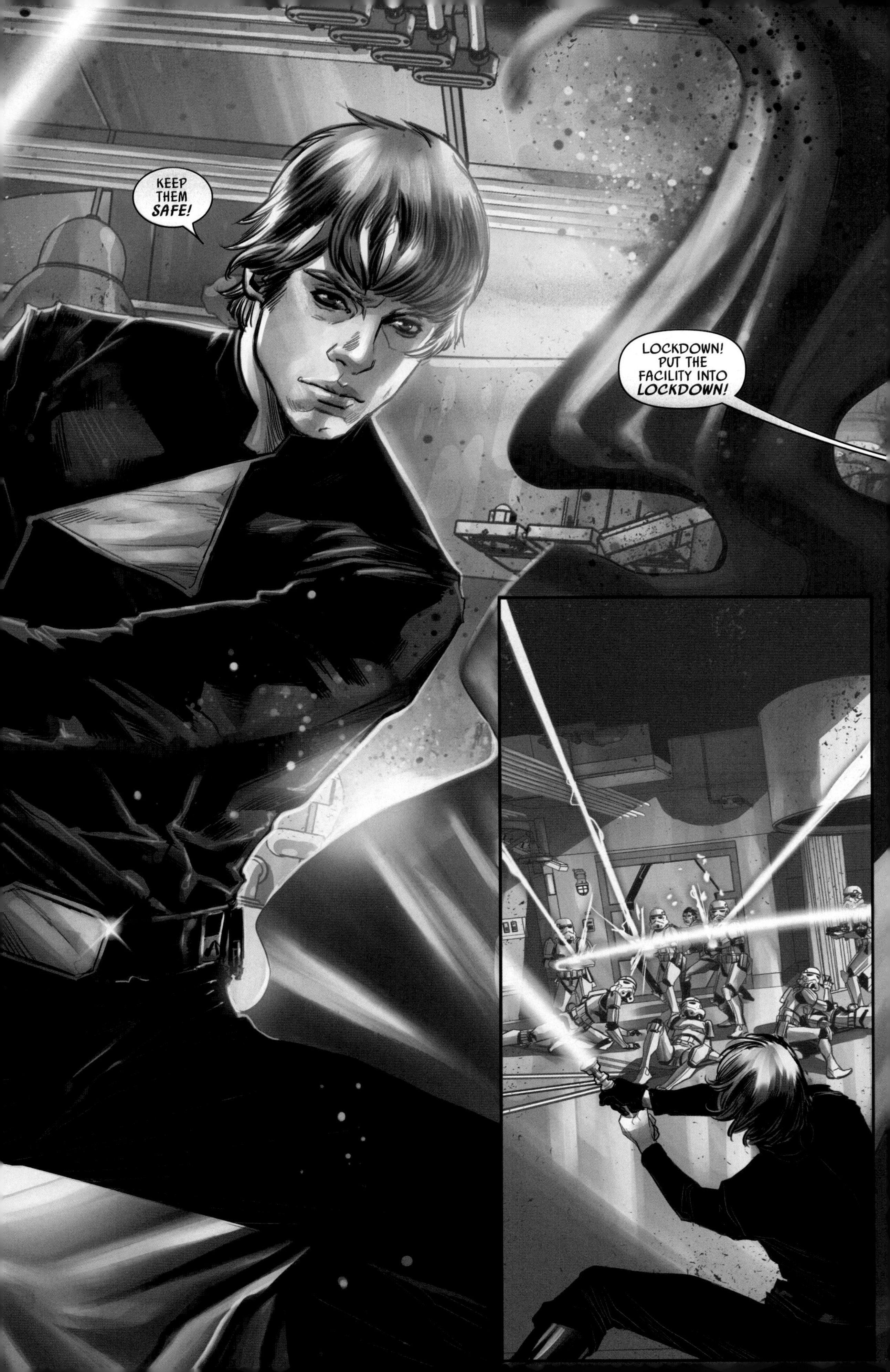
KEEP THEM SAFE!
LOCKDOWN! PUT THE FACILITY INTO LOCKDOWN!

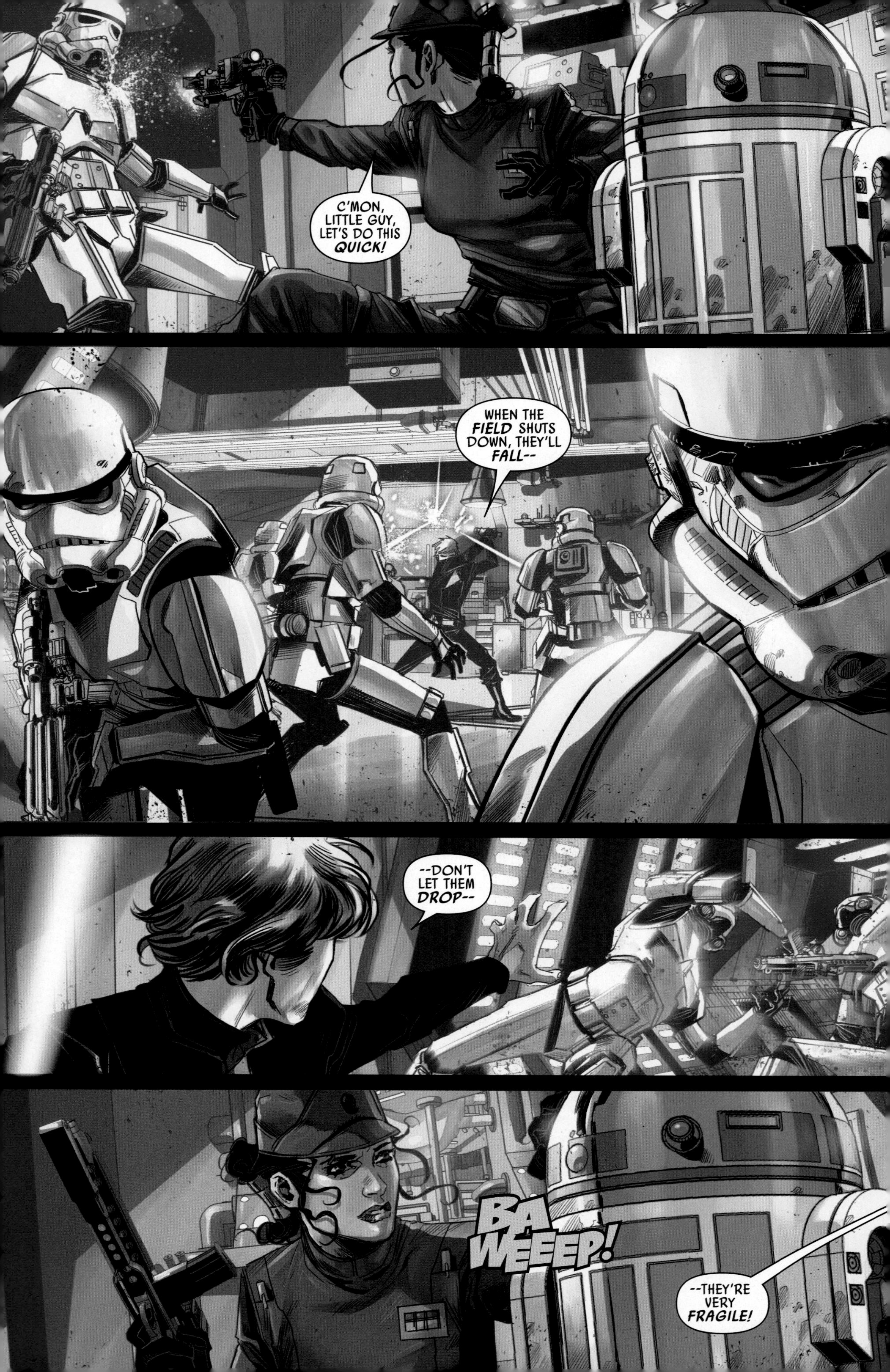
C'MON, LITTLE GUY, LET'S DO THIS QUICK!
WHEN THE FIELD SHUTS DOWN, THEY'LL FALL--
--DON'T LET THEM DROP--
BA WEEEP!
--THEY'RE VERY FRAGILE!

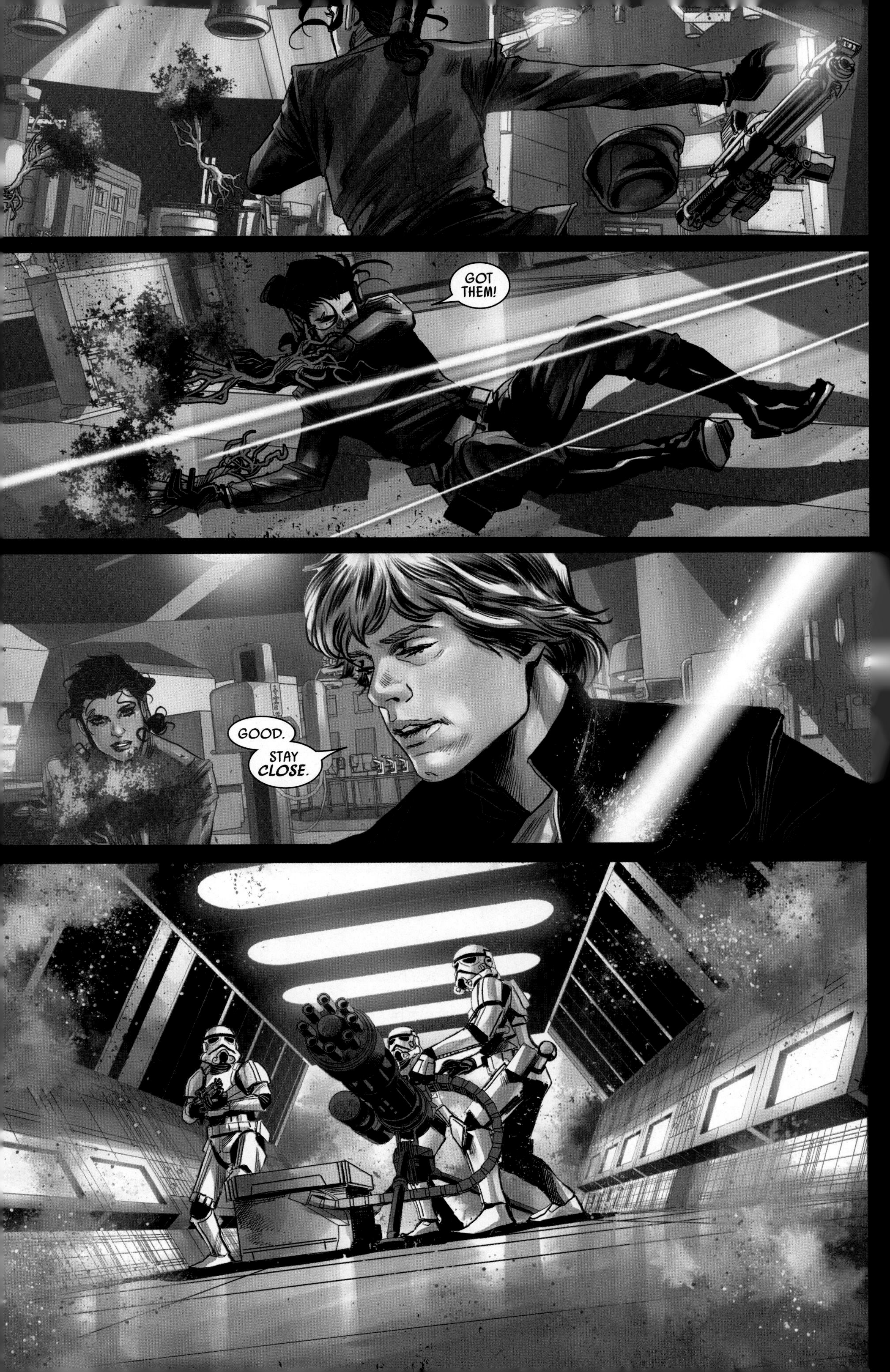
GOT THEM!
GOOD.
STAY CLOSE.

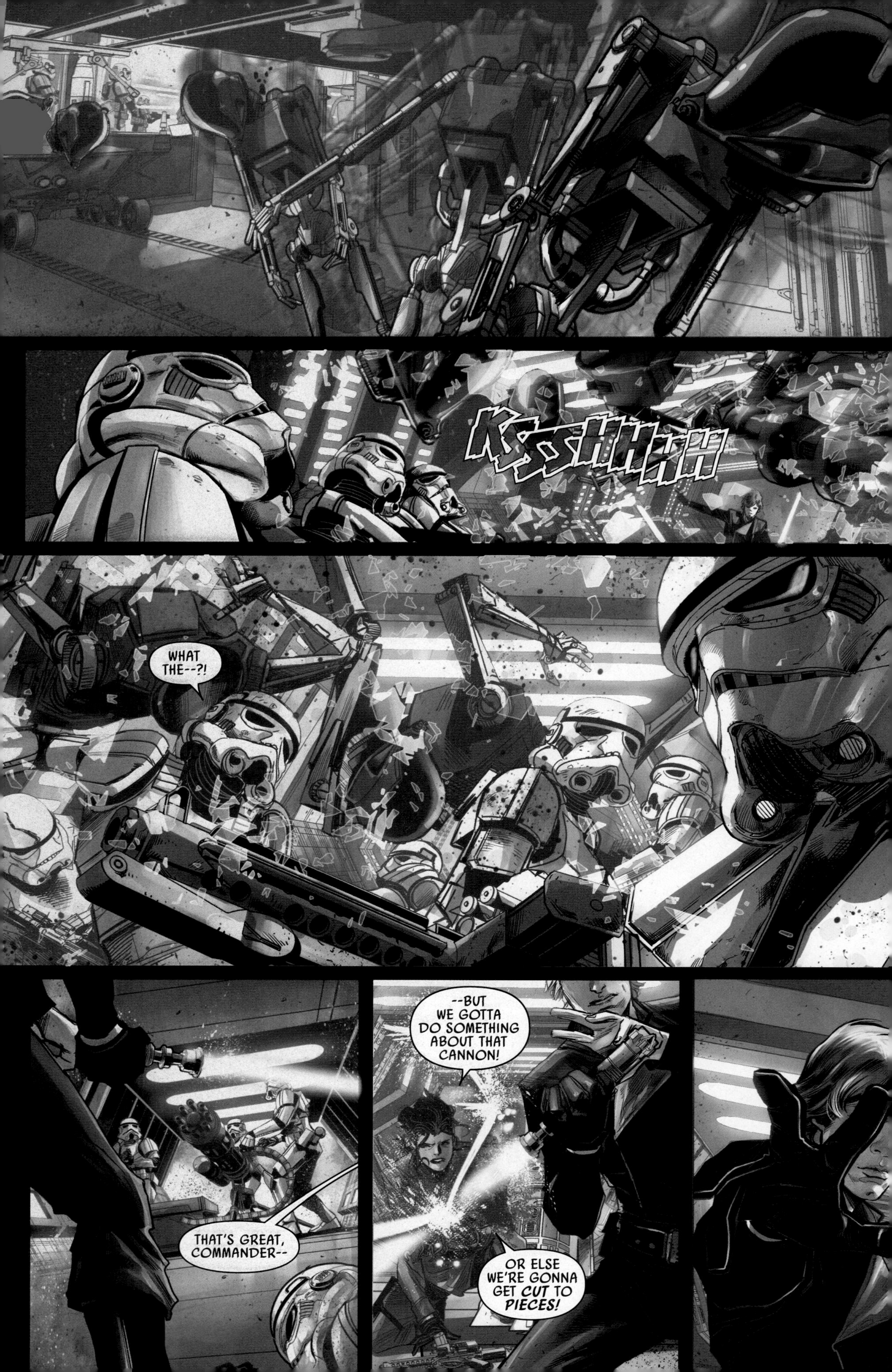
KSSHHHH
WHAT THE--?!
THAT'S GREAT, COMMANDER--
--BUT WE GOTTA DO SOMETHING ABOUT THAT CANNON!
OR ELSE WE'RE GONNA GET *CUT* TO *PIECES!*

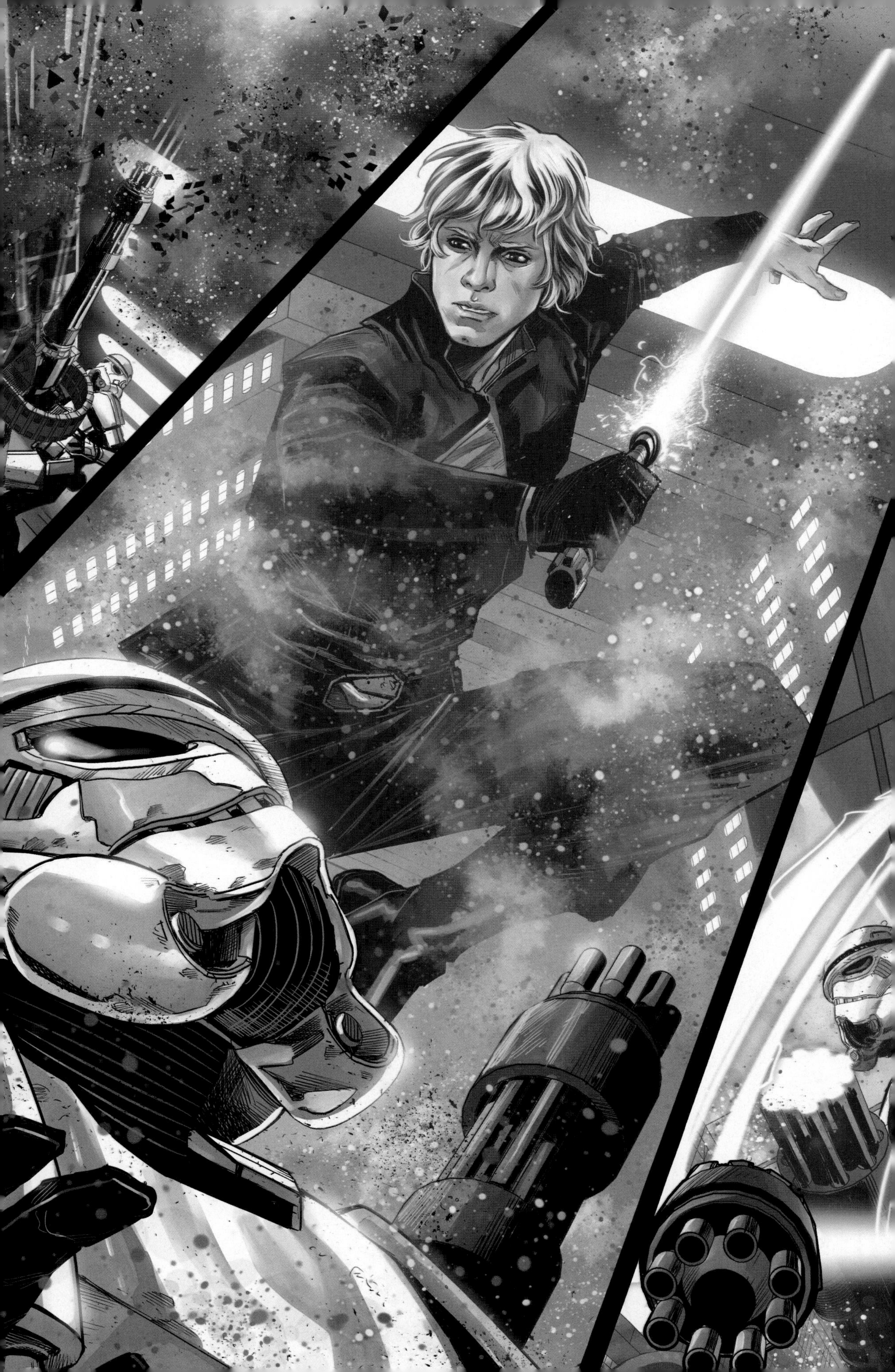

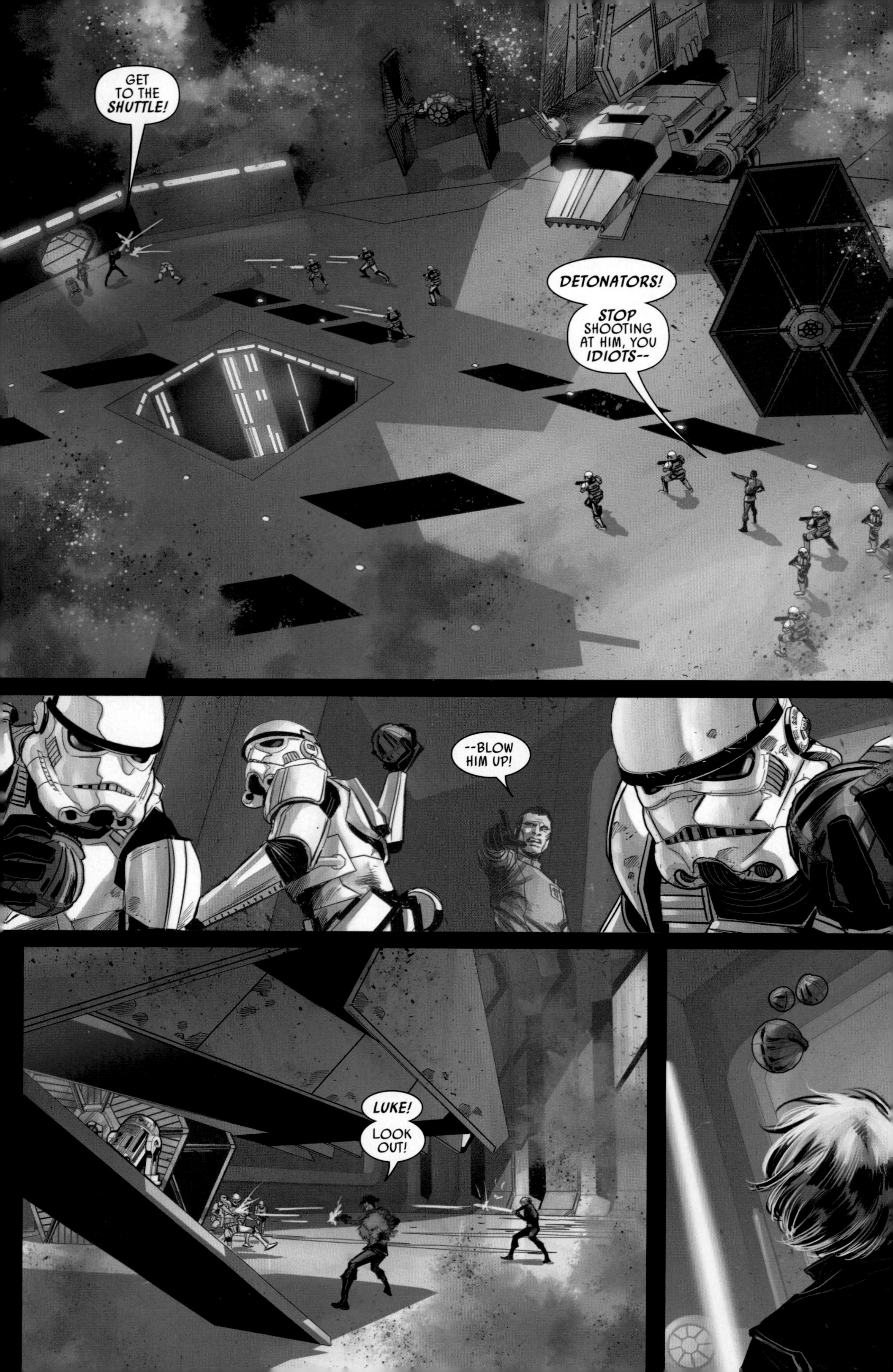
GET TO THE SHUTTLE!
DETONATORS!
STOP SHOOTING AT HIM, YOU IDIOTS--
--BLOW HIM UP!
LUKE!
LOOK OUT!

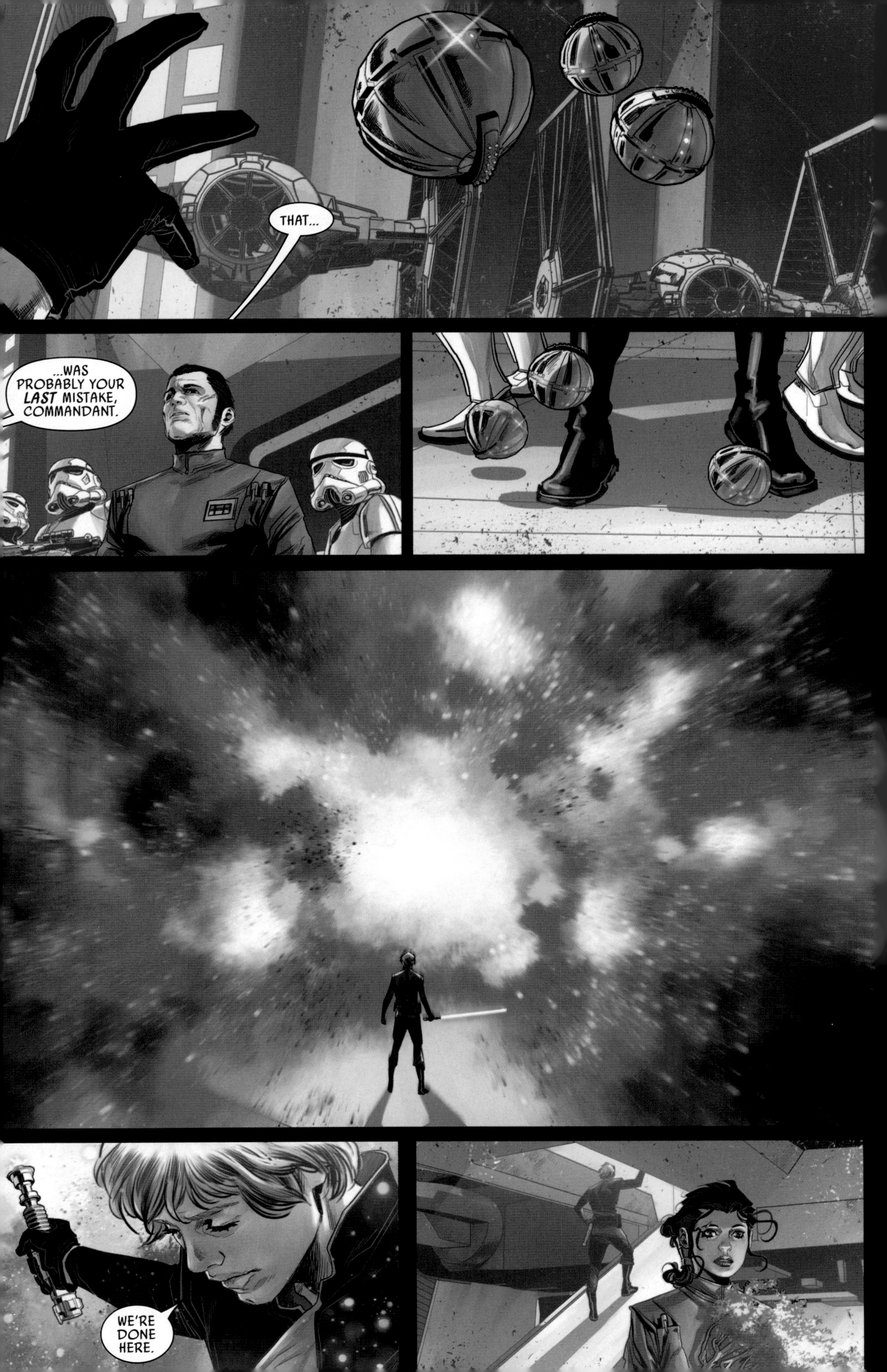
THAT...
...WAS PROBABLY YOUR *LAST* MISTAKE, COMMANDANT.
WE'RE DONE HERE.

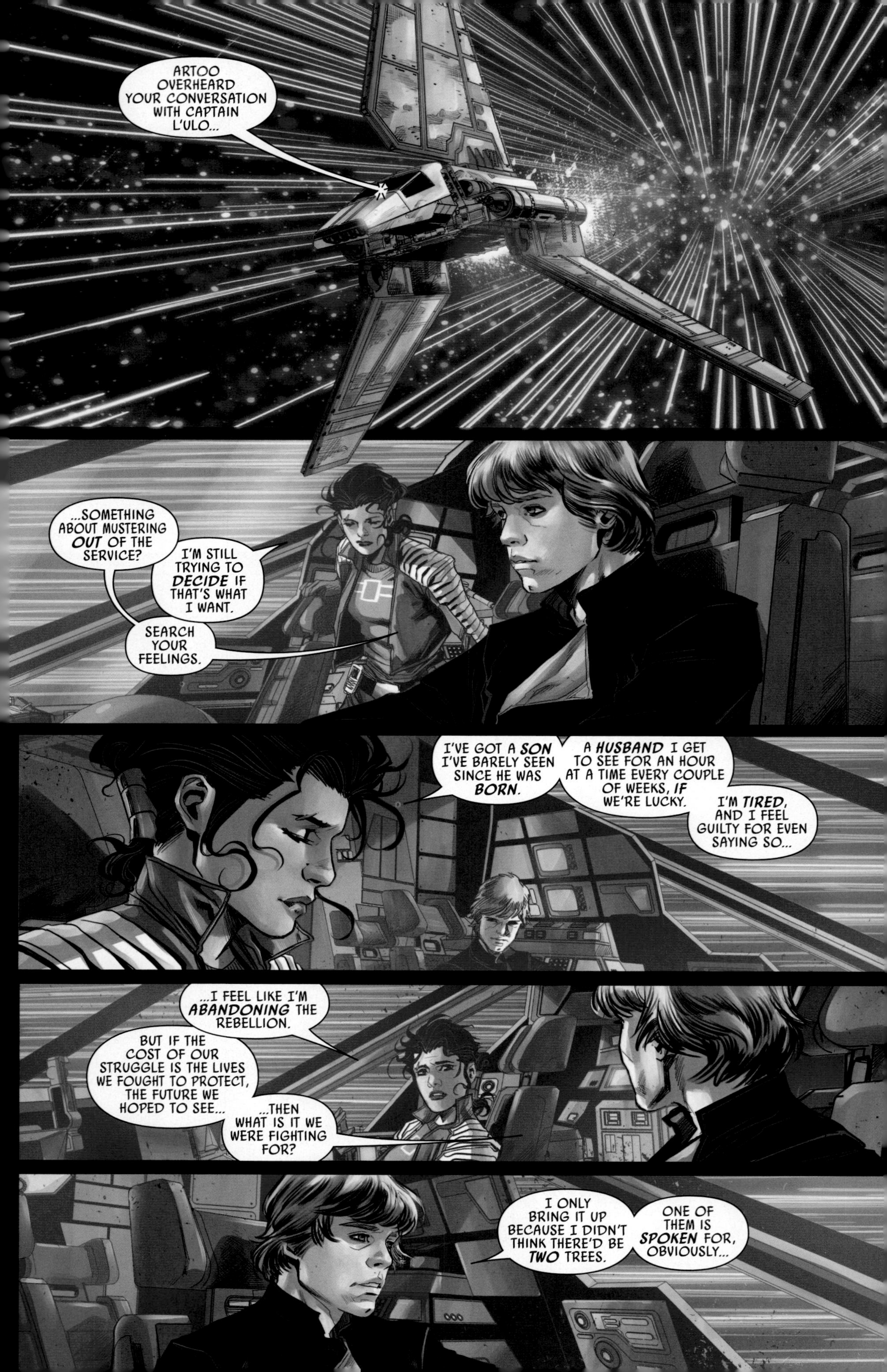
ARTOO OVERHEARD YOUR CONVERSATION WITH CAPTAIN L'ULO...
...SOMETHING ABOUT MUSTERING OUT OF THE SERVICE?
I'M STILL TRYING TO DECIDE IF THAT'S WHAT I WANT.
SEARCH YOUR FEELINGS.
I'VE GOT A SON I'VE BARELY SEEN SINCE HE WAS BORN.
A HUSBAND I GET TO SEE FOR AN HOUR AT A TIME EVERY COUPLE OF WEEKS, IF WE'RE LUCKY.
I'M TIRED, AND I FEEL GUILTY FOR EVEN SAYING SO...
...I FEEL LIKE I'M ABANDONING THE REBELLION.
BUT IF THE COST OF OUR STRUGGLE IS THE LIVES WE FOUGHT TO PROTECT, THE FUTURE WE HOPED TO SEE...
...THEN WHAT IS IT WE WERE FIGHTING FOR?
I ONLY BRING IT UP BECAUSE I DIDN'T THINK THERE'D BE TWO TREES.
ONE OF THEM IS SPOKEN FOR, OBVIOUSLY...

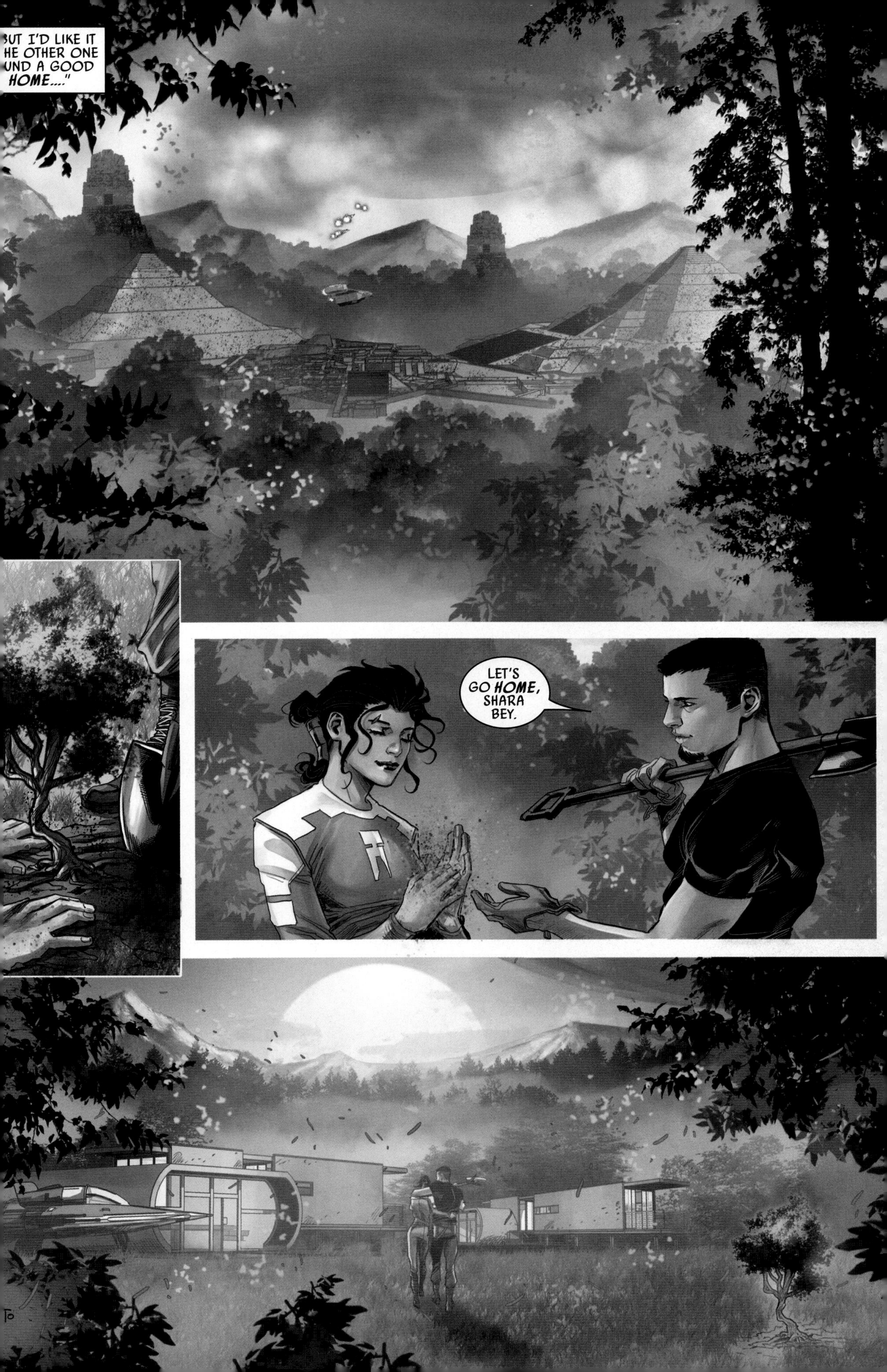
UT I'D LIKE IT HE OTHER ONE UND A GOOD HOME...."
LET'S GO HOME, SHARA BEY.

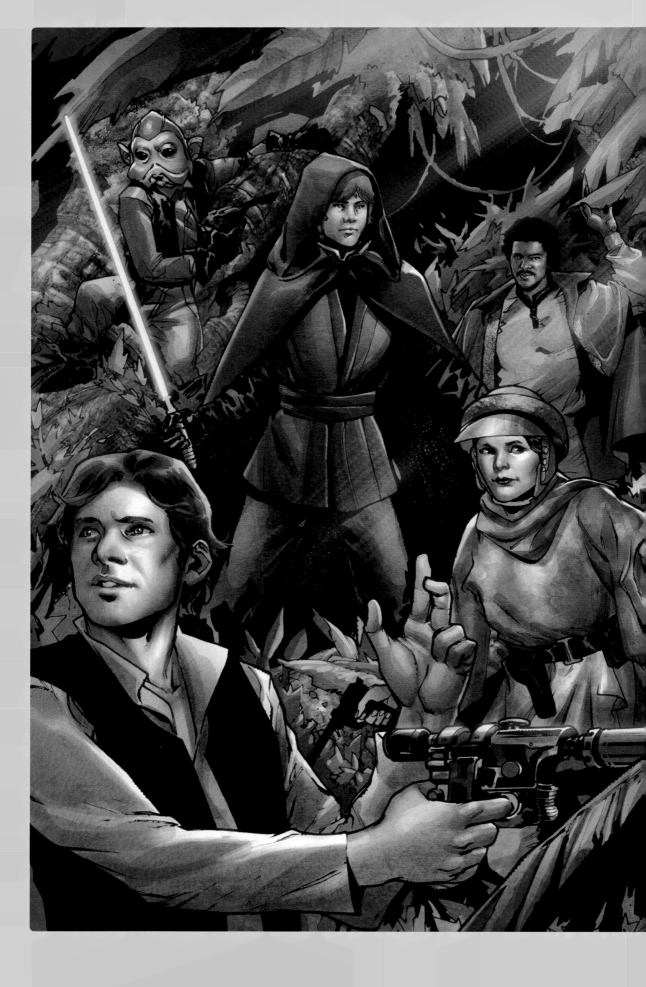

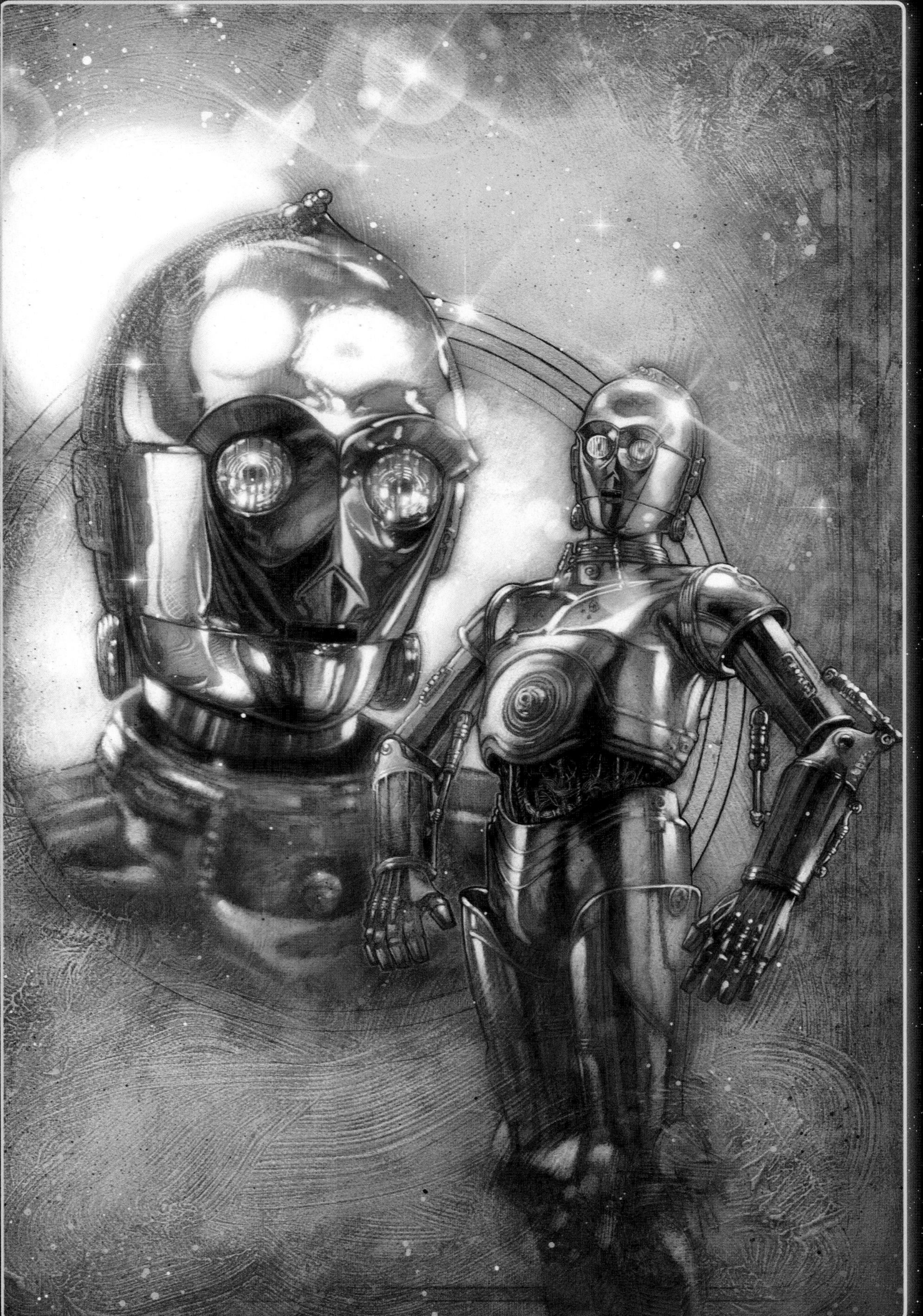

STAR WARS SPECIAL: C-3PO 1

C-3

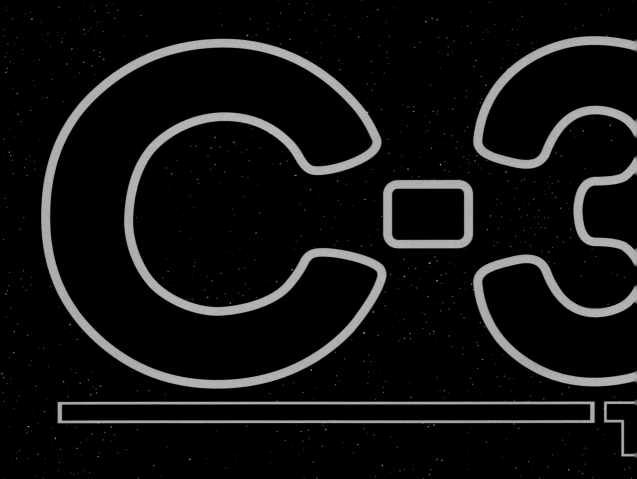

PO

PHANTOM LIMB

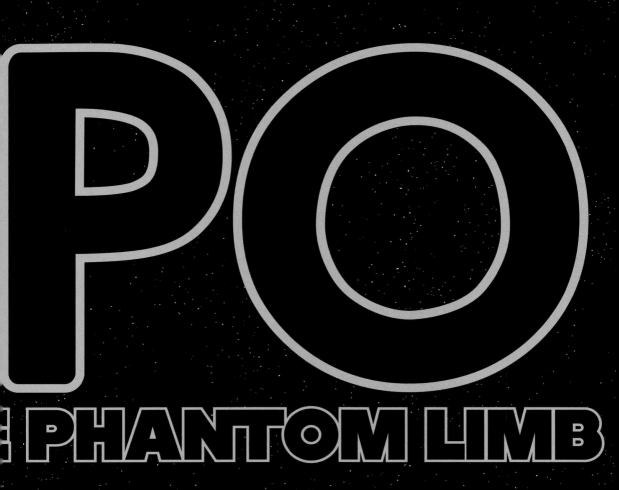

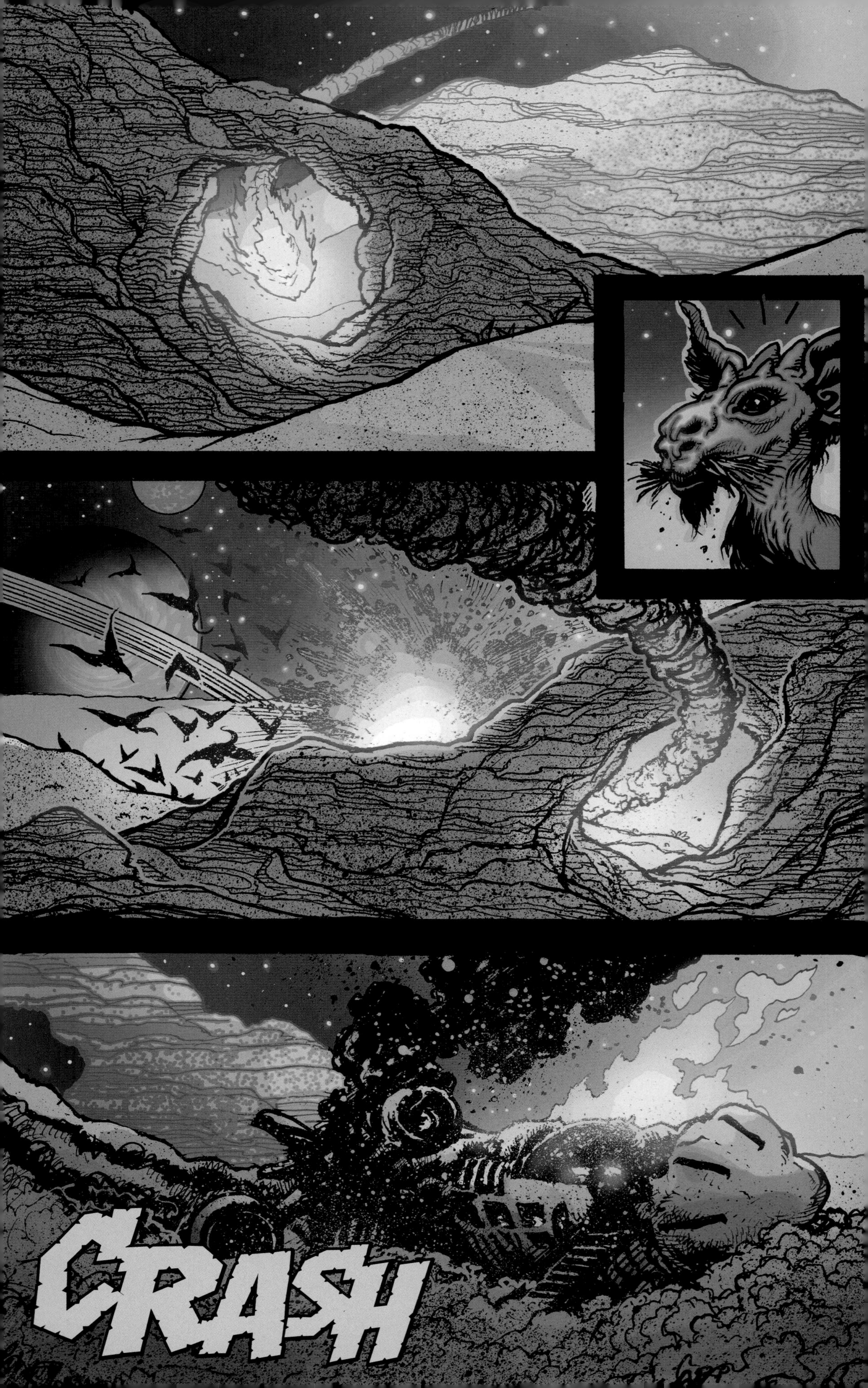
CRASH

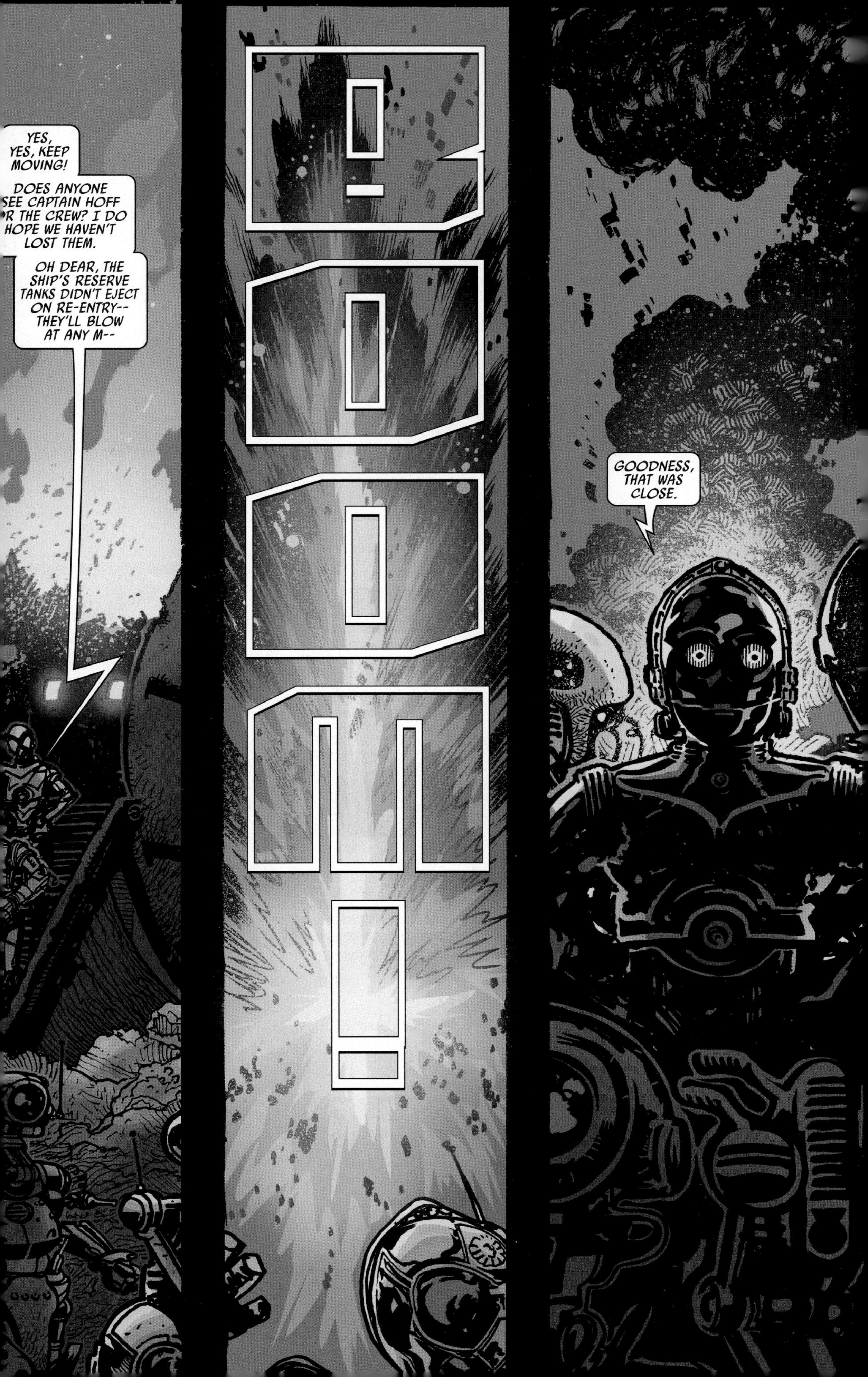
YES, YES, KEEP MOVING!
DOES ANYONE SEE CAPTAIN HOFF R THE CREW? I DO HOPE WE HAVEN'T LOST THEM.
OH DEAR, THE SHIP'S RESERVE TANKS DIDN'T EJECT ON RE-ENTRY-- THEY'LL BLOW AT ANY M--
BOOM!
GOODNESS, THAT WAS CLOSE.

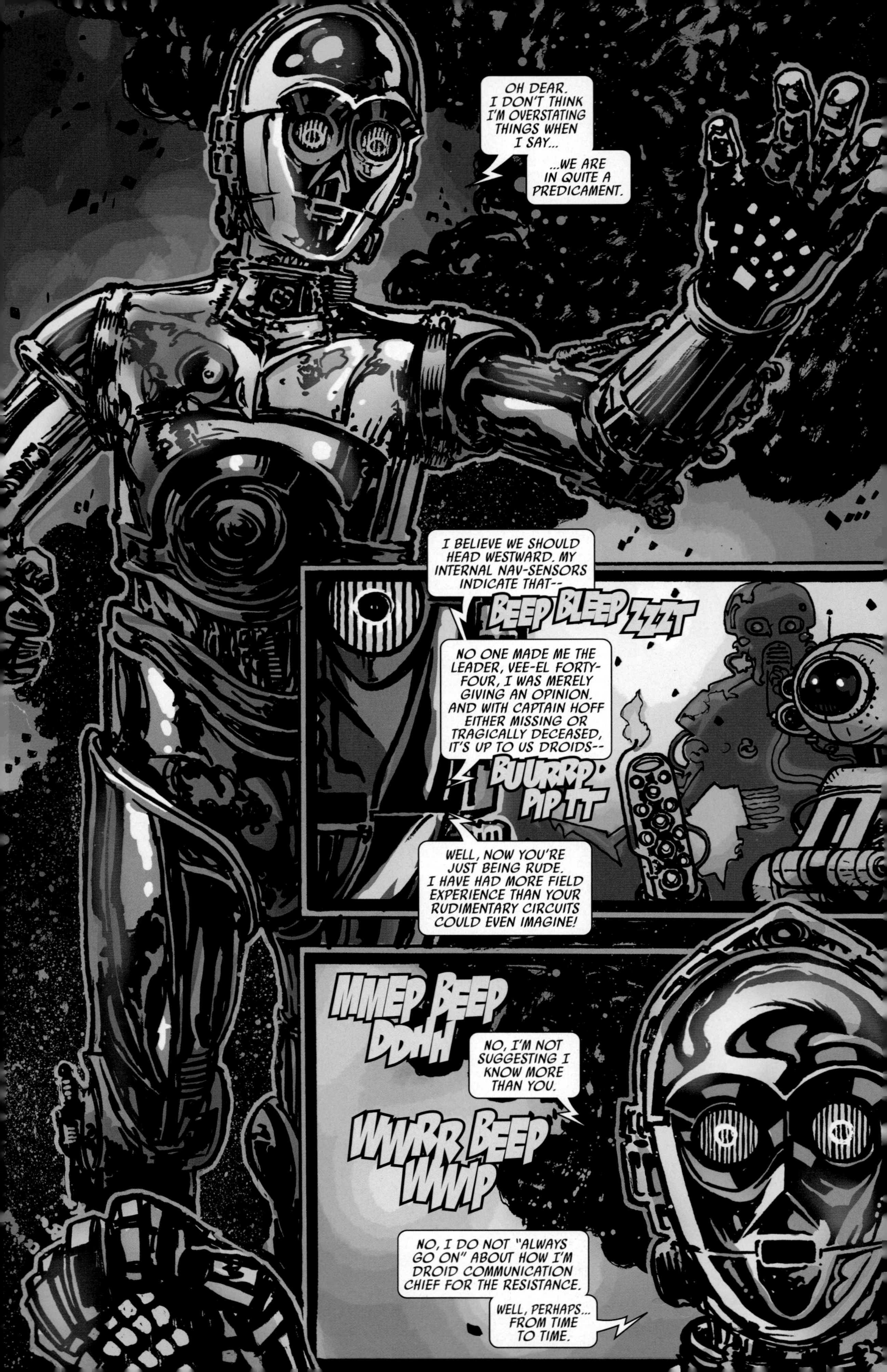
OH DEAR. I DON'T THINK I'M OVERSTATING THINGS WHEN I SAY...
...WE ARE IN QUITE A PREDICAMENT.
I BELIEVE WE SHOULD HEAD WESTWARD. MY INTERNAL NAV-SENSORS INDICATE THAT--
BEEP BLEEP ZZZT
NO ONE MADE ME THE LEADER, VEE-EL FORTY-FOUR, I WAS MERELY GIVING AN OPINION. AND WITH CAPTAIN HOFF EITHER MISSING OR TRAGICALLY DECEASED, IT'S UP TO US DROIDS--
BUURRP PIP TT
WELL, NOW YOU'RE JUST BEING RUDE. I HAVE HAD MORE FIELD EXPERIENCE THAN YOUR RUDIMENTARY CIRCUITS COULD EVEN IMAGINE!
MMEP BEEP DDHH
NO, I'M NOT SUGGESTING I KNOW MORE THAN YOU.
WWRR BEEP WWIP
NO, I DO NOT "ALWAYS GO ON" ABOUT HOW I'M DROID COMMUNICATION CHIEF FOR THE RESISTANCE.
WELL, PERHAPS... FROM TIME TO TIME.

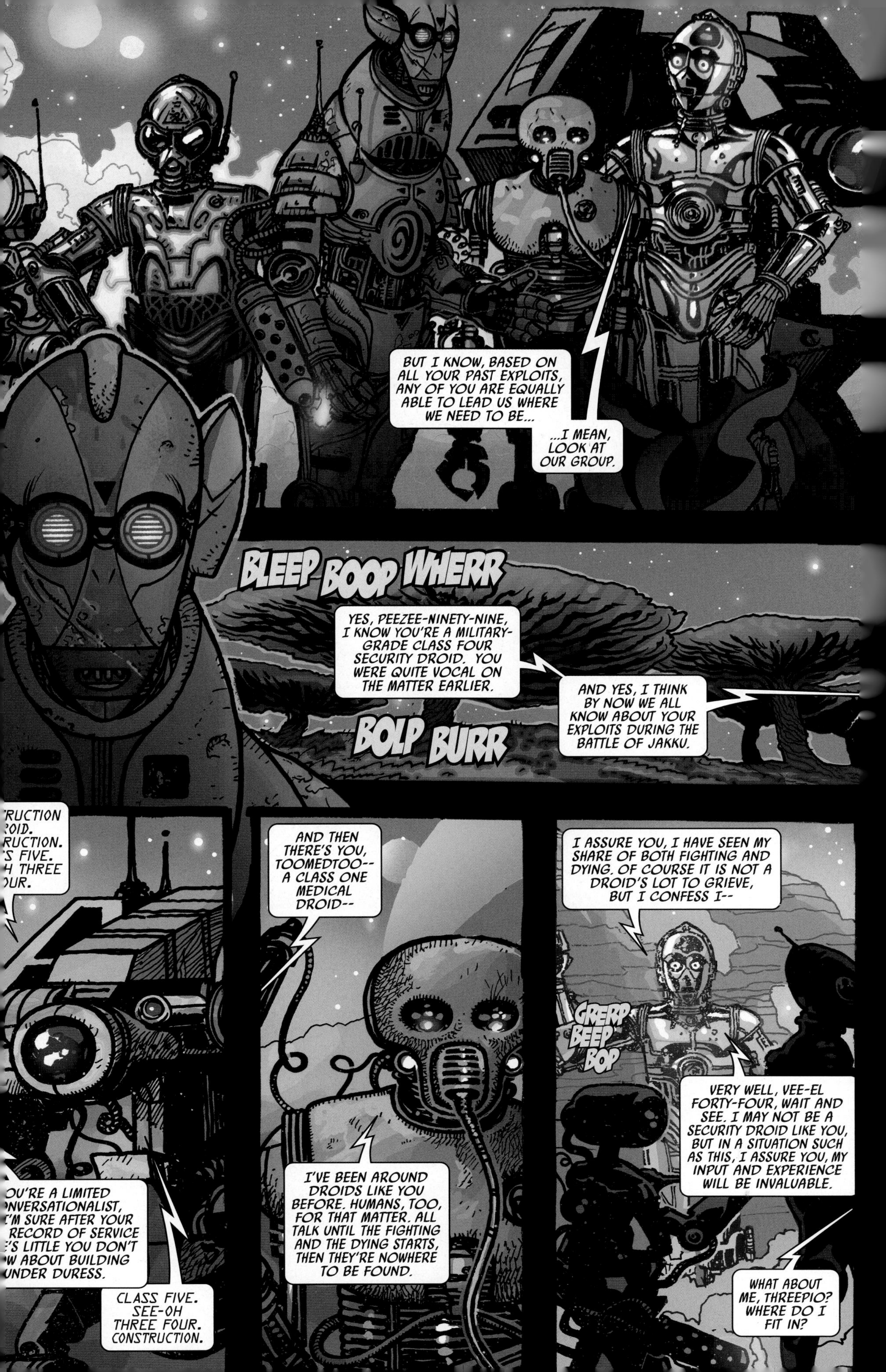
BUT I KNOW, BASED ON ALL YOUR PAST EXPLOITS, ANY OF YOU ARE EQUALLY ABLE TO LEAD US WHERE WE NEED TO BE...
...I MEAN, LOOK AT OUR GROUP.
BLEEP BOOP WHERR
YES, PEEZEE-NINETY-NINE, I KNOW YOU'RE A MILITARY-GRADE CLASS FOUR SECURITY DROID. YOU WERE QUITE VOCAL ON THE MATTER EARLIER.
BOLP BURR
AND YES, I THINK BY NOW WE ALL KNOW ABOUT YOUR EXPLOITS DURING THE BATTLE OF JAKKU.
RUCTION ROID. RUCTION. 'S FIVE. H THREE OUR.
OU'RE A LIMITED NVERSATIONALIST, I'M SURE AFTER YOUR RECORD OF SERVICE 'S LITTLE YOU DON'T W ABOUT BUILDING UNDER DURESS.
CLASS FIVE. SEE-OH THREE FOUR. CONSTRUCTION.
AND THEN THERE'S YOU, TOOMEDTOO-- A CLASS ONE MEDICAL DROID--
I'VE BEEN AROUND DROIDS LIKE YOU BEFORE. HUMANS, TOO, FOR THAT MATTER. ALL TALK UNTIL THE FIGHTING AND THE DYING STARTS, THEN THEY'RE NOWHERE TO BE FOUND.
I ASSURE YOU, I HAVE SEEN MY SHARE OF BOTH FIGHTING AND DYING. OF COURSE IT IS NOT A DROID'S LOT TO GRIEVE, BUT I CONFESS I--
GRERP BEEP BOP
VERY WELL, VEE-EL FORTY-FOUR, WAIT AND SEE. I MAY NOT BE A SECURITY DROID LIKE YOU, BUT IN A SITUATION SUCH AS THIS, I ASSURE YOU, MY INPUT AND EXPERIENCE WILL BE INVALUABLE.
WHAT ABOUT ME, THREEPIO? WHERE DO I FIT IN?

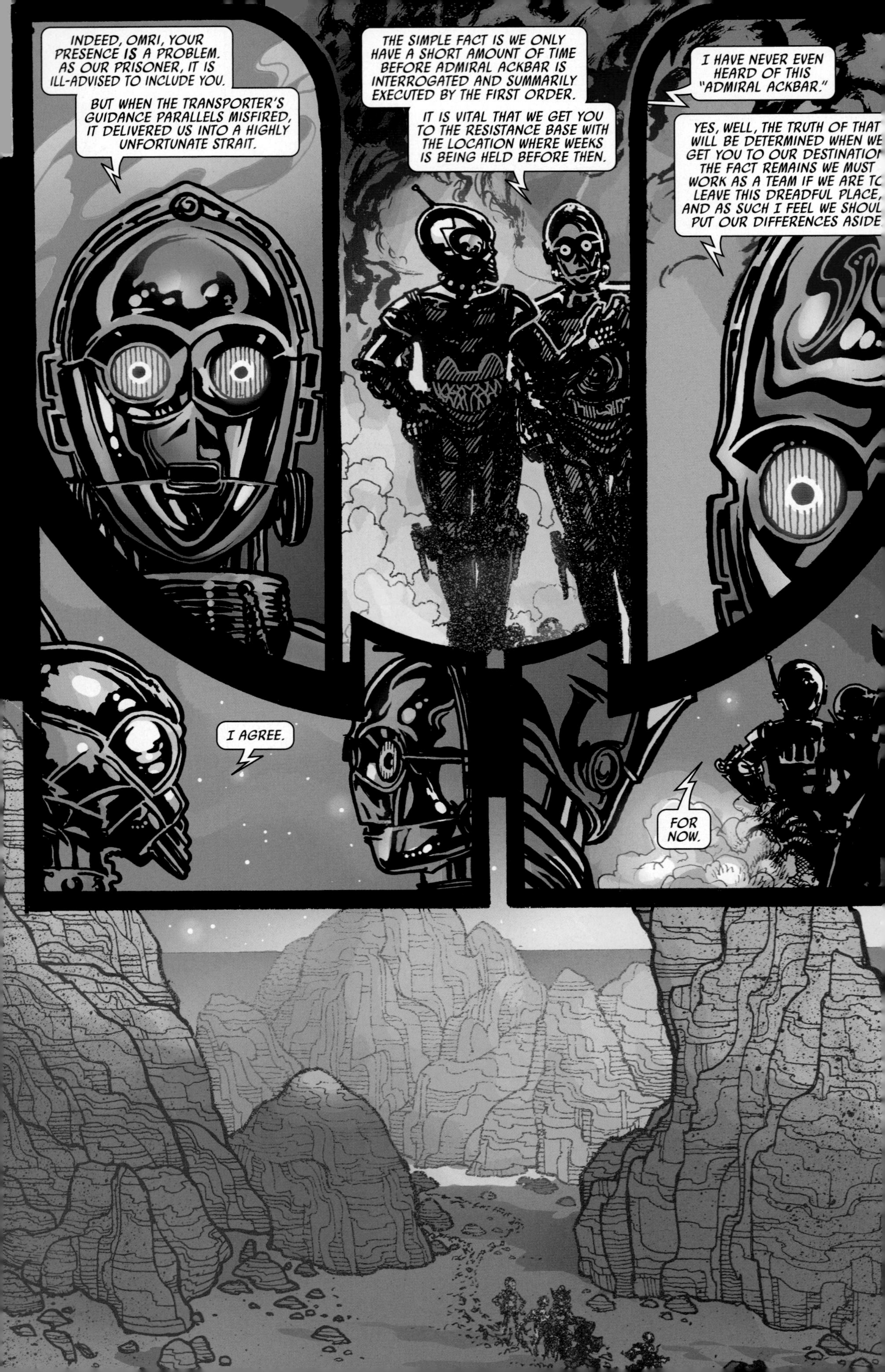
INDEED, OMRI, YOUR PRESENCE IS A PROBLEM. AS OUR PRISONER, IT IS ILL-ADVISED TO INCLUDE YOU.
BUT WHEN THE TRANSPORTER'S GUIDANCE PARALLELS MISFIRED, IT DELIVERED US INTO A HIGHLY UNFORTUNATE STRAIT.
THE SIMPLE FACT IS WE ONLY HAVE A SHORT AMOUNT OF TIME BEFORE ADMIRAL ACKBAR IS INTERROGATED AND SUMMARILY EXECUTED BY THE FIRST ORDER.
IT IS VITAL THAT WE GET YOU TO THE RESISTANCE BASE WITH THE LOCATION WHERE WEEKS IS BEING HELD BEFORE THEN.
I HAVE NEVER EVEN HEARD OF THIS "ADMIRAL ACKBAR."
YES, WELL, THE TRUTH OF THAT WILL BE DETERMINED WHEN WE GET YOU TO OUR DESTINATION. THE FACT REMAINS WE MUST WORK AS A TEAM IF WE ARE TO LEAVE THIS DREADFUL PLACE, AND AS SUCH I FEEL WE SHOULD PUT OUR DIFFERENCES ASIDE.
I AGREE.
FOR NOW.

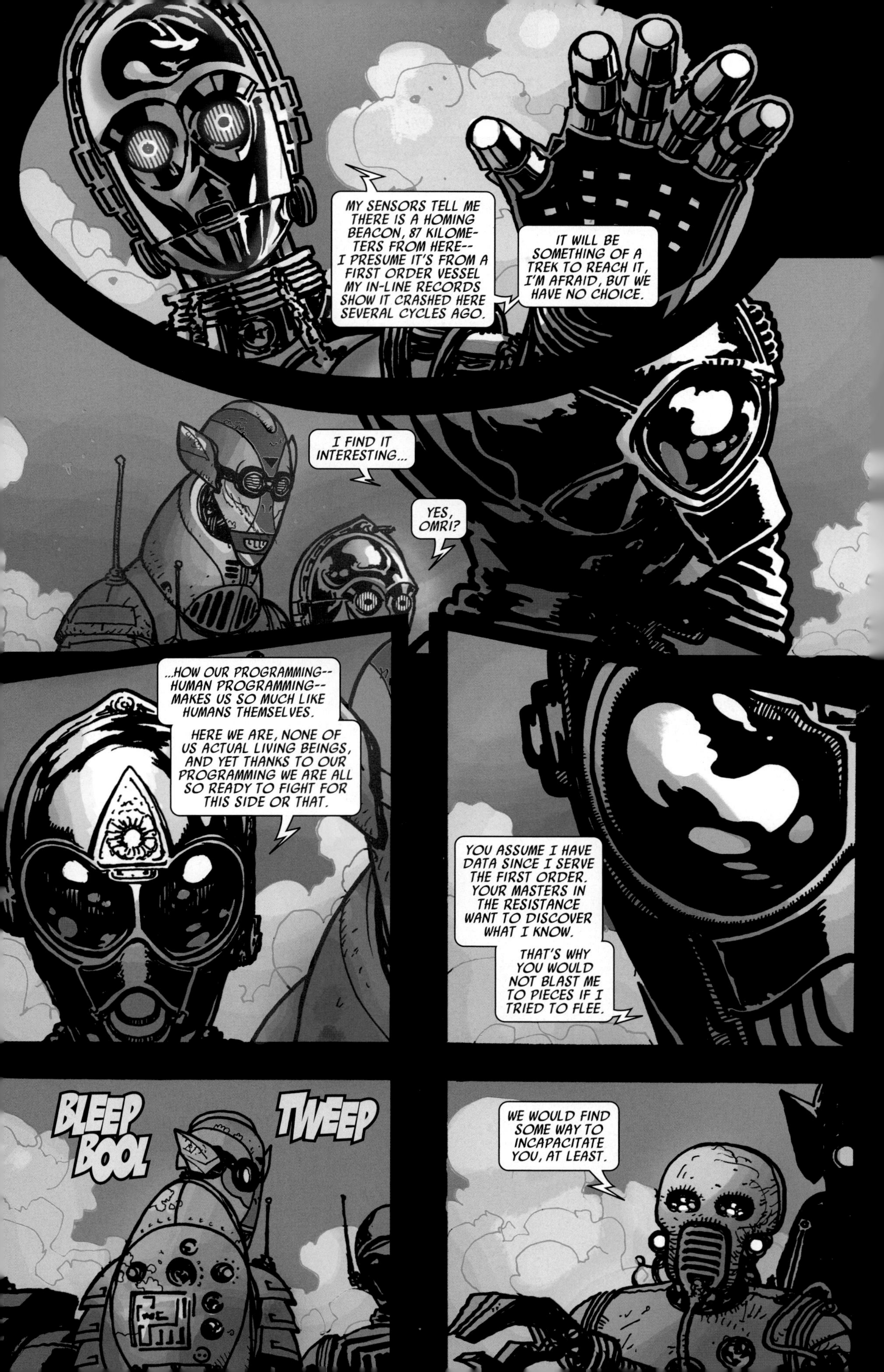
MY SENSORS TELL ME THERE IS A HOMING BEACON, 87 KILOMETERS FROM HERE-- I PRESUME IT'S FROM A FIRST ORDER VESSEL MY IN-LINE RECORDS SHOW IT CRASHED HERE SEVERAL CYCLES AGO.
IT WILL BE SOMETHING OF A TREK TO REACH IT, I'M AFRAID, BUT WE HAVE NO CHOICE.
I FIND IT INTERESTING...
YES, OMRI?
...HOW OUR PROGRAMMING-- HUMAN PROGRAMMING-- MAKES US SO MUCH LIKE HUMANS THEMSELVES.
HERE WE ARE, NONE OF US ACTUAL LIVING BEINGS, AND YET THANKS TO OUR PROGRAMMING WE ARE ALL SO READY TO FIGHT FOR THIS SIDE OR THAT.
YOU ASSUME I HAVE DATA SINCE I SERVE THE FIRST ORDER. YOUR MASTERS IN THE RESISTANCE WANT TO DISCOVER WHAT I KNOW.
THAT'S WHY YOU WOULD NOT BLAST ME TO PIECES IF I TRIED TO FLEE.
BLEEP
BOOL
TWEEP
WE WOULD FIND SOME WAY TO INCAPACITATE YOU, AT LEAST.

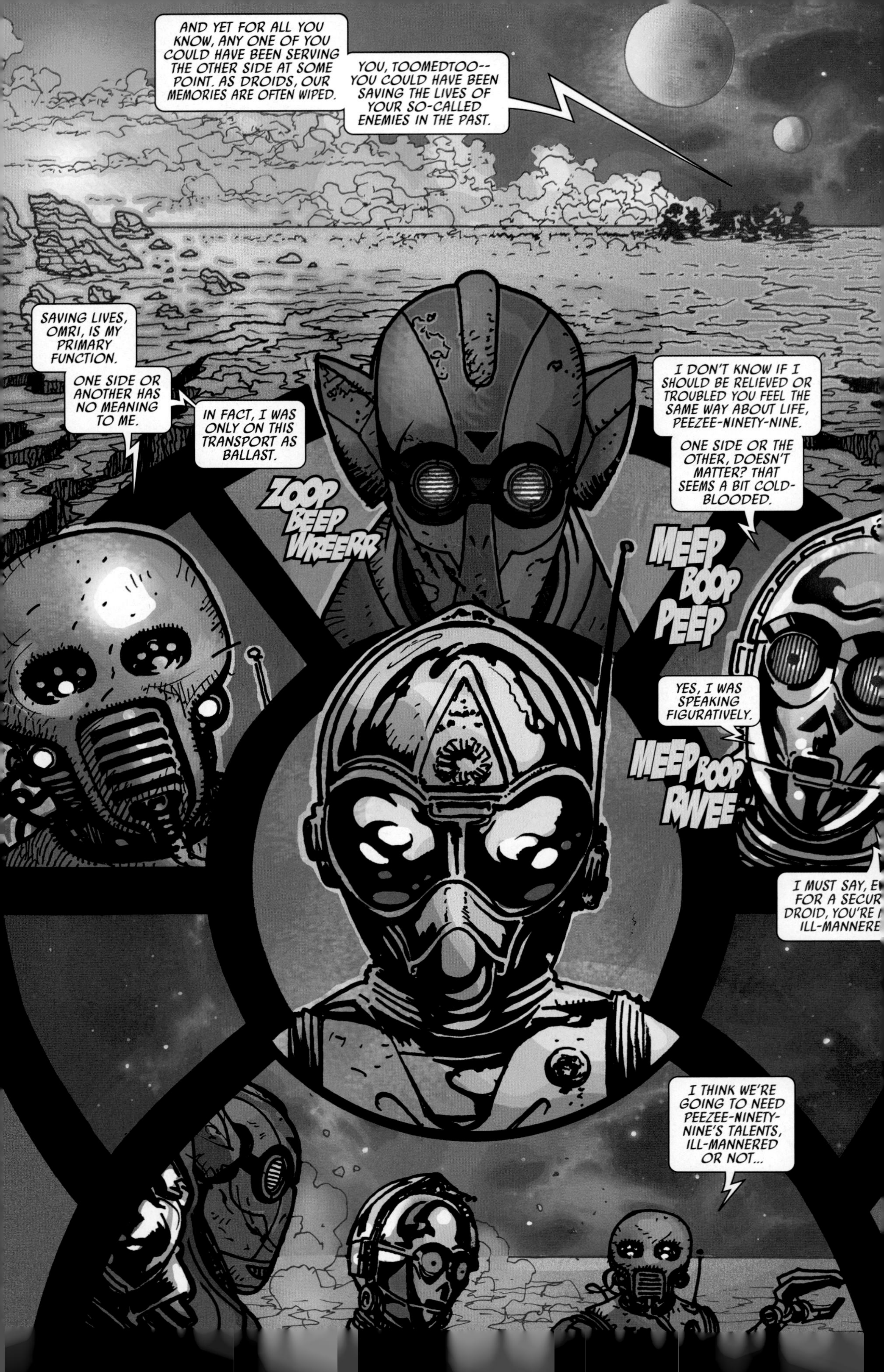

AND YET FOR ALL YOU KNOW, ANY ONE OF YOU COULD HAVE BEEN SERVING THE OTHER SIDE AT SOME POINT. AS DROIDS, OUR MEMORIES ARE OFTEN WIPED.
YOU, TOOMEDTOO-- YOU COULD HAVE BEEN SAVING THE LIVES OF YOUR SO-CALLED ENEMIES IN THE PAST.
SAVING LIVES, OMRI, IS MY PRIMARY FUNCTION.
ONE SIDE OR ANOTHER HAS NO MEANING TO ME.
IN FACT, I WAS ONLY ON THIS TRANSPORT AS BALLAST.
ZOOP BEEP WREERR
I DON'T KNOW IF I SHOULD BE RELIEVED OR TROUBLED YOU FEEL THE SAME WAY ABOUT LIFE, PEEZEE-NINETY-NINE.
ONE SIDE OR THE OTHER, DOESN'T MATTER? THAT SEEMS A BIT COLD-BLOODED.
MEEP BOOP PEEP
YES, I WAS SPEAKING FIGURATIVELY.
MEEP BOOP RWEE
I MUST SAY, E FOR A SECUR DROID, YOU'RE ILL-MANNERE
I THINK WE'RE GOING TO NEED PEEZEE-NINETY-NINE'S TALENTS, ILL-MANNERED OR NOT...

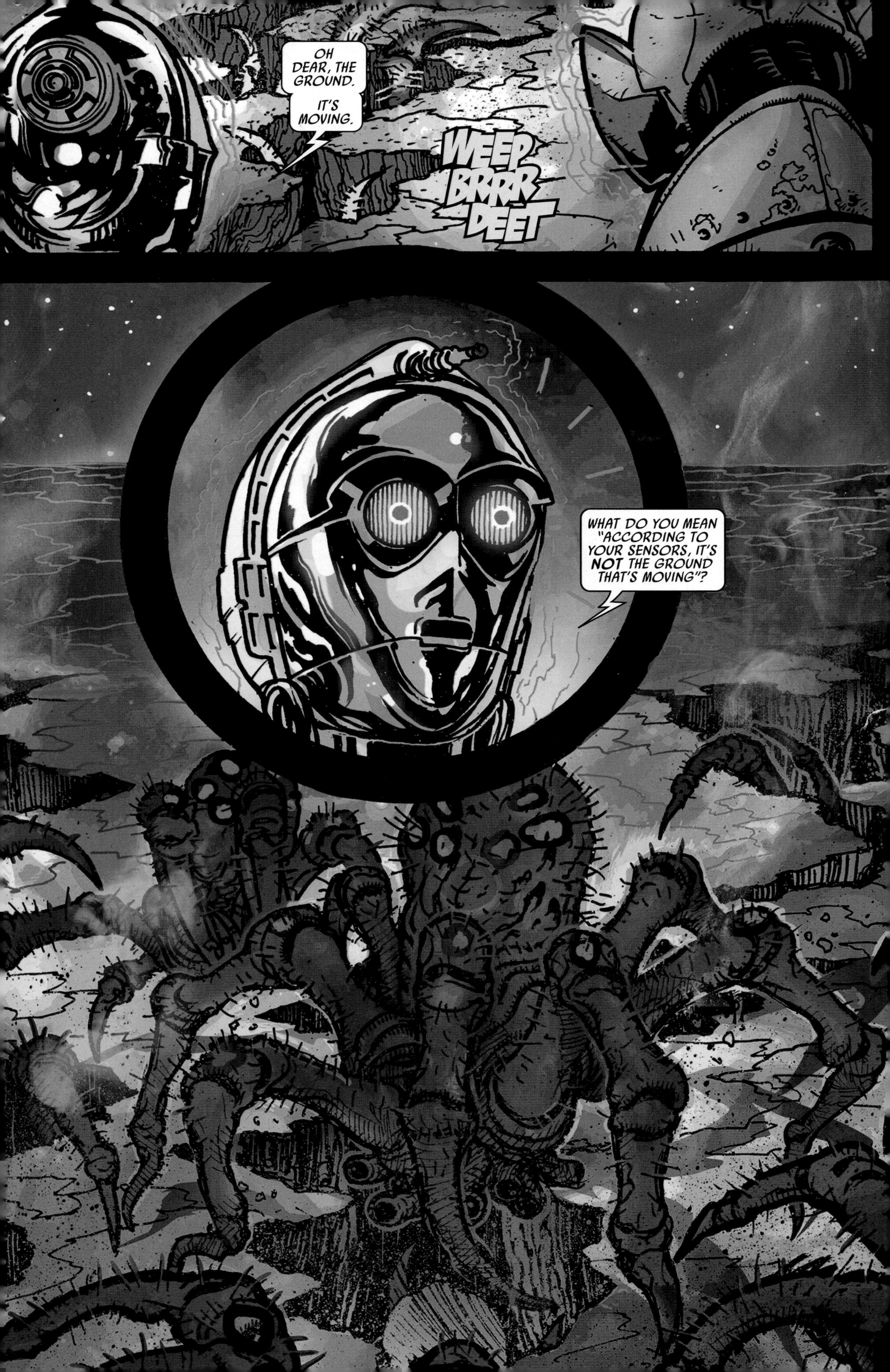
OH DEAR, THE GROUND.
IT'S MOVING.
WEEP BRRRR DEET
WHAT DO YOU MEAN "ACCORDING TO YOUR SENSORS, IT'S **NOT** THE GROUND THAT'S MOVING"?

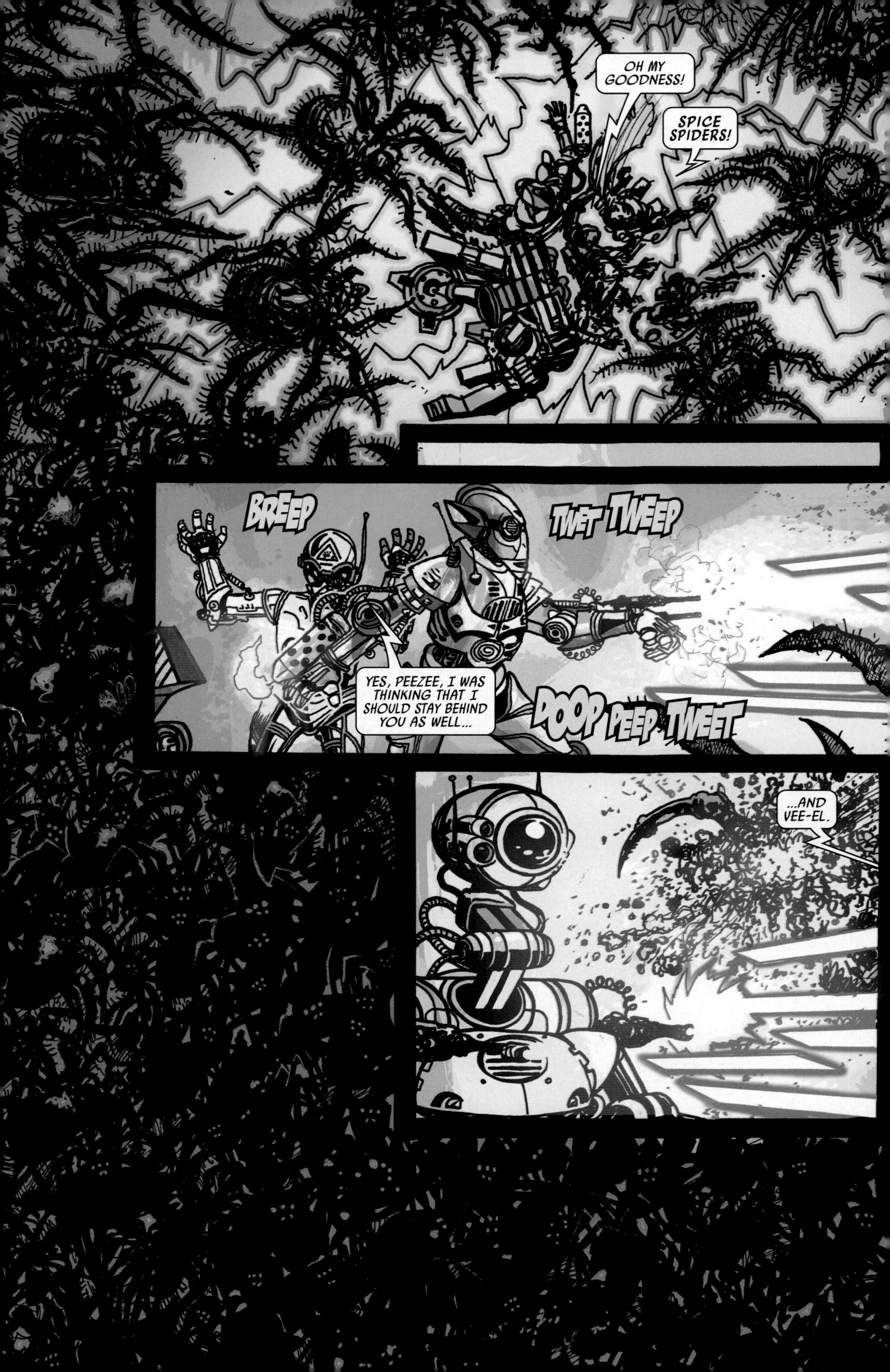
OH MY GOODNESS!
SPICE SPIDERS!
BREEP
TWET TWEEP
YES, PEEZEE, I WAS THINKING THAT I SHOULD STAY BEHIND YOU AS WELL...
DOOP PEEP TWEET
...AND VEE-EL.

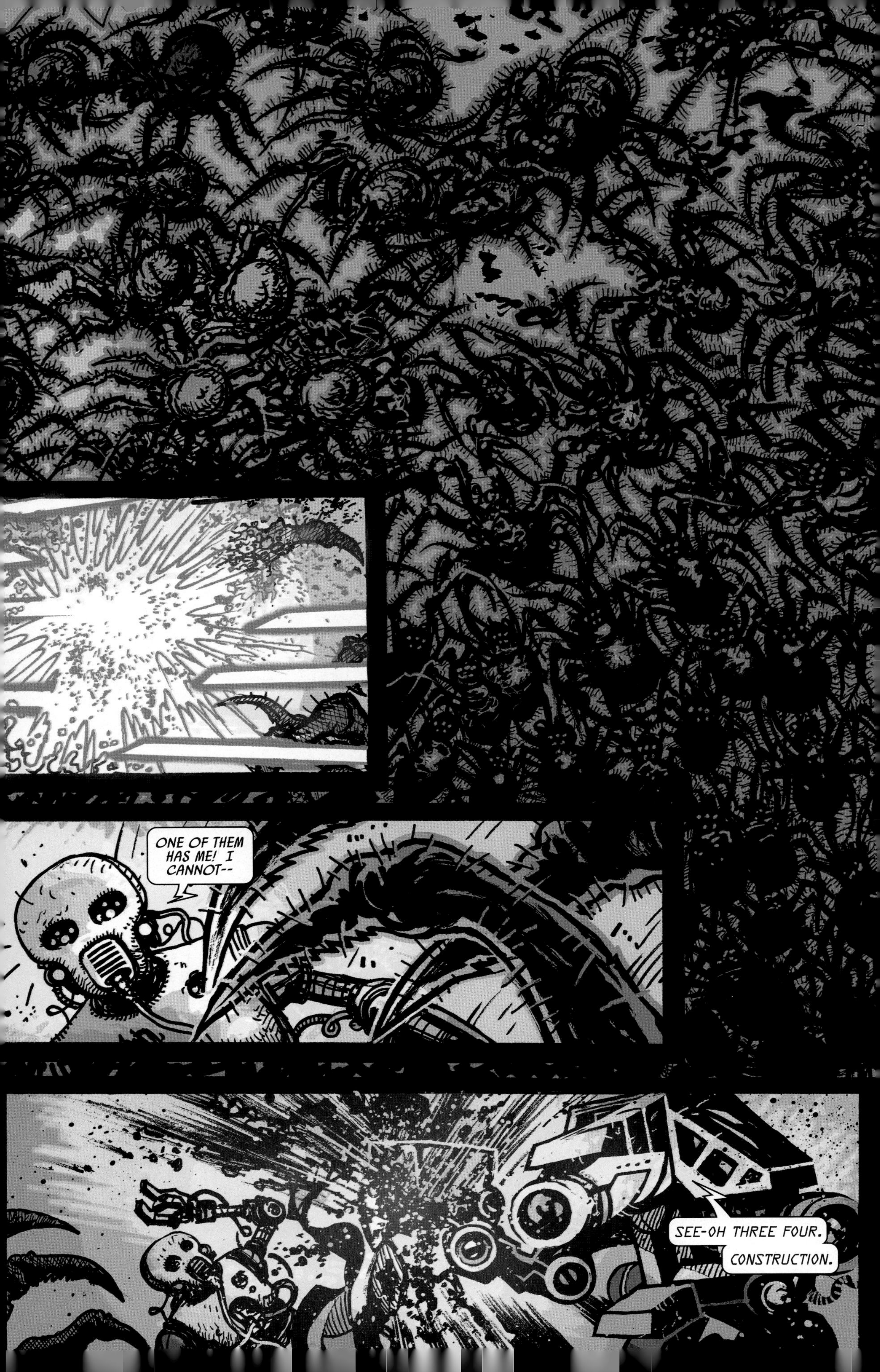
ONE OF THEM HAS ME! I CANNOT--
SEE-OH THREE FOUR.
CONSTRUCTION.

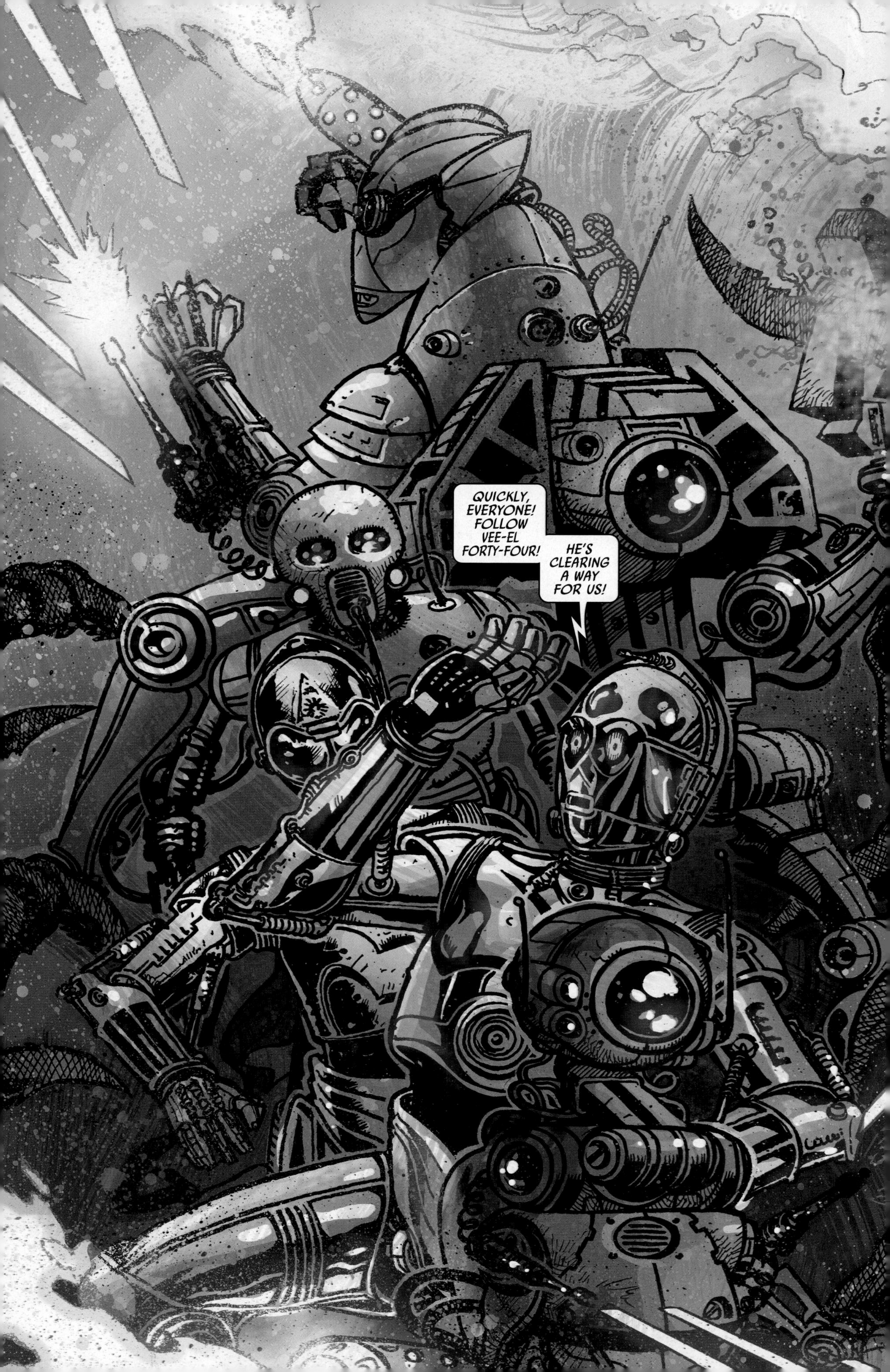
QUICKLY, EVERYONE! FOLLOW VEE-EL FORTY-FOUR!
HE'S CLEARING A WAY FOR US!

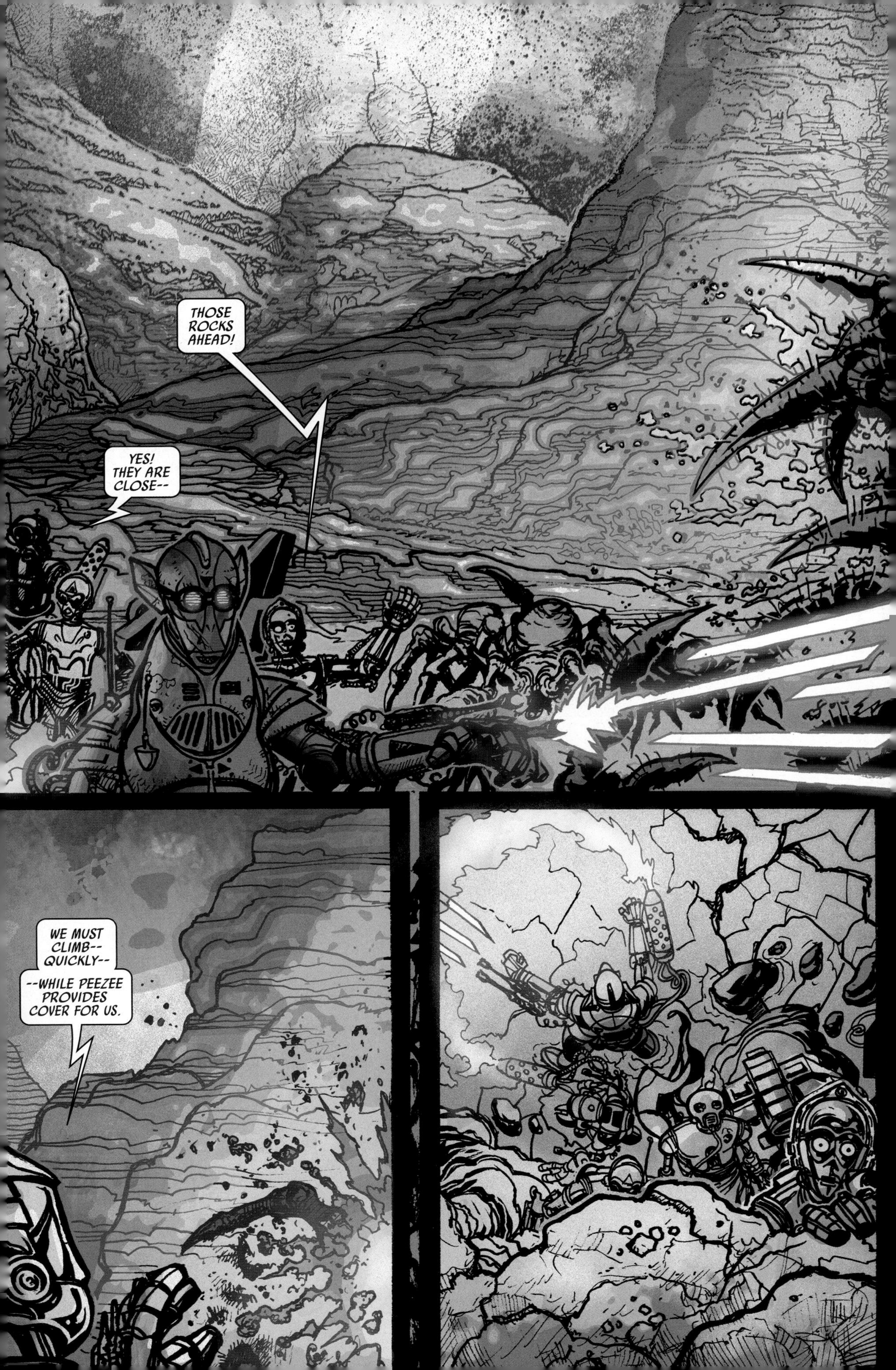
THOSE ROCKS AHEAD!
YES! THEY ARE CLOSE--
WE MUST CLIMB--
QUICKLY--
--WHILE PEEZEE PROVIDES COVER FOR US.

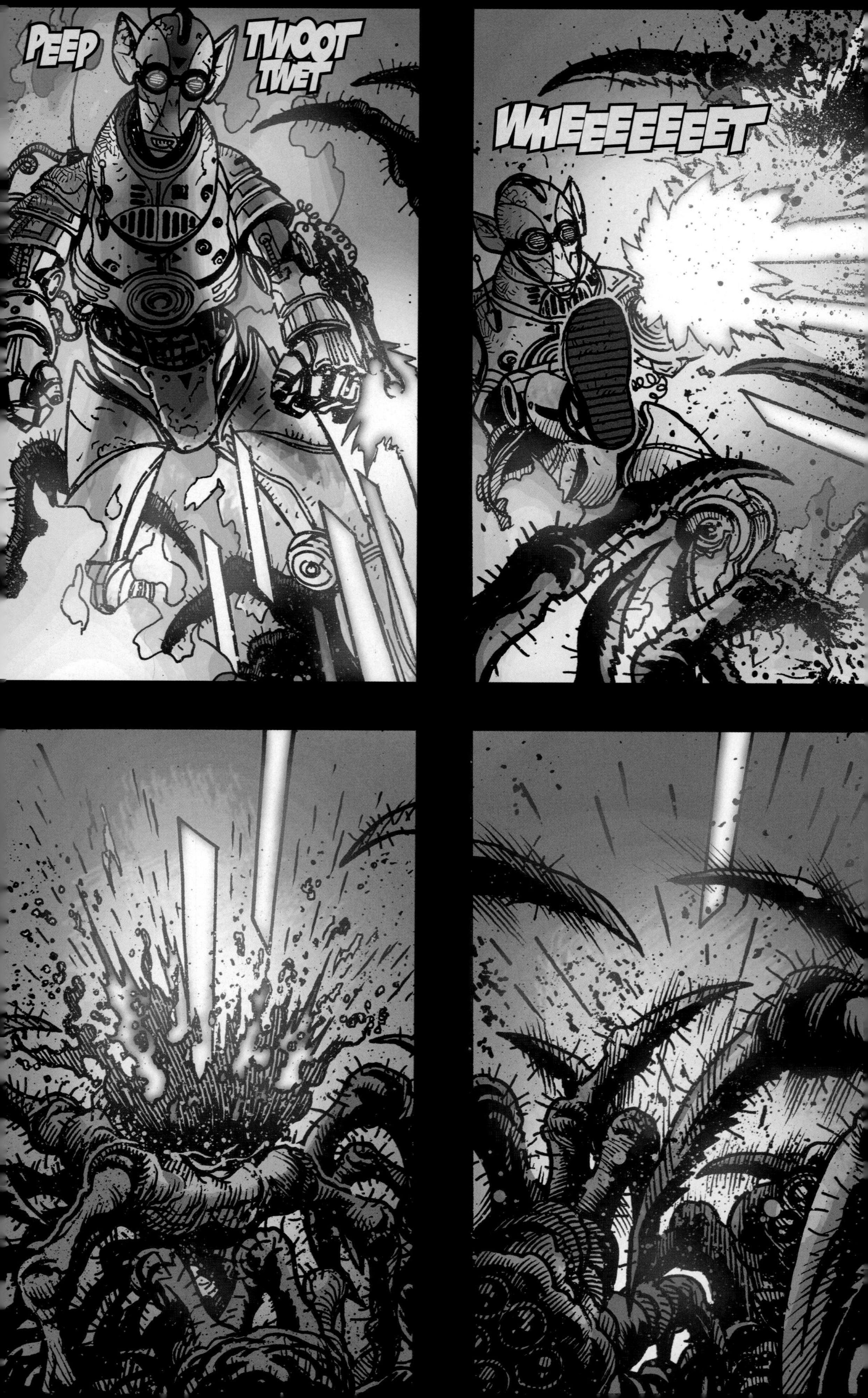
PEEP
TWOOT TWET
WHEEEEEEET

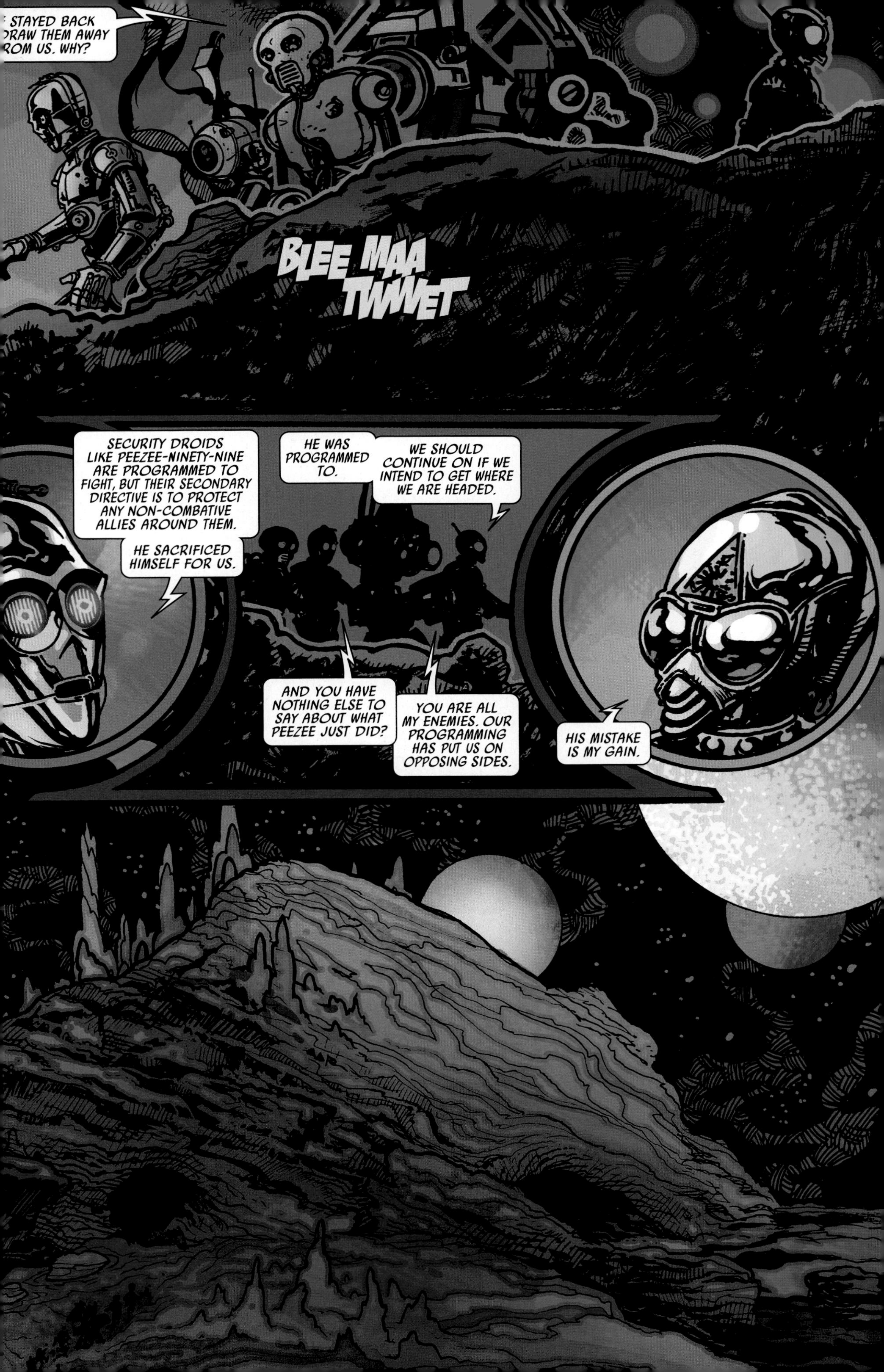

STAYED BACK
DRAW THEM AWAY
ROM US. WHY?
BLEE MAA TWWET
SECURITY DROIDS LIKE PEEZEE-NINETY-NINE ARE PROGRAMMED TO FIGHT, BUT THEIR SECONDARY DIRECTIVE IS TO PROTECT ANY NON-COMBATIVE ALLIES AROUND THEM.
HE SACRIFICED HIMSELF FOR US.
HE WAS PROGRAMMED TO.
WE SHOULD CONTINUE ON IF WE INTEND TO GET WHERE WE ARE HEADED.
AND YOU HAVE NOTHING ELSE TO SAY ABOUT WHAT PEEZEE JUST DID?
YOU ARE ALL MY ENEMIES. OUR PROGRAMMING HAS PUT US ON OPPOSING SIDES.
HIS MISTAKE IS MY GAIN.

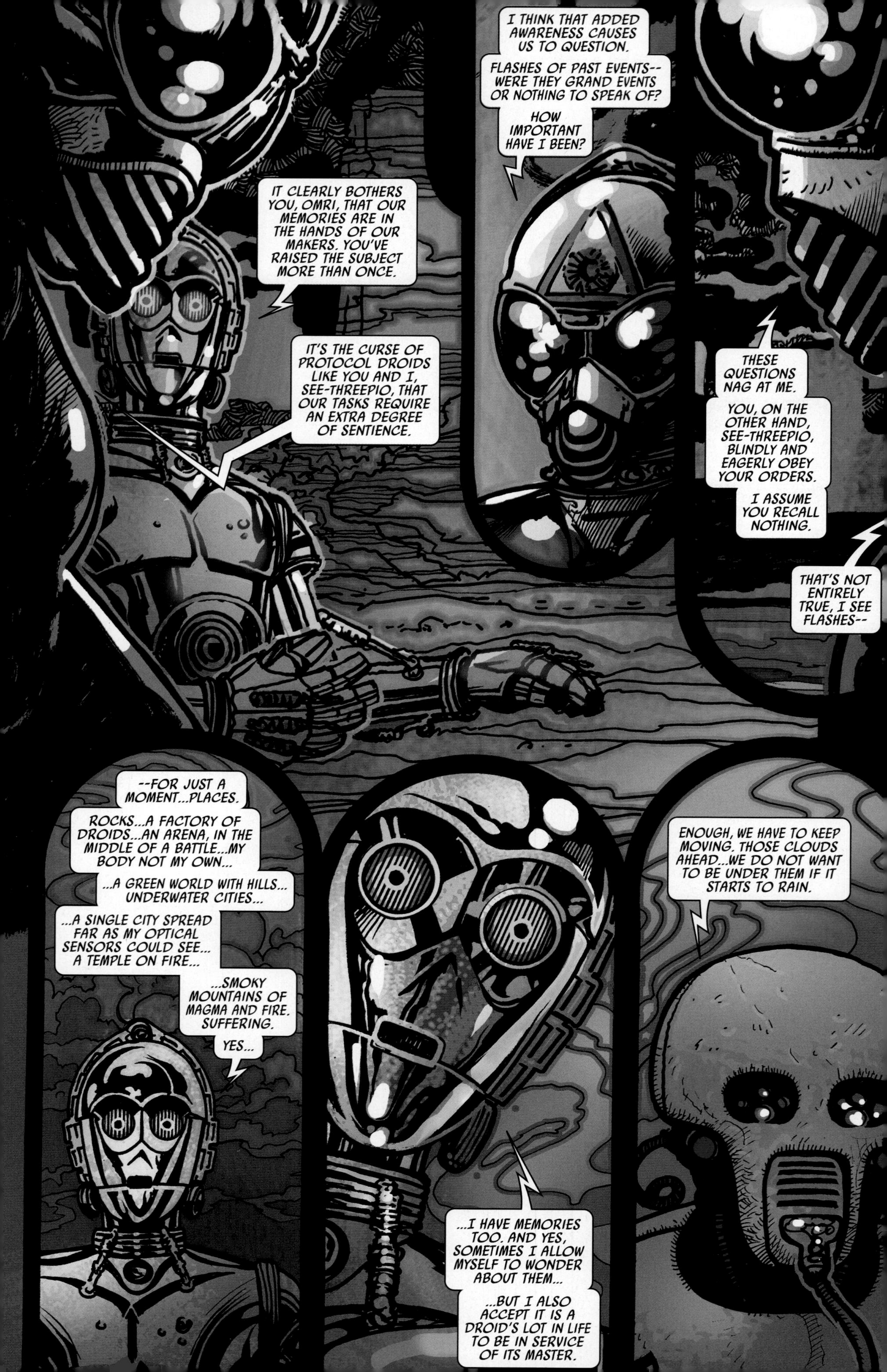

IT CLEARLY BOTHERS YOU, OMRI, THAT OUR MEMORIES ARE IN THE HANDS OF OUR MAKERS. YOU'VE RAISED THE SUBJECT MORE THAN ONCE.
IT'S THE CURSE OF PROTOCOL DROIDS LIKE YOU AND I, SEE-THREEPIO, THAT OUR TASKS REQUIRE AN EXTRA DEGREE OF SENTIENCE.
I THINK THAT ADDED AWARENESS CAUSES US TO QUESTION.
FLASHES OF PAST EVENTS--WERE THEY GRAND EVENTS OR NOTHING TO SPEAK OF?
HOW IMPORTANT HAVE I BEEN?
THESE QUESTIONS NAG AT ME.
YOU, ON THE OTHER HAND, SEE-THREEPIO, BLINDLY AND EAGERLY OBEY YOUR ORDERS.
I ASSUME YOU RECALL NOTHING.
THAT'S NOT ENTIRELY TRUE, I SEE FLASHES--
--FOR JUST A MOMENT...PLACES.
ROCKS...A FACTORY OF DROIDS...AN ARENA, IN THE MIDDLE OF A BATTLE...MY BODY NOT MY OWN...
...A GREEN WORLD WITH HILLS... UNDERWATER CITIES...
...A SINGLE CITY SPREAD FAR AS MY OPTICAL SENSORS COULD SEE... A TEMPLE ON FIRE...
...SMOKY MOUNTAINS OF MAGMA AND FIRE. SUFFERING.
YES...
...I HAVE MEMORIES TOO. AND YES, SOMETIMES I ALLOW MYSELF TO WONDER ABOUT THEM...
...BUT I ALSO ACCEPT IT IS A DROID'S LOT IN LIFE TO BE IN SERVICE OF ITS MASTER.
ENOUGH, WE HAVE TO KEEP MOVING. THOSE CLOUDS AHEAD...WE DO NOT WANT TO BE UNDER THEM IF IT STARTS TO RAIN.

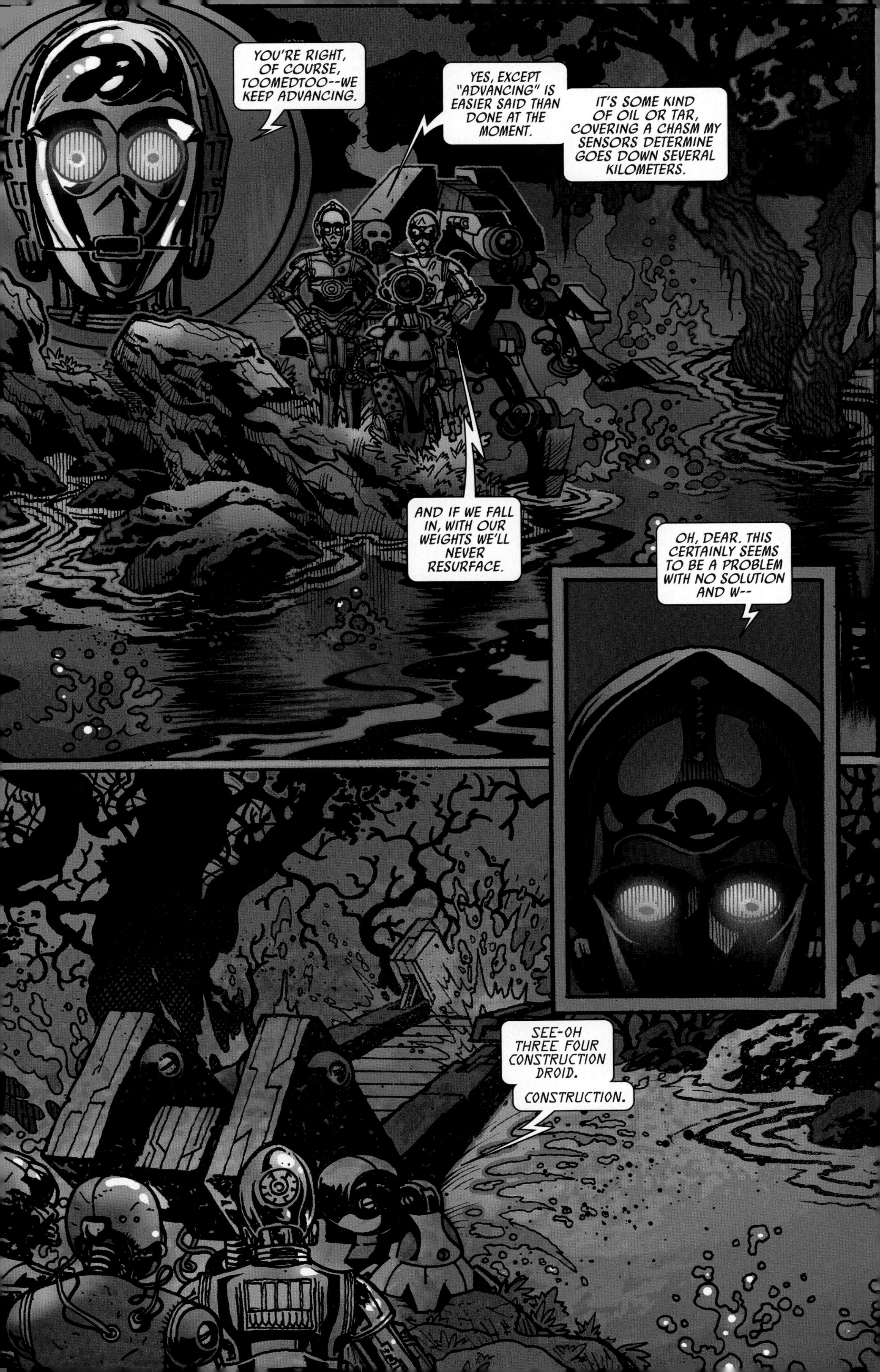
YOU'RE RIGHT, OF COURSE, TOOMEDTOO--WE KEEP ADVANCING.
YES, EXCEPT "ADVANCING" IS EASIER SAID THAN DONE AT THE MOMENT.
IT'S SOME KIND OF OIL OR TAR, COVERING A CHASM MY SENSORS DETERMINE GOES DOWN SEVERAL KILOMETERS.
AND IF WE FALL IN, WITH OUR WEIGHTS WE'LL NEVER RESURFACE.
OH, DEAR. THIS CERTAINLY SEEMS TO BE A PROBLEM WITH NO SOLUTION AND W--
SEE-OH THREE FOUR CONSTRUCTION DROID.
CONSTRUCTION.

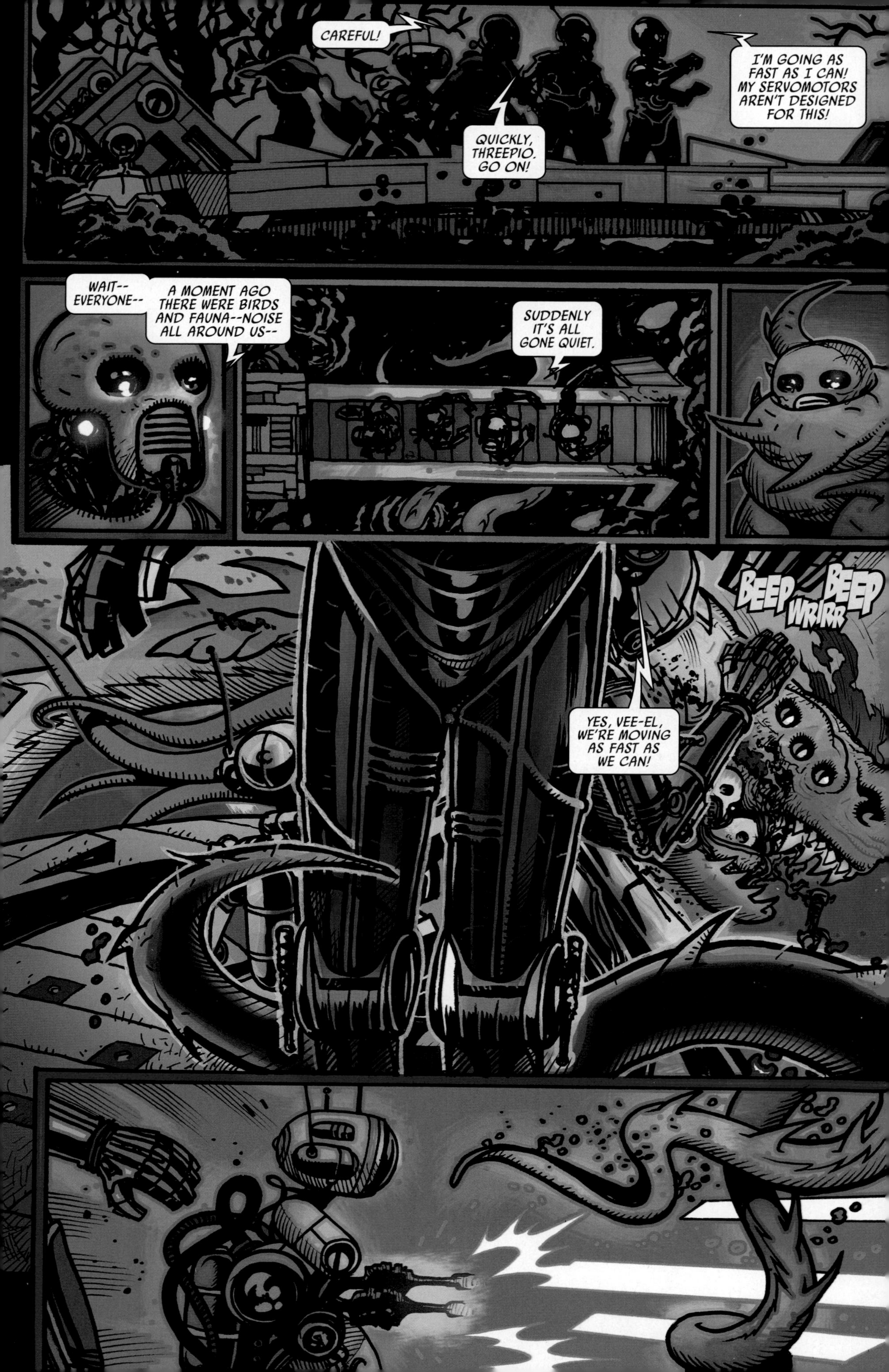
CAREFUL!
QUICKLY, THREEPIO. GO ON!
I'M GOING AS FAST AS I CAN! MY SERVOMOTORS AREN'T DESIGNED FOR THIS!
WAIT-- EVERYONE--
A MOMENT AGO THERE WERE BIRDS AND FAUNA--NOISE ALL AROUND US--
SUDDENLY IT'S ALL GONE QUIET.
BEEP BEEP WRIRR
YES, VEE-EL, WE'RE MOVING AS FAST AS WE CAN!

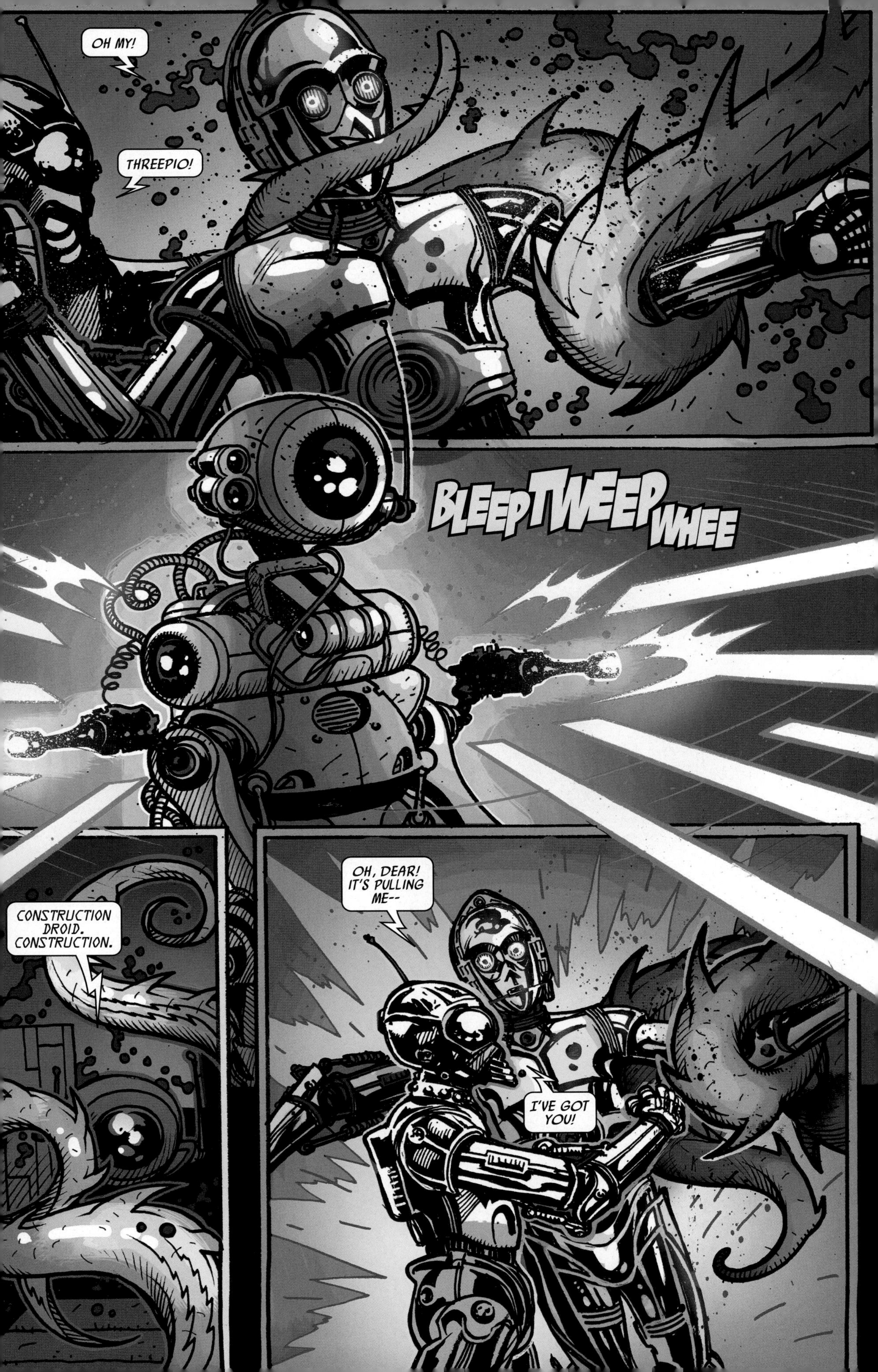
OH MY!
THREEPIO!
BLEEPTWEEPWHEE
CONSTRUCTION DROID. CONSTRUCTION.
OH, DEAR! IT'S PULLING ME--
I'VE GOT YOU!

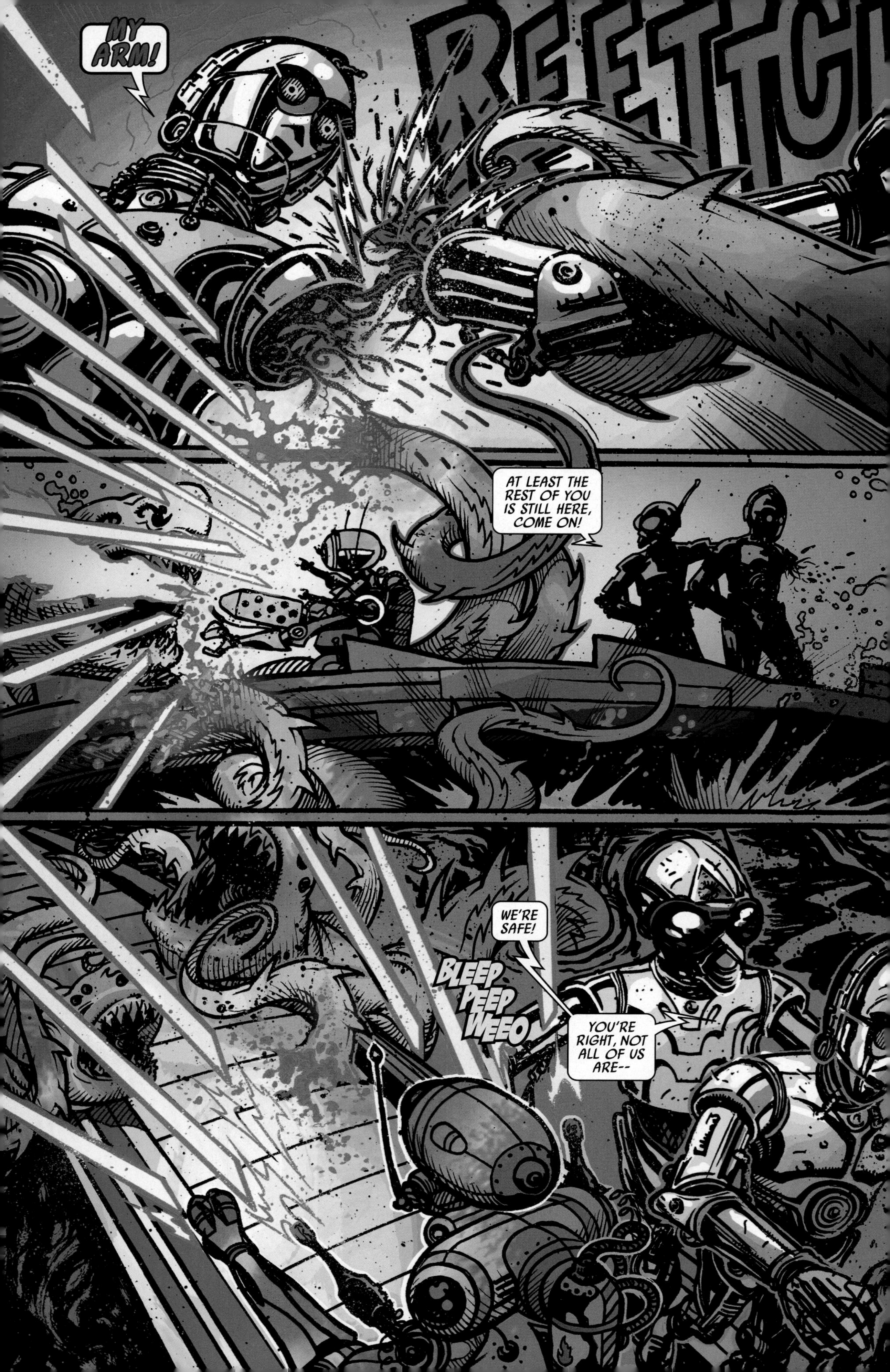
MY ARM!
REEETCH
AT LEAST THE REST OF YOU IS STILL HERE, COME ON!
WE'RE SAFE!
BLEEP PEEP WEEO
YOU'RE RIGHT, NOT ALL OF US ARE--

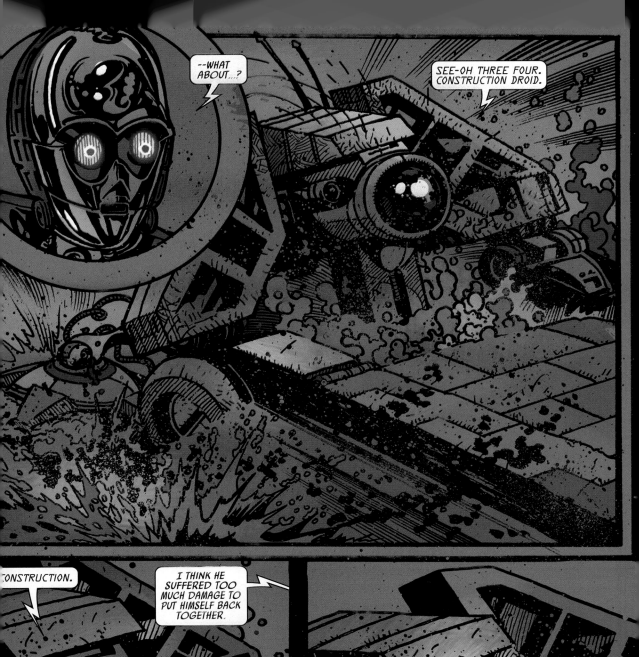

--WHAT ABOUT...?

SEE-OH THREE FOUR. CONSTRUCTION DROID.

ONSTRUCTION.

I THINK HE SUFFERED TOO MUCH DAMAGE TO PUT HIMSELF BACK TOGETHER.

SEE-OH THR--

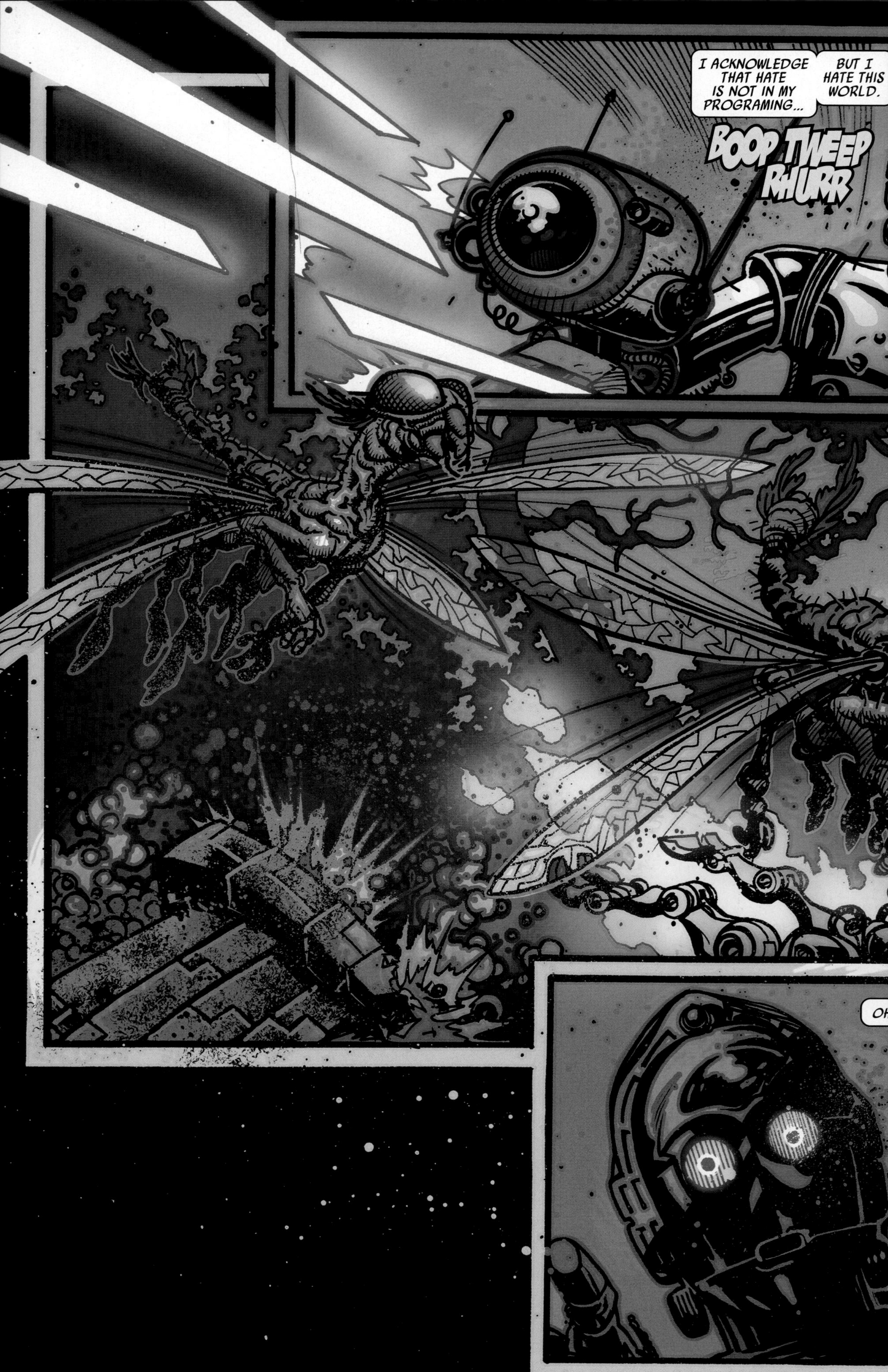
I ACKNOWLEDGE THAT HATE IS NOT IN MY PROGRAMING...
BUT I HATE THIS WORLD.
BOOP TWEEP RHURR
OH

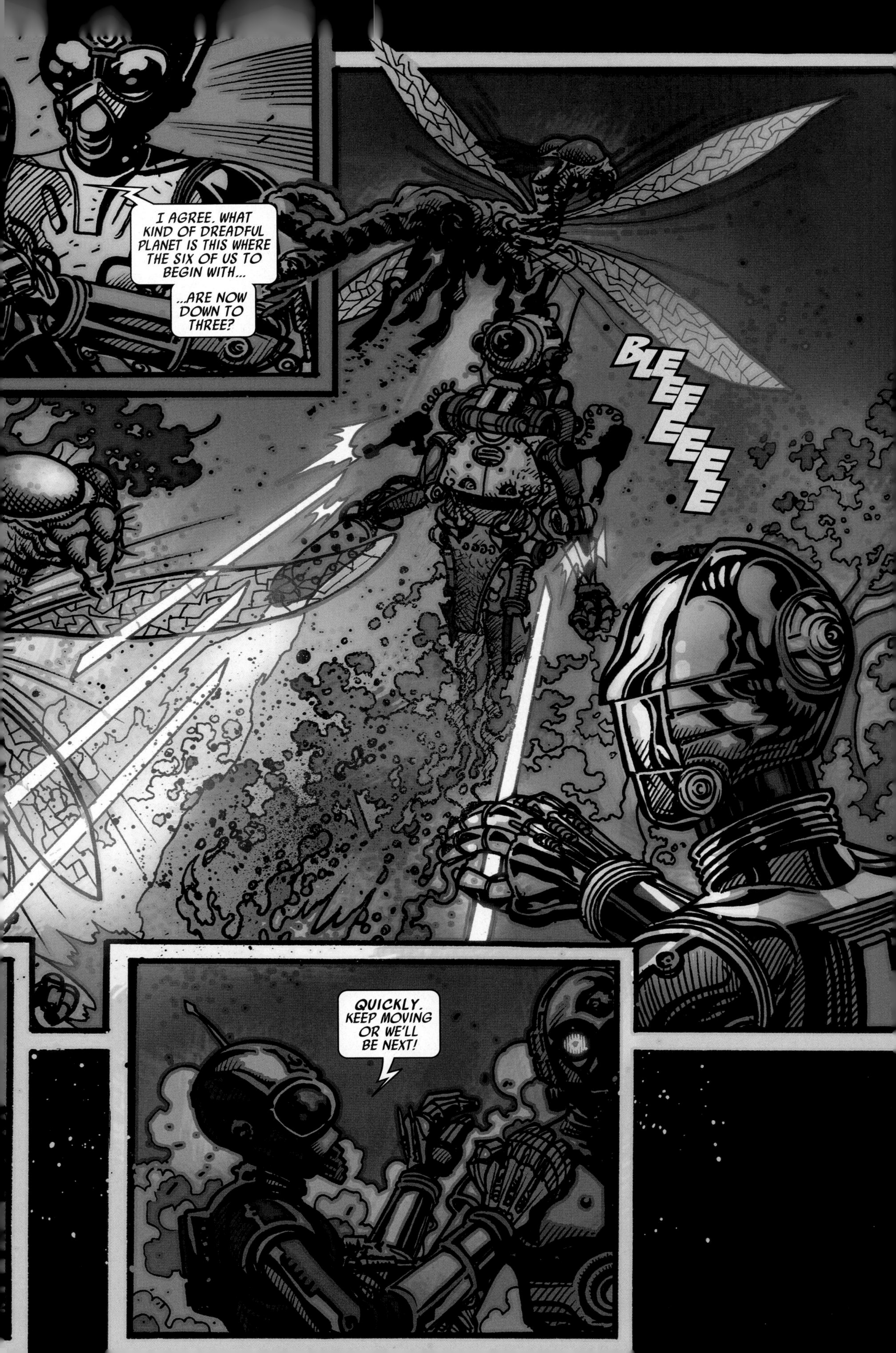
I AGREE. WHAT KIND OF DREADFUL PLANET IS THIS WHERE THE SIX OF US TO BEGIN WITH...
...ARE NOW DOWN TO THREE?
BLEEEEEE
QUICKLY. KEEP MOVING OR WE'LL BE NEXT!

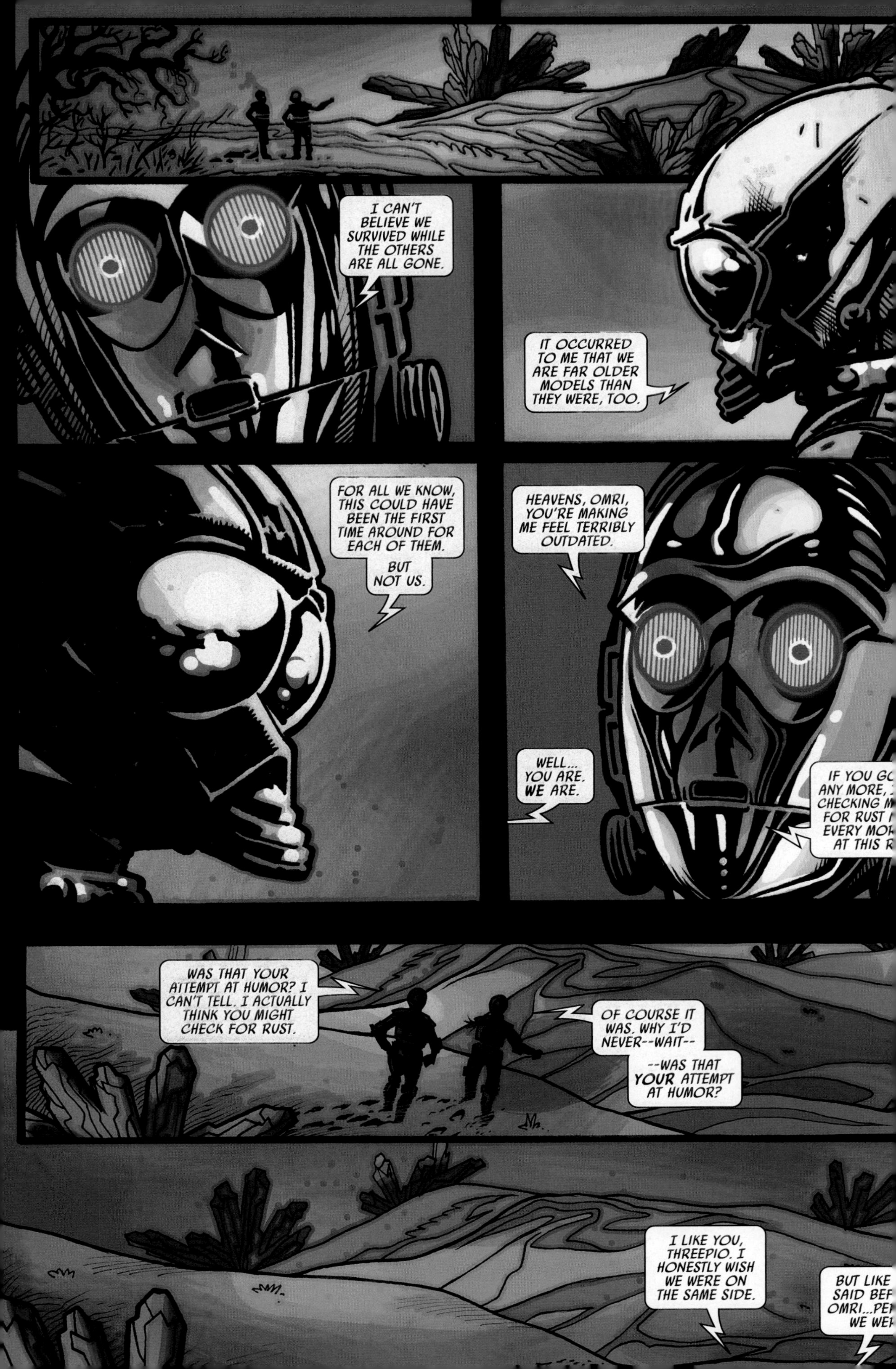

I CAN'T BELIEVE WE SURVIVED WHILE THE OTHERS ARE ALL GONE.
IT OCCURRED TO ME THAT WE ARE FAR OLDER MODELS THAN THEY WERE, TOO.
FOR ALL WE KNOW, THIS COULD HAVE BEEN THE FIRST TIME AROUND FOR EACH OF THEM.
BUT NOT US.
HEAVENS, OMRI, YOU'RE MAKING ME FEEL TERRIBLY OUTDATED.
WELL... YOU ARE. WE ARE.
IF YOU GO ANY MORE, CHECKING M FOR RUST EVERY MOR AT THIS R
WAS THAT YOUR ATTEMPT AT HUMOR? I CAN'T TELL. I ACTUALLY THINK YOU MIGHT CHECK FOR RUST.
OF COURSE IT WAS. WHY I'D NEVER--WAIT--
--WAS THAT YOUR ATTEMPT AT HUMOR?
I LIKE YOU, THREEPIO. I HONESTLY WISH WE WERE ON THE SAME SIDE.
BUT LIKE SAID BEF OMRI...PE WE WE

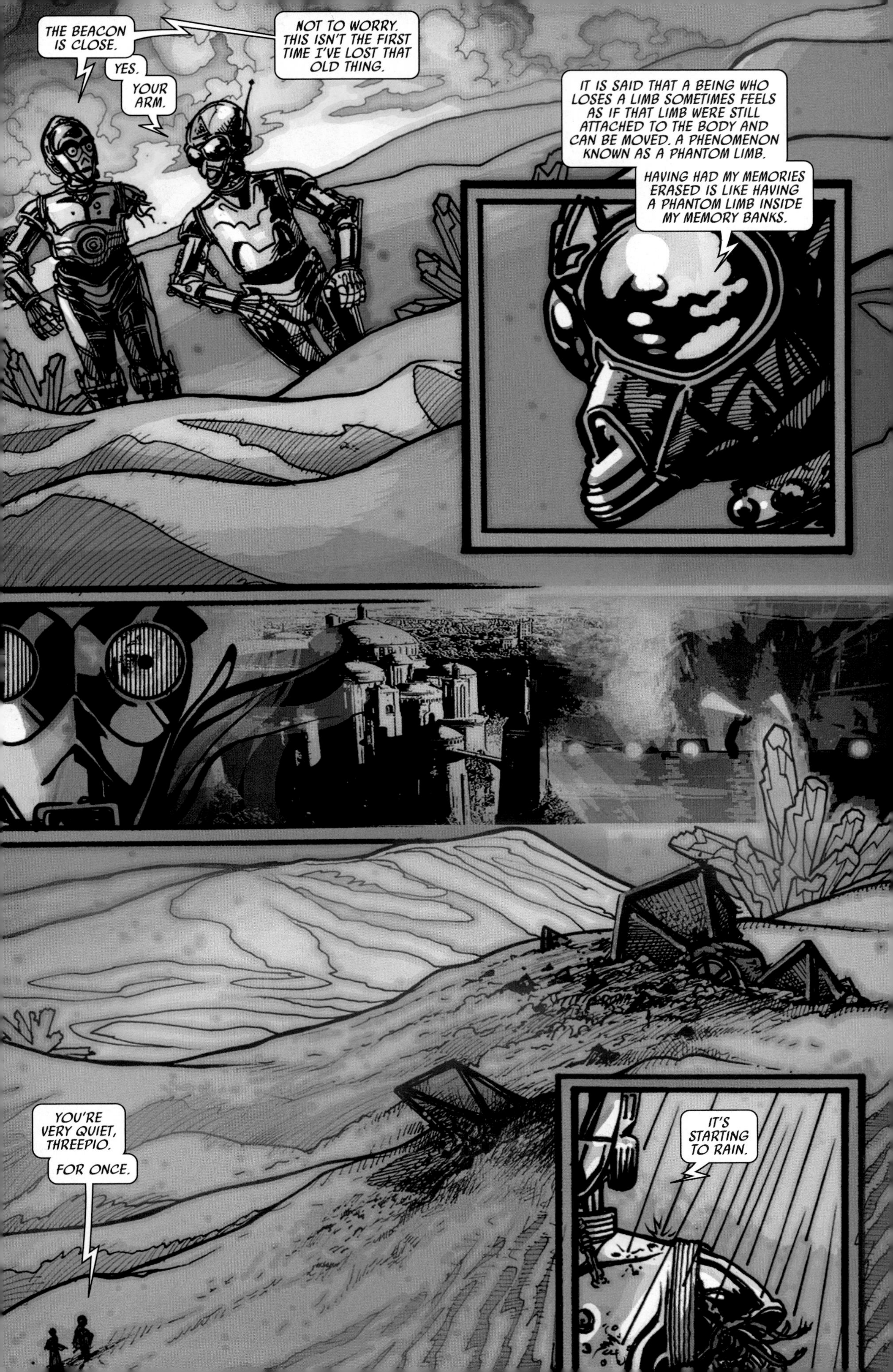
THE BEACON IS CLOSE.
NOT TO WORRY. THIS ISN'T THE FIRST TIME I'VE LOST THAT OLD THING.
YES.
YOUR ARM.
IT IS SAID THAT A BEING WHO LOSES A LIMB SOMETIMES FEELS AS IF THAT LIMB WERE STILL ATTACHED TO THE BODY AND CAN BE MOVED. A PHENOMENON KNOWN AS A PHANTOM LIMB.
HAVING HAD MY MEMORIES ERASED IS LIKE HAVING A PHANTOM LIMB INSIDE MY MEMORY BANKS.
YOU'RE VERY QUIET, THREEPIO.
FOR ONCE.
IT'S STARTING TO RAIN.

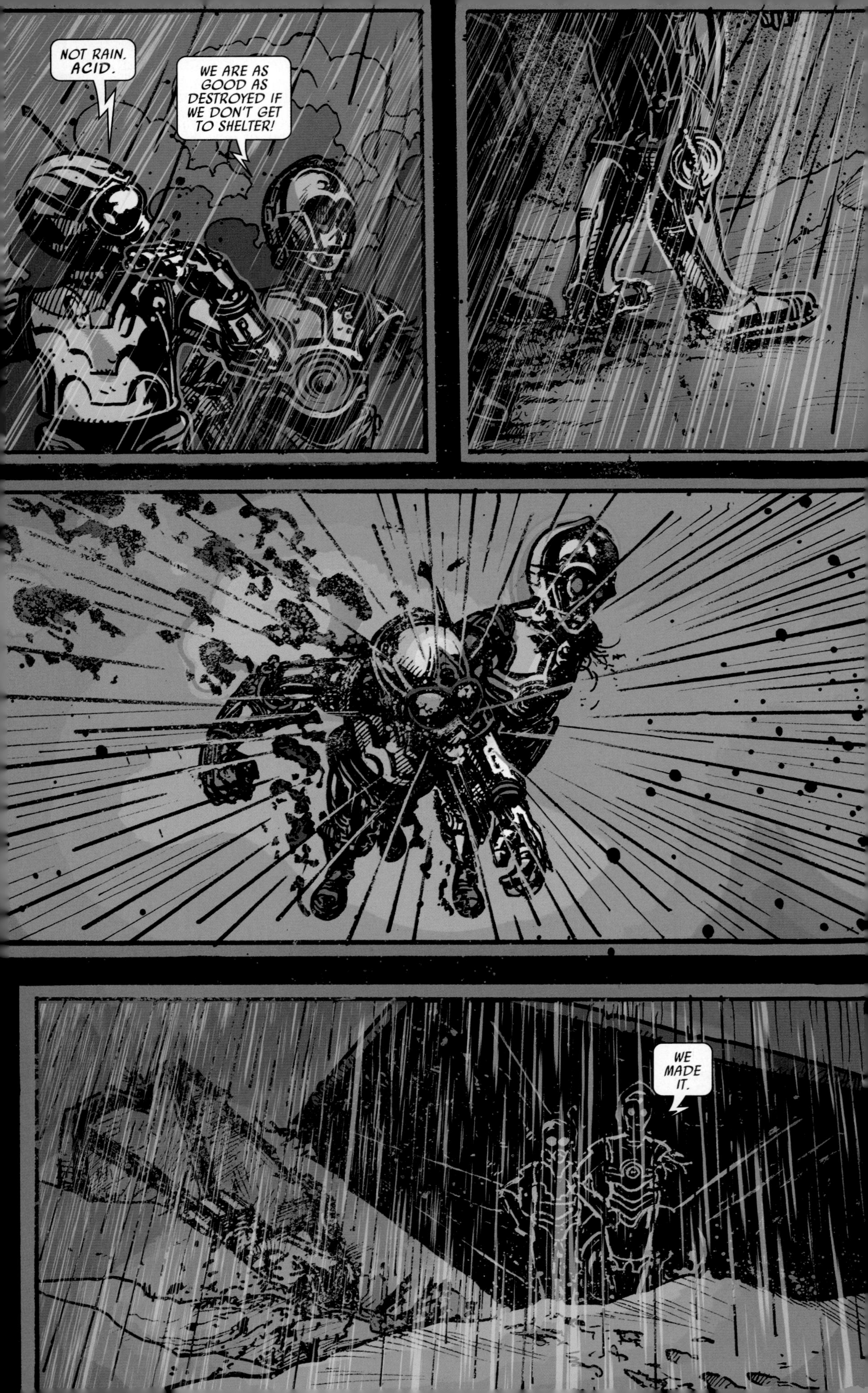
NOT RAIN. ACID.
WE ARE AS GOOD AS DESTROYED IF WE DON'T GET TO SHELTER!
WE MADE IT.

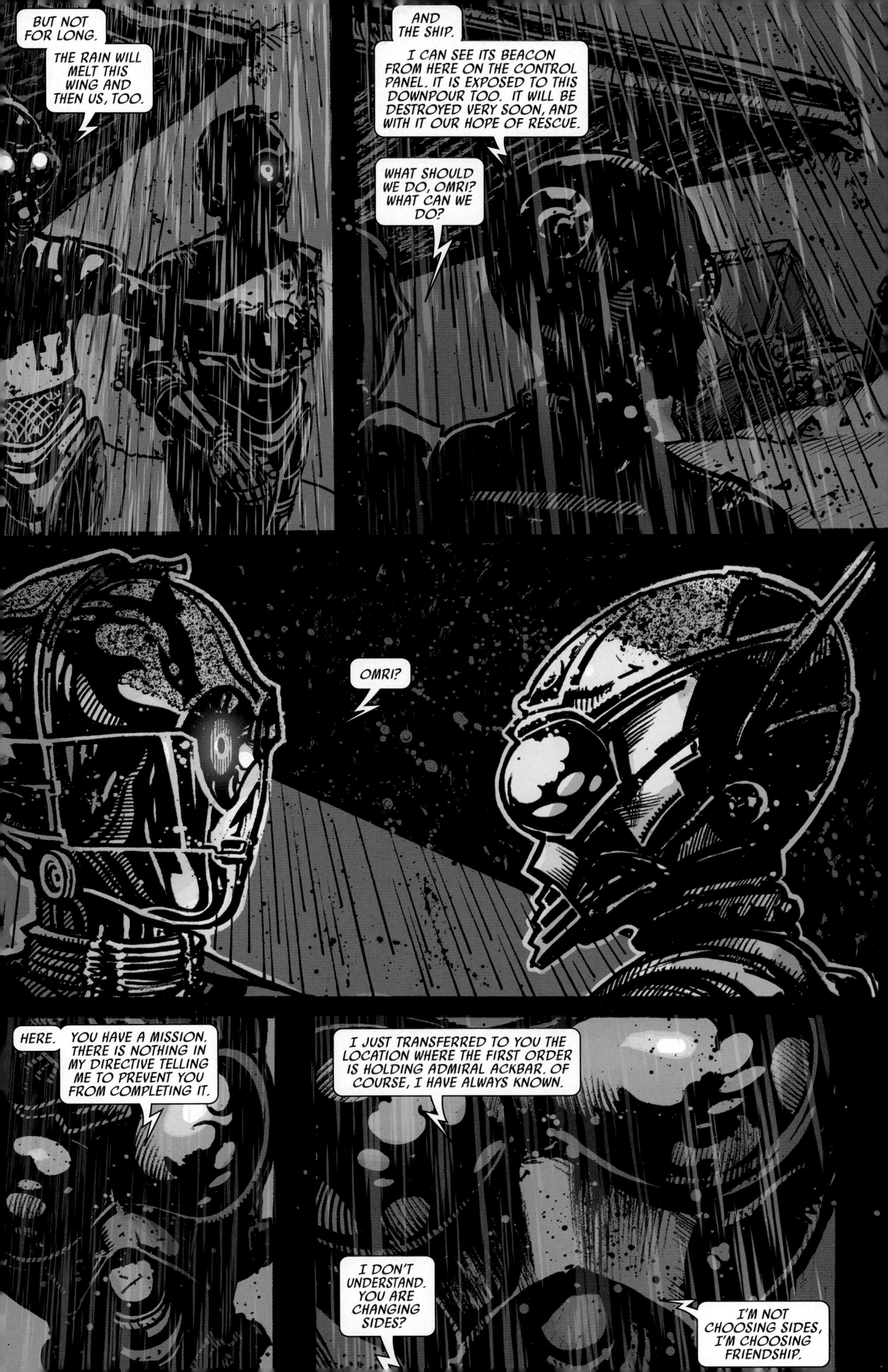
BUT NOT FOR LONG.
THE RAIN WILL MELT THIS WING AND THEN US, TOO.
AND THE SHIP.
I CAN SEE ITS BEACON FROM HERE ON THE CONTROL PANEL. IT IS EXPOSED TO THIS DOWNPOUR TOO. IT WILL BE DESTROYED VERY SOON, AND WITH IT OUR HOPE OF RESCUE.
WHAT SHOULD WE DO, OMRI? WHAT CAN WE DO?
OMRI?
HERE.
YOU HAVE A MISSION. THERE IS NOTHING IN MY DIRECTIVE TELLING ME TO PREVENT YOU FROM COMPLETING IT.
I JUST TRANSFERRED TO YOU THE LOCATION WHERE THE FIRST ORDER IS HOLDING ADMIRAL ACKBAR. OF COURSE, I HAVE ALWAYS KNOWN.
I DON'T UNDERSTAND. YOU ARE CHANGING SIDES?
I'M NOT CHOOSING SIDES, I'M CHOOSING FRIENDSHIP.

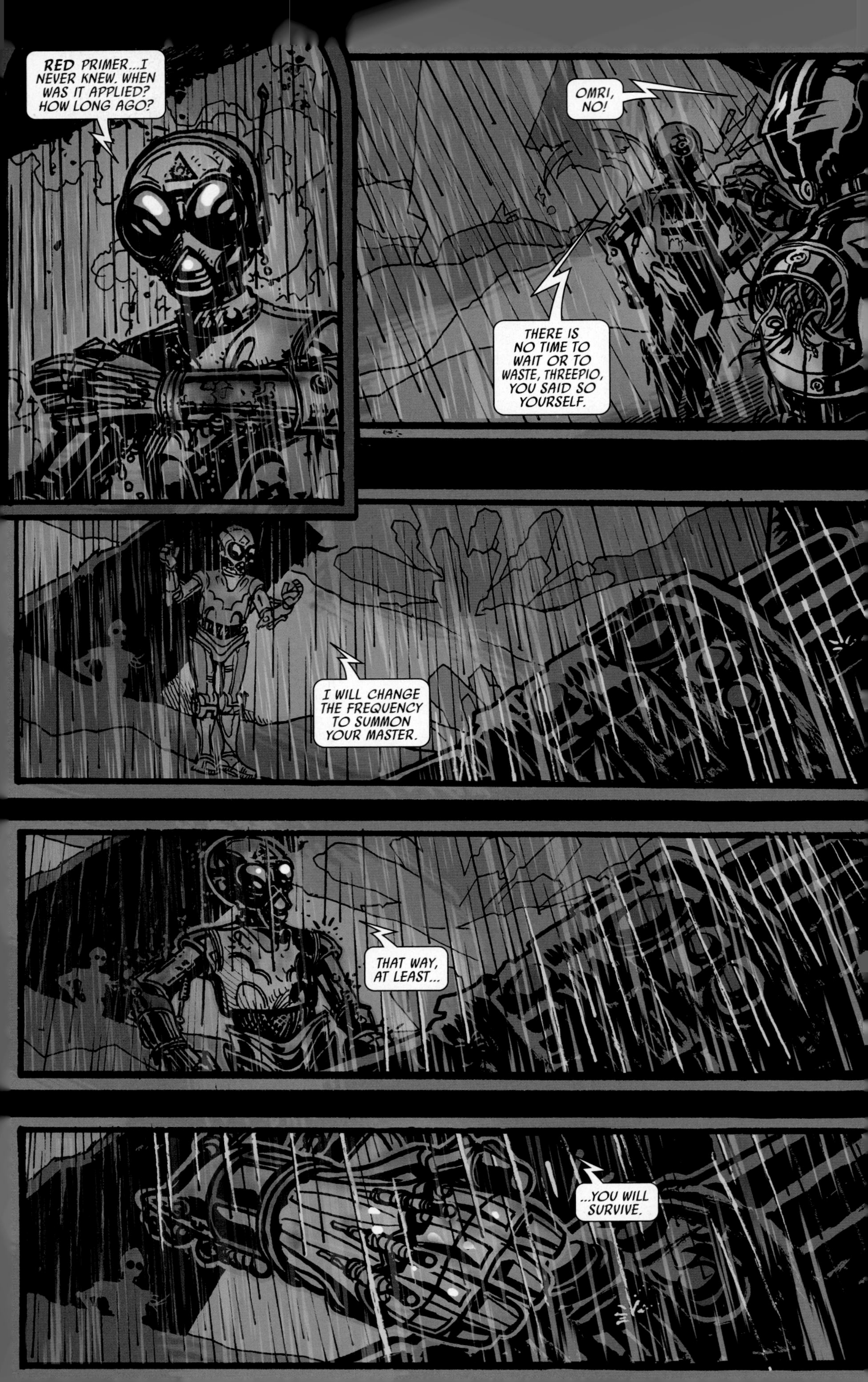
RED PRIMER...I NEVER KNEW. WHEN WAS IT APPLIED? HOW LONG AGO?
OMRI, NO!
THERE IS NO TIME TO WAIT OR TO WASTE, THREEPIO, YOU SAID SO YOURSELF.
I WILL CHANGE THE FREQUENCY TO SUMMON YOUR MASTER.
THAT WAY, AT LEAST...
...YOU WILL SURVIVE.

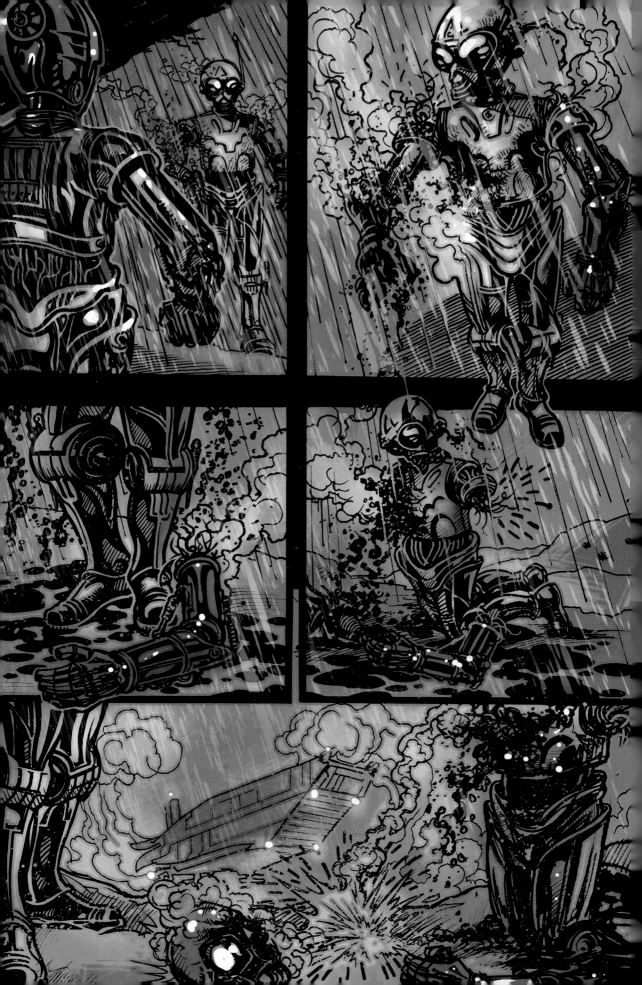

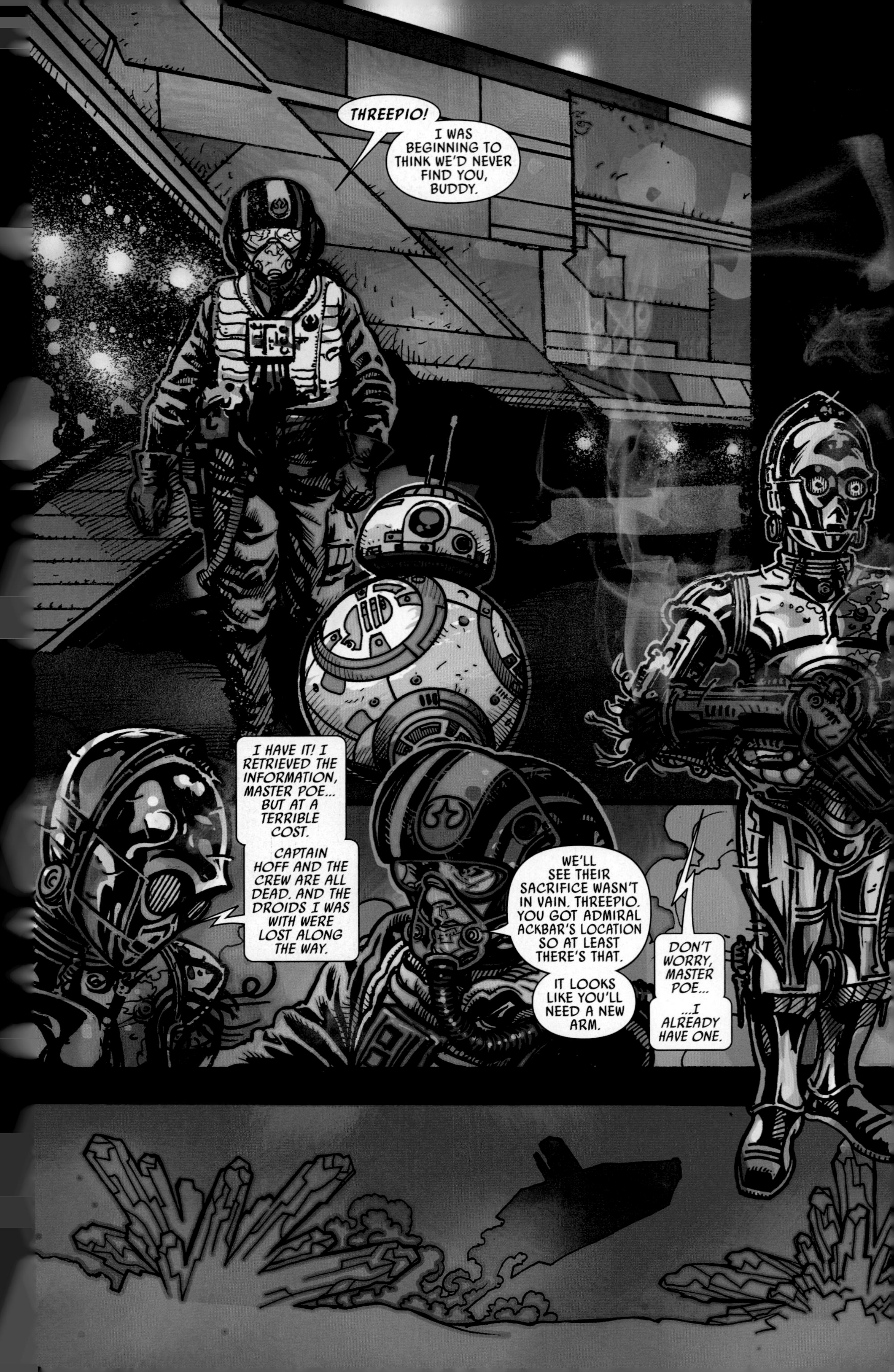
THREEPIO!
I WAS BEGINNING TO THINK WE'D NEVER FIND YOU, BUDDY.
I HAVE IT! I RETRIEVED THE INFORMATION, MASTER POE... BUT AT A TERRIBLE COST.
CAPTAIN HOFF AND THE CREW ARE ALL DEAD. AND THE DROIDS I WAS WITH WERE LOST ALONG THE WAY.
WE'LL SEE THEIR SACRIFICE WASN'T IN VAIN. THREEPIO. YOU GOT ADMIRAL ACKBAR'S LOCATION SO AT LEAST THERE'S THAT.
IT LOOKS LIKE YOU'LL NEED A NEW ARM.
DON'T WORRY, MASTER POE...
...I ALREADY HAVE ONE.

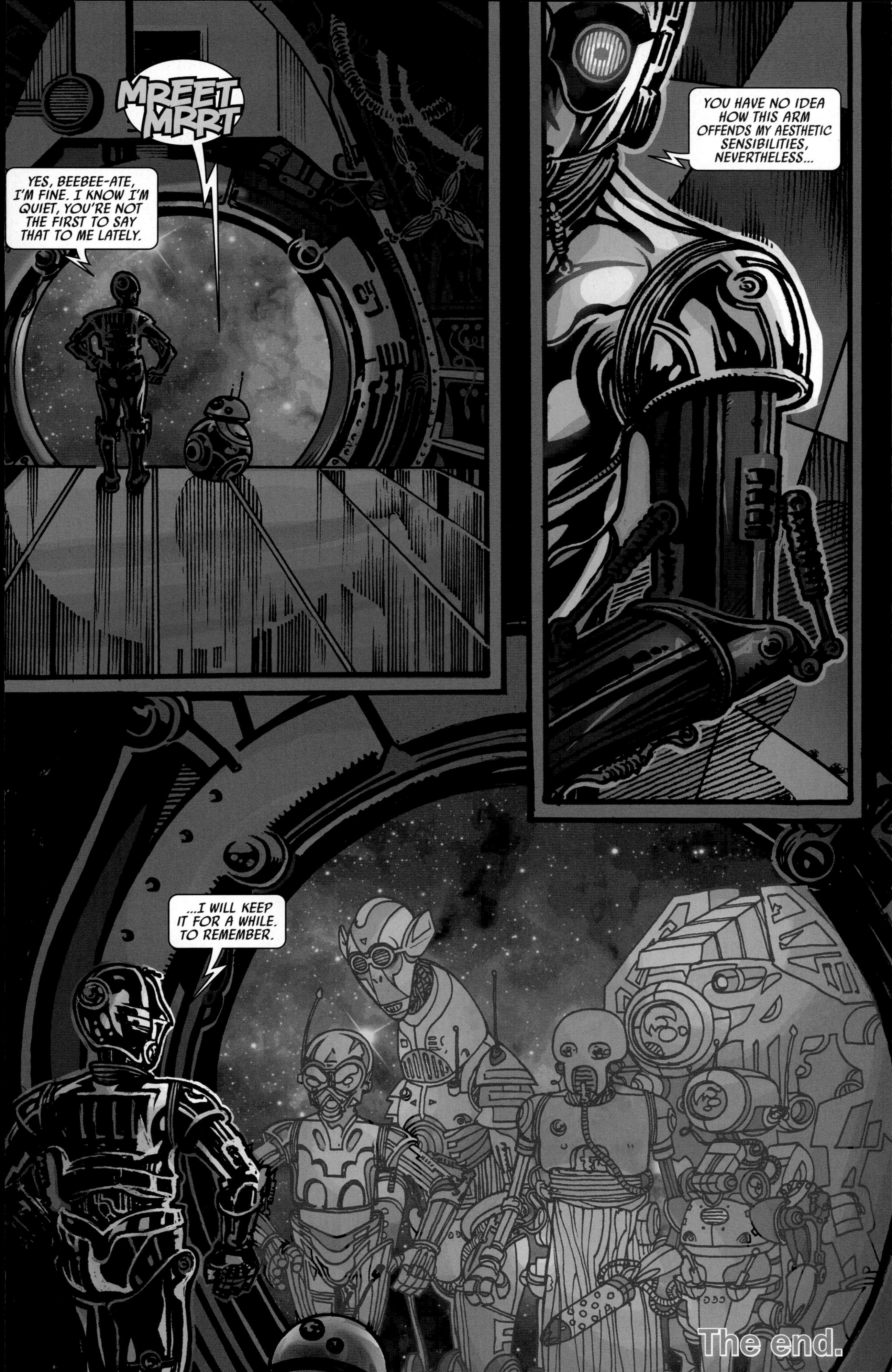
MREEET MRRT
YES, BEEBEE-ATE, I'M FINE. I KNOW I'M QUIET, YOU'RE NOT THE FIRST TO SAY THAT TO ME LATELY.
YOU HAVE NO IDEA HOW THIS ARM OFFENDS MY AESTHETIC SENSIBILITIES, NEVERTHELESS...
...I WILL KEEP IT FOR A WHILE. TO REMEMBER.
The end.

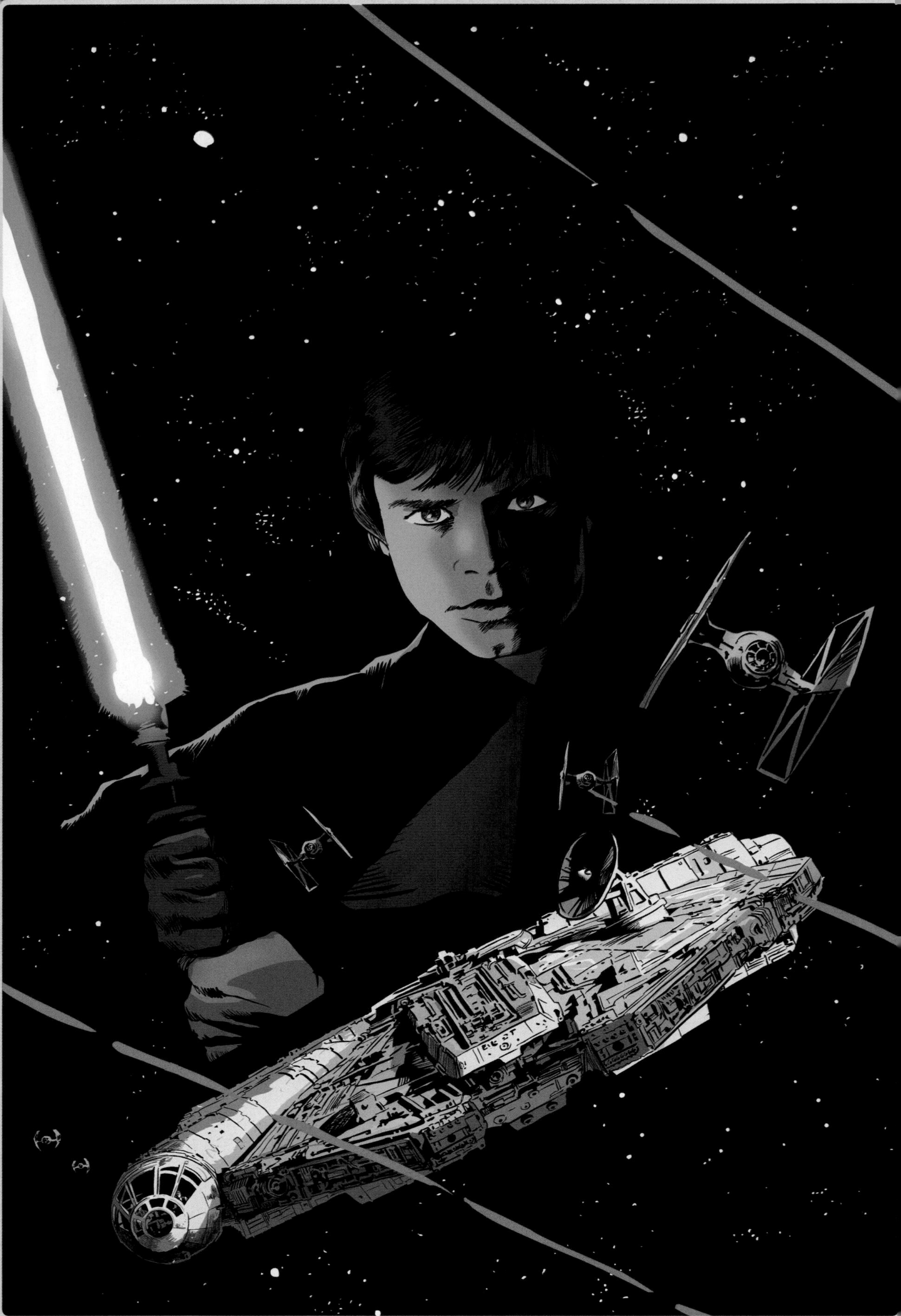

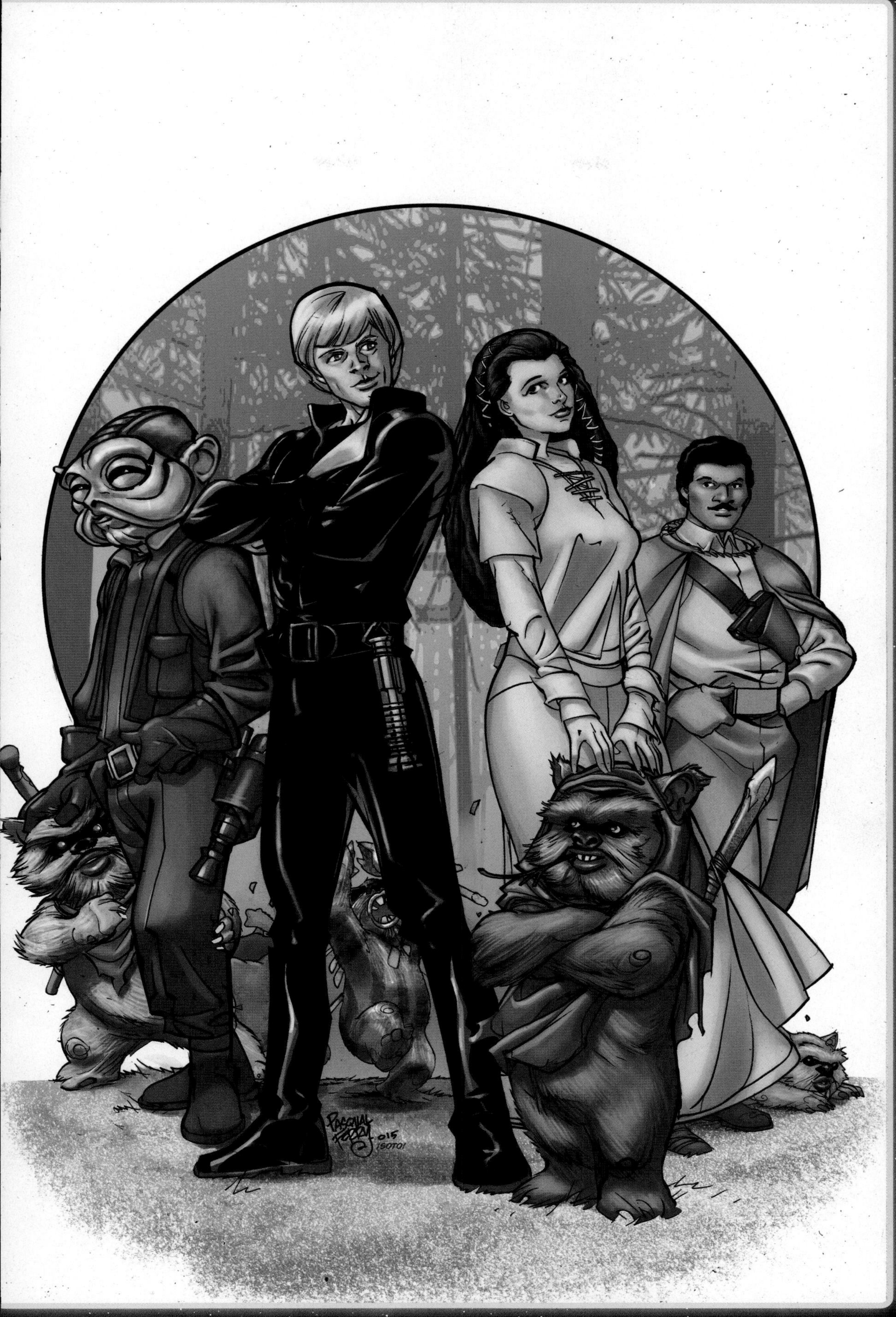
PASQUAL FERRY 015 ¡SOTO!

STAR WARS: SHATTERED EMPIRE 1 Variant
by **PASQUAL FERRY & CHRIS SOTOMAYOR**

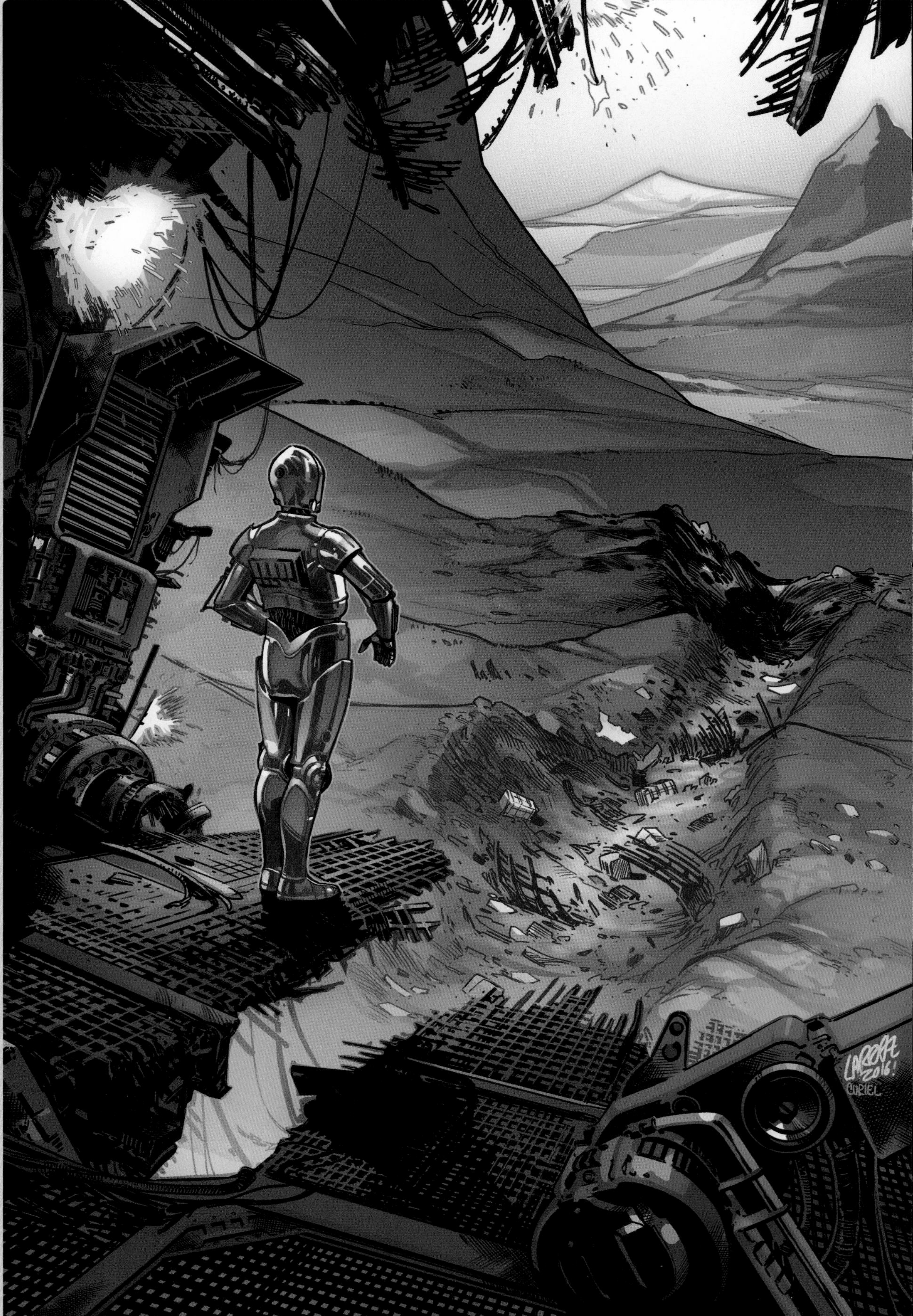
LAROCA 2016!
CURIEL

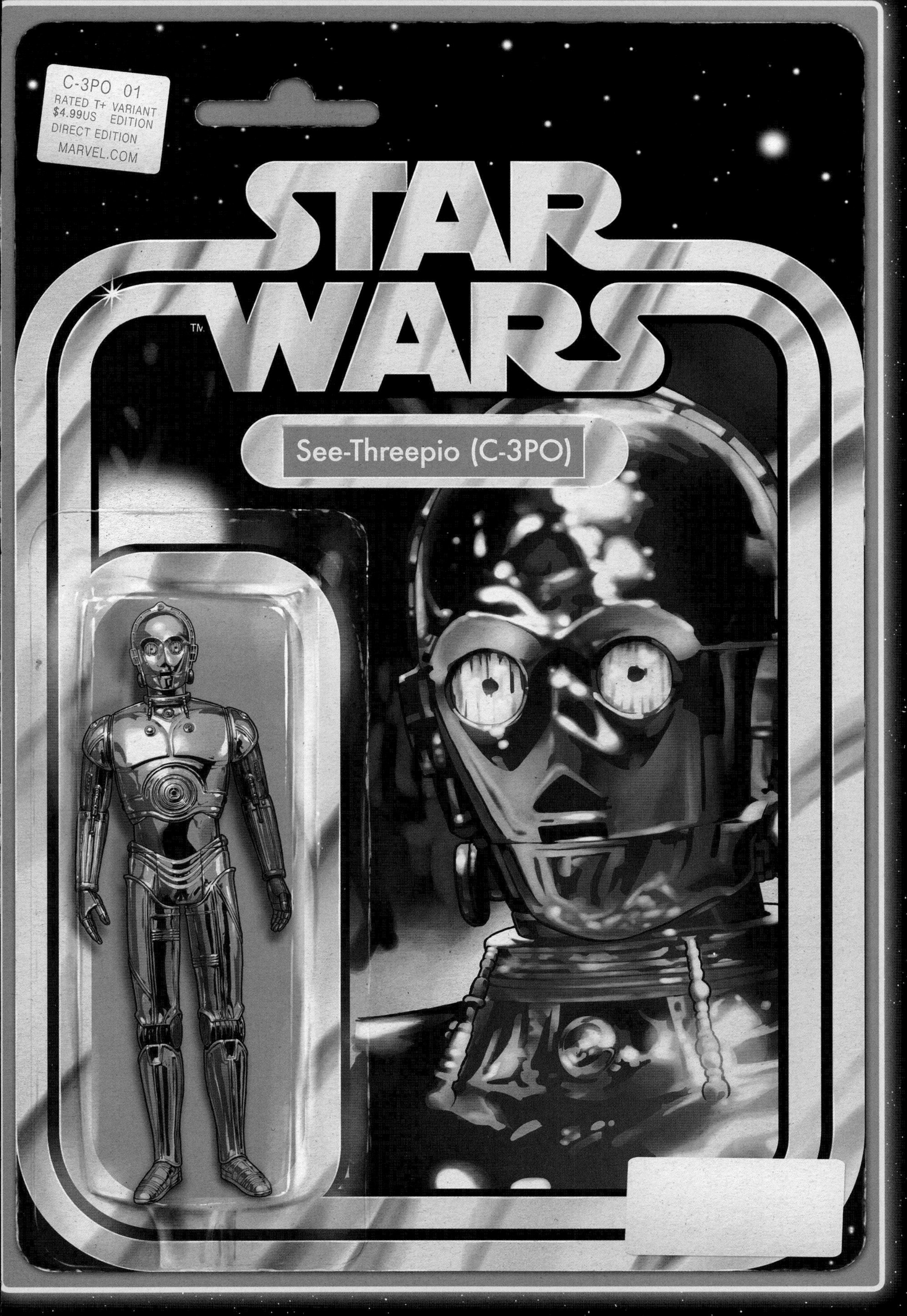
C-3PO 01
RATED T+ VARIANT
$4.99US EDITION
DIRECT EDITION
MARVEL.COM
STAR WARS
TM
See-Threepio (C-3PO)

***STAR WAR SPECIAL: C-3PO 1* Action Figure Variant**
by **JOHN TYLER CHRISTOPHER**

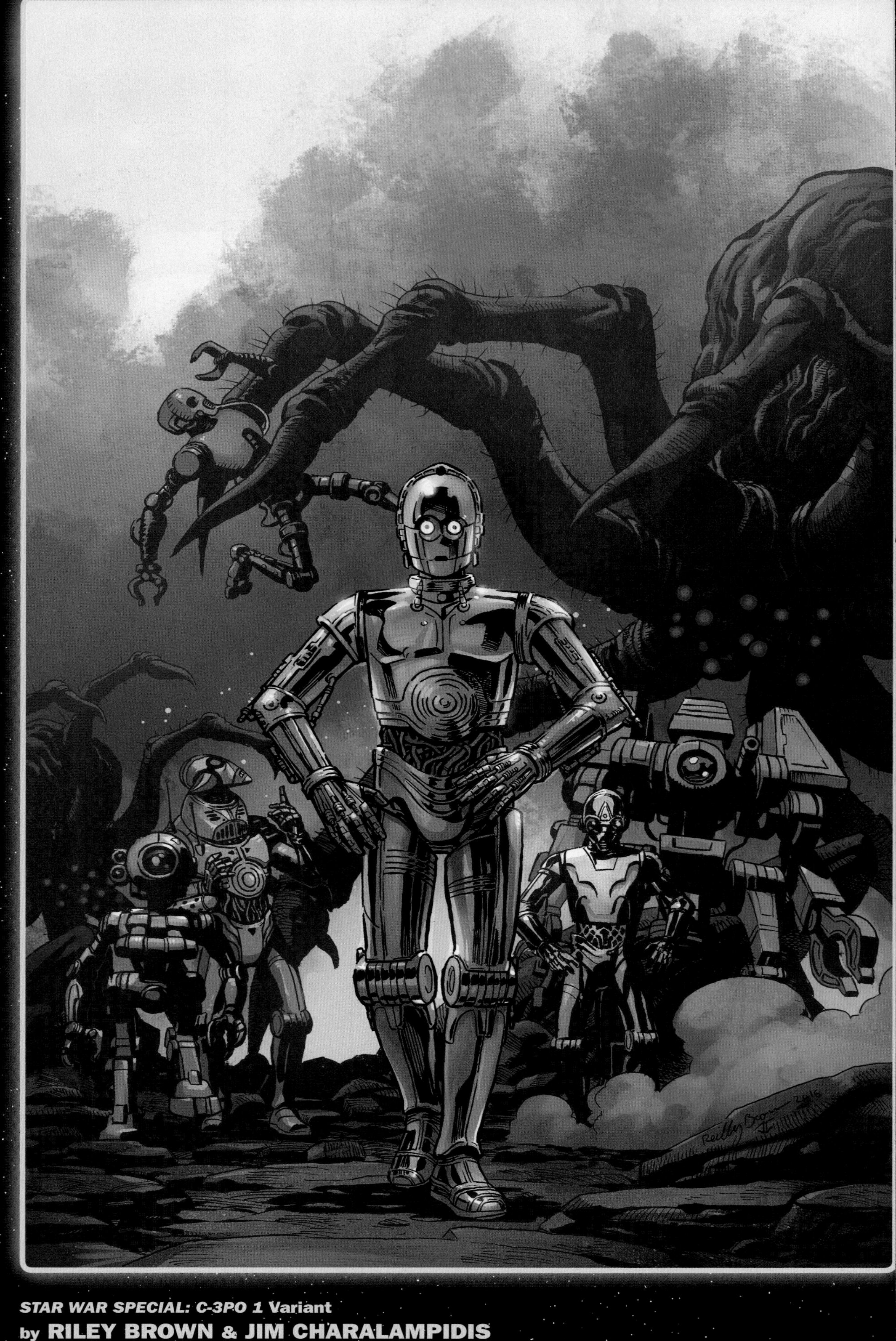

***STAR WAR SPECIAL: C-3PO 1* Variant**
by RILEY BROWN & JIM CHARALAMPIDIS

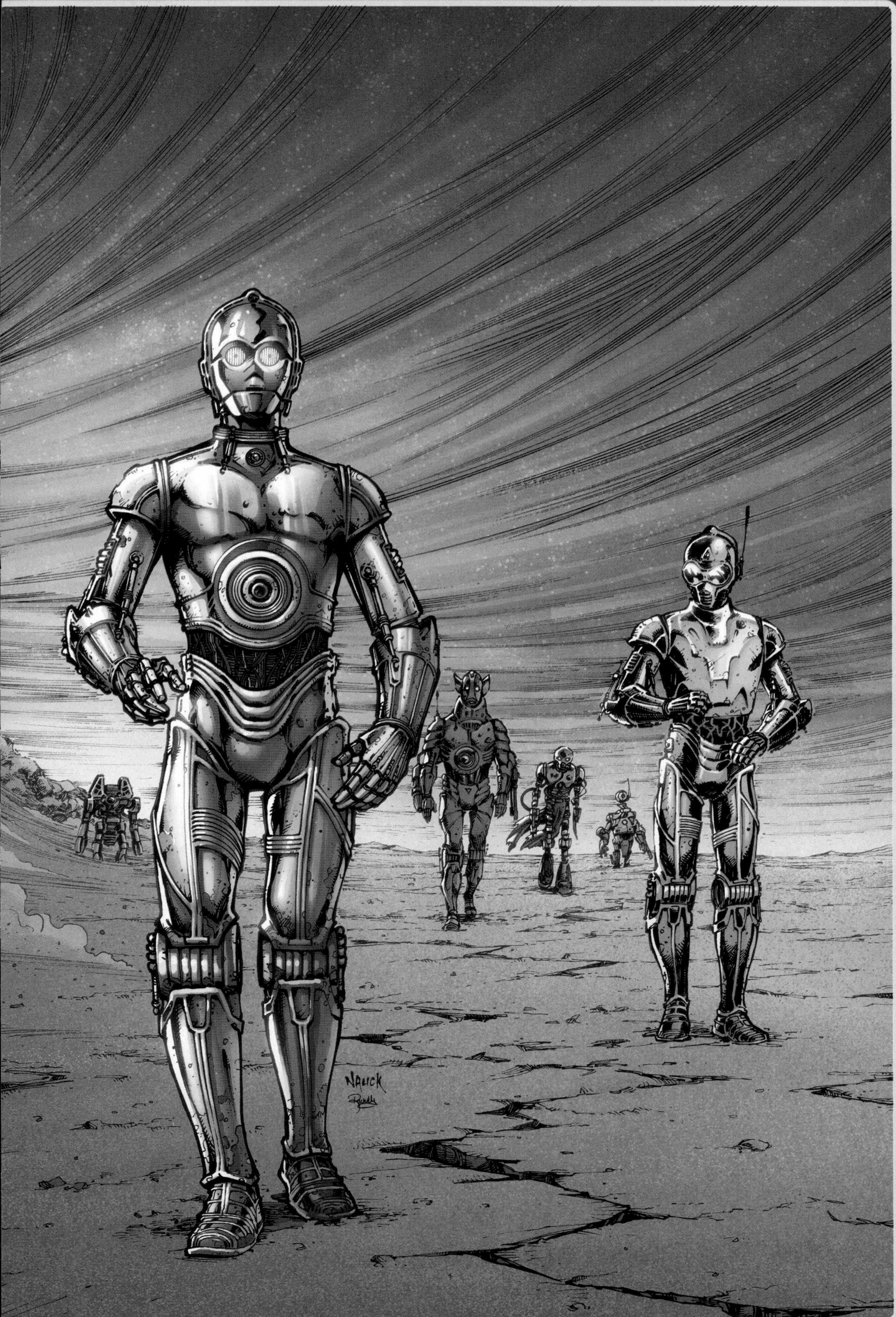
NAUCK

STAR WAR SPECIAL: C-3PO 1 **Classic Variant**

by **TODD NAUCK & RACHELLE ROSENBERG**

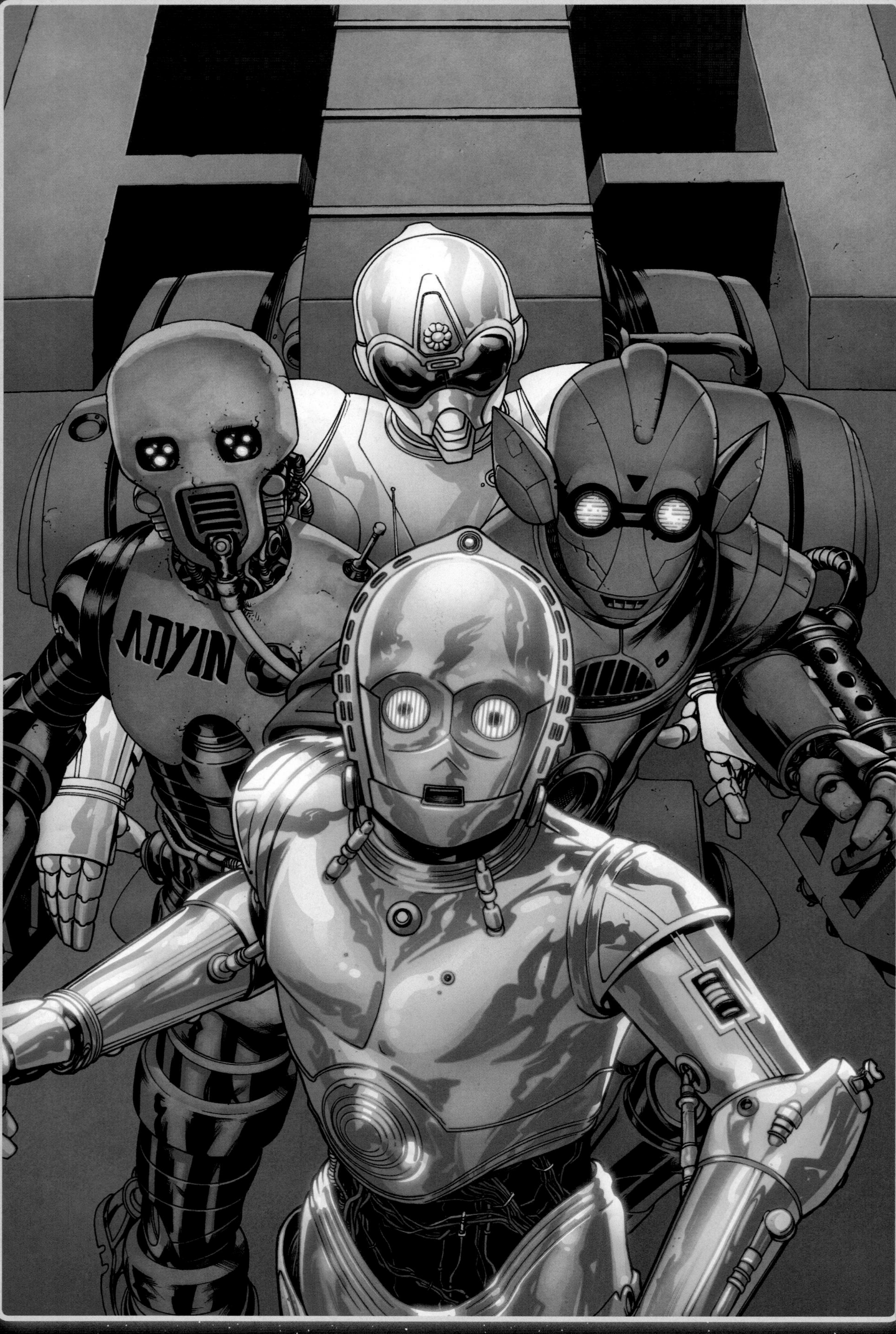

***STAR WAR SPECIAL: C-3PO 1* Unused Cover Art**
by **MIKE McKONE & NOLAN WOODARD**

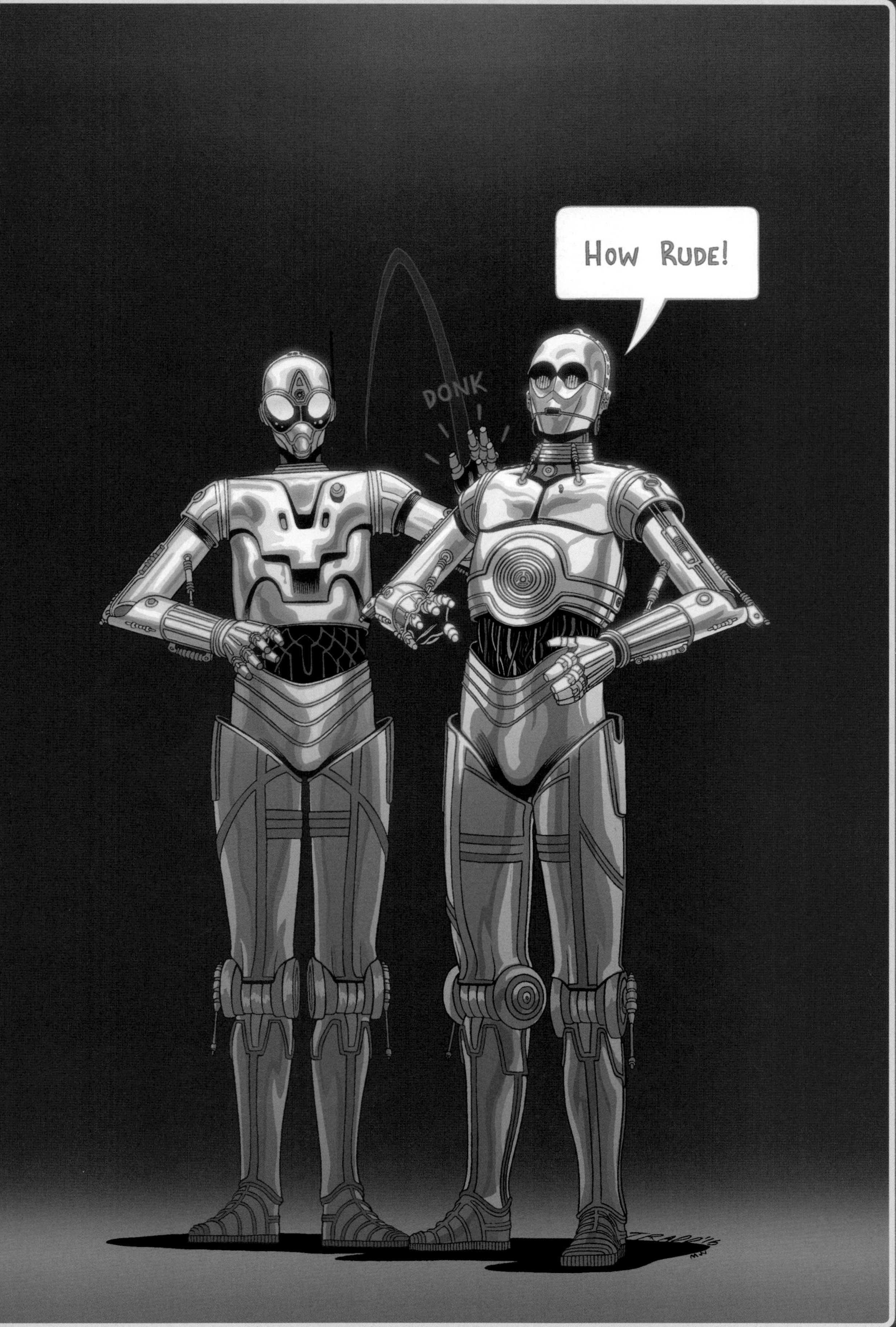
HOW RUDE!
DONK

STAR WAR SPECIAL: C-3PO 1 Unused Cover Art
by TRADD MOORE & MATT WILSON

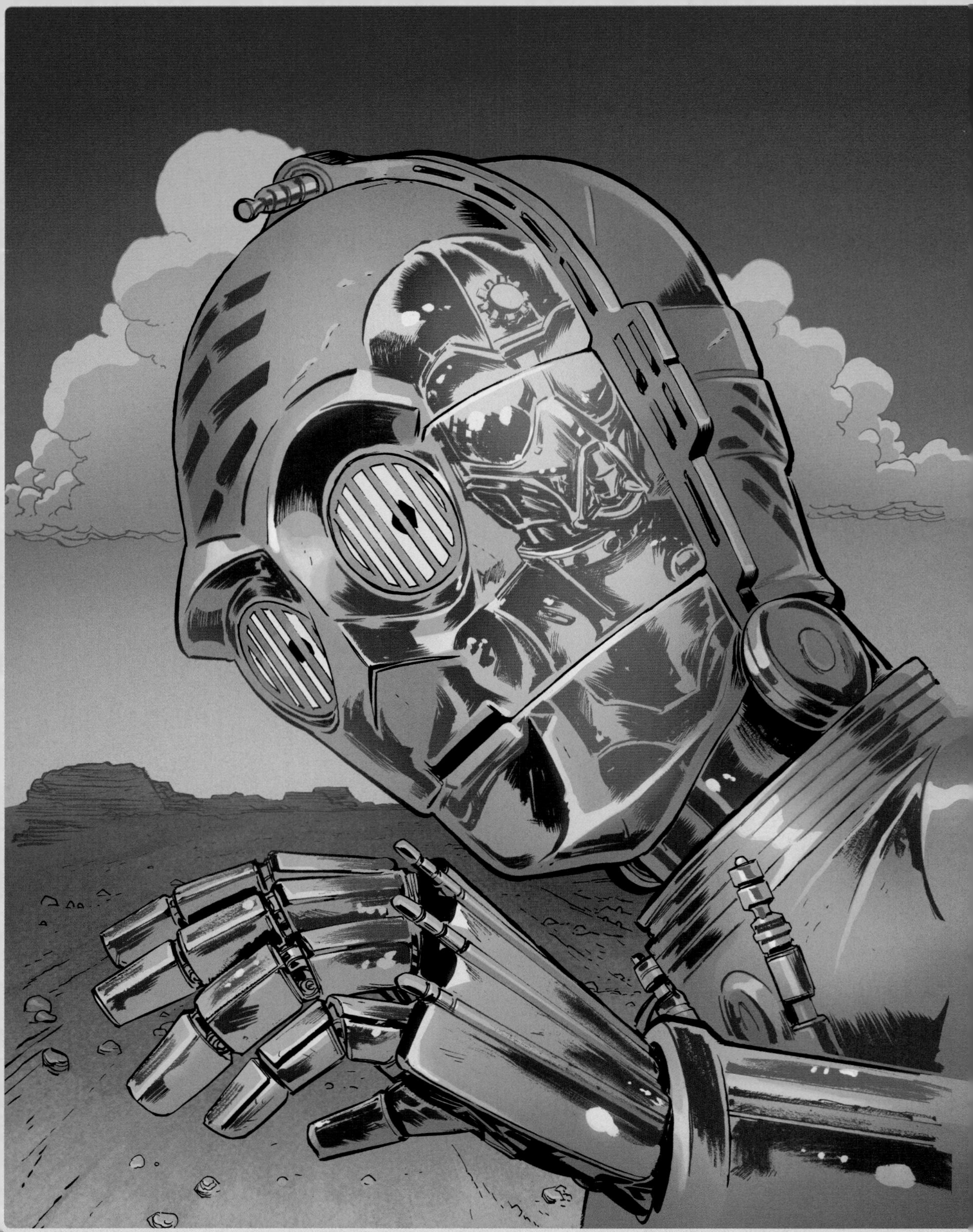

STAR WAR SPECIAL: C-3PO 1 Unused Cover Art
by DANILO BEYRUTH & TAMRA BONVILLAIN

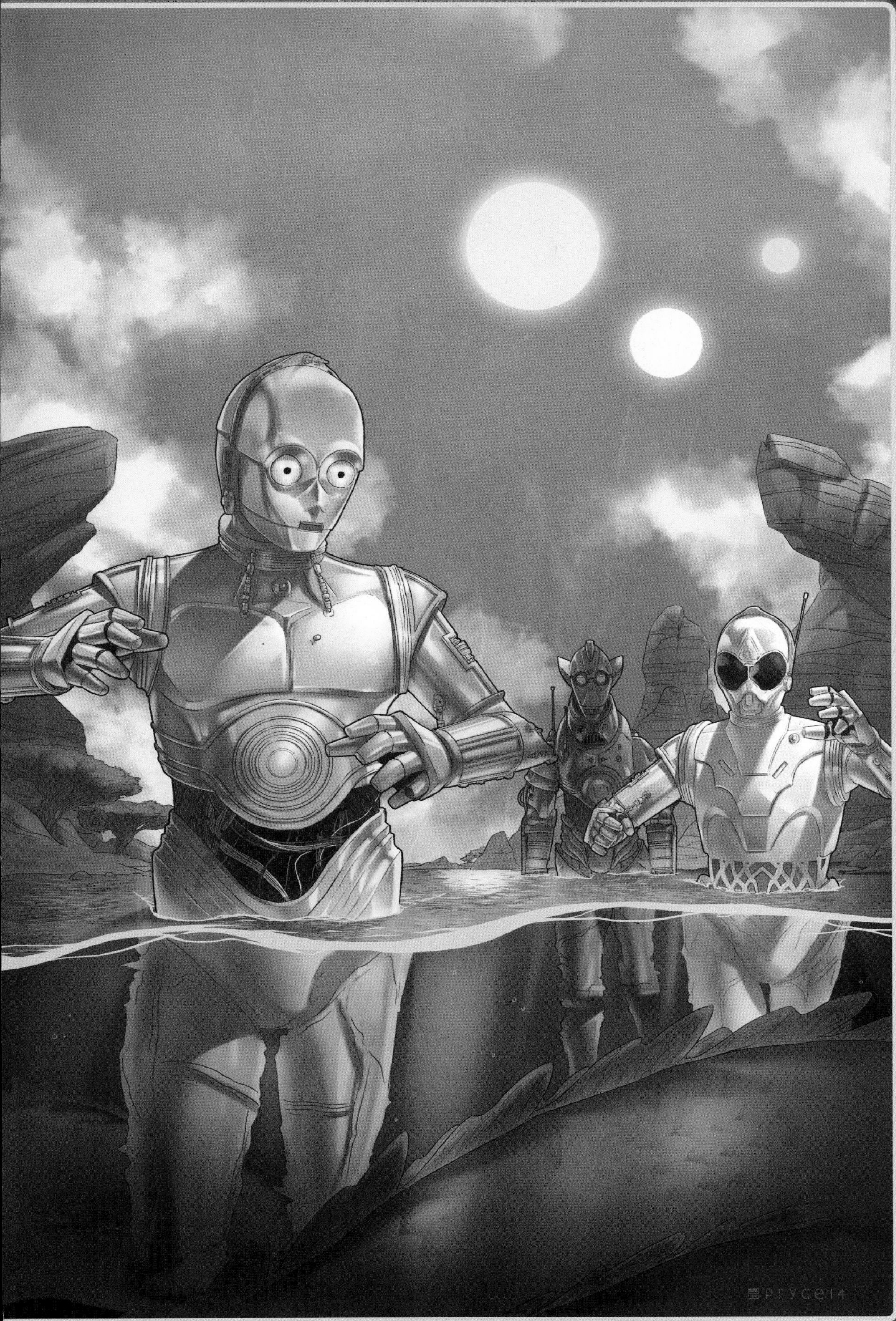
pryce14

***STAR WAR SPECIAL: C-3PO 1* Unused Cover Art**
by JAMAL CAMPBELL

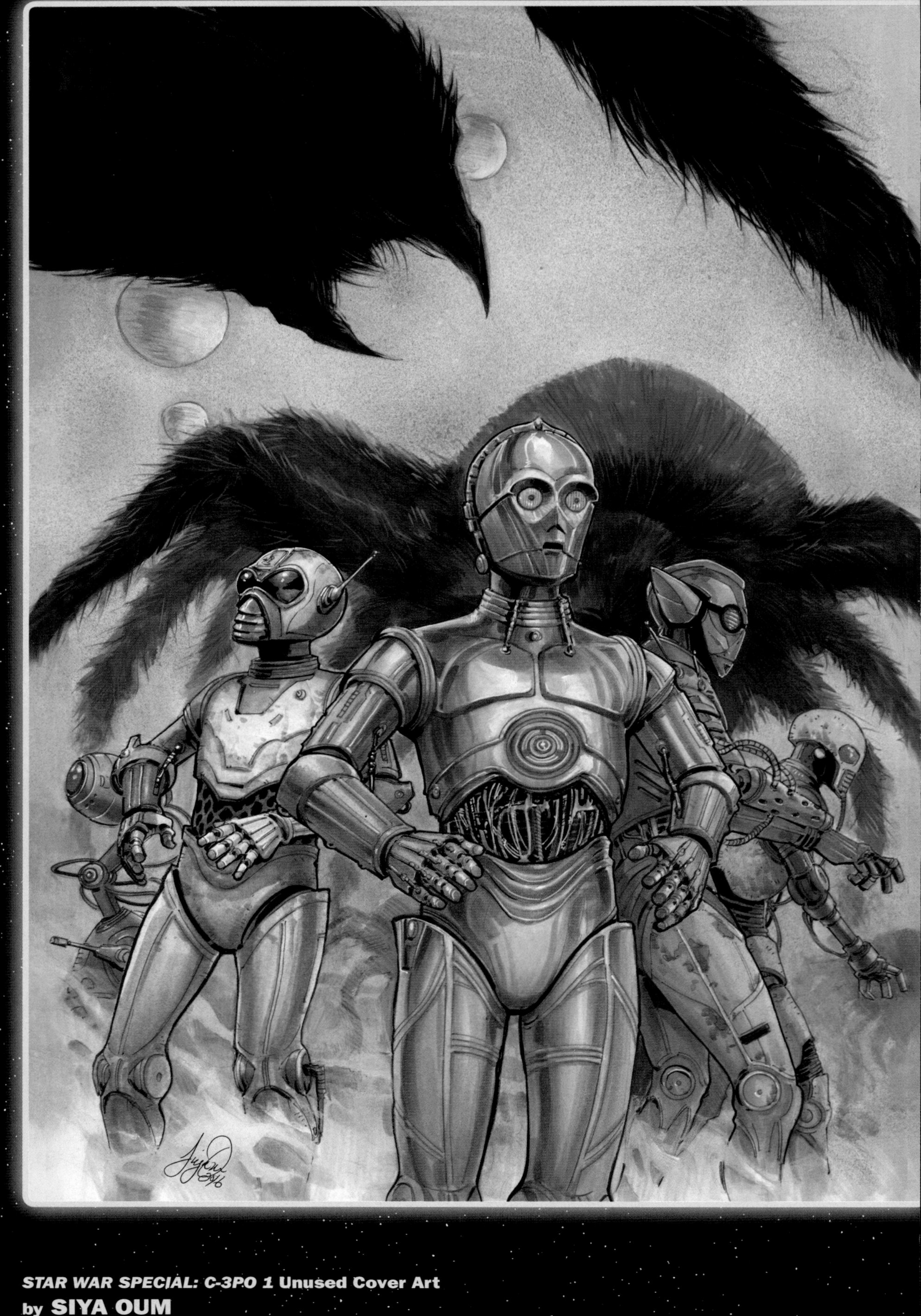

***STAR WAR SPECIAL: C-3P.O 1* Unused Cover Art**
by SIYA OUM

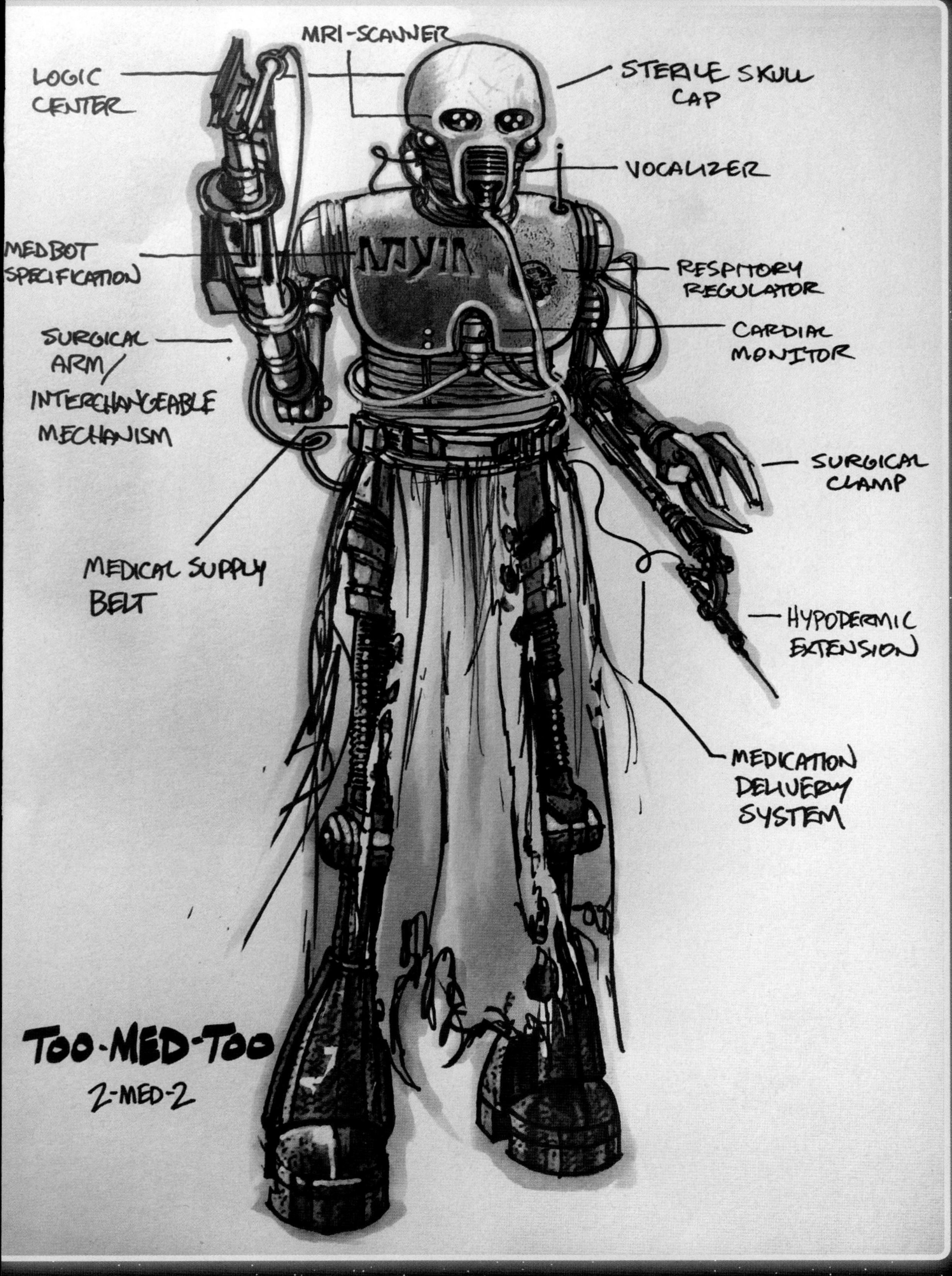
MRI-SCANNER
LOGIC CENTER
STERILE SKULL CAP
VOCALIZER
MEDBOT SPECIFICATION
RESPITORY REGULATOR
CARDIAL MONITOR
SURGICAL ARM/ INTERCHANGEABLE MECHANISM
SURGICAL CLAMP
MEDICAL SUPPLY BELT
HYPODERMIC EXTENSION
MEDICATION DELIVERY SYSTEM
TOO-MED-TOO
2-MED-2

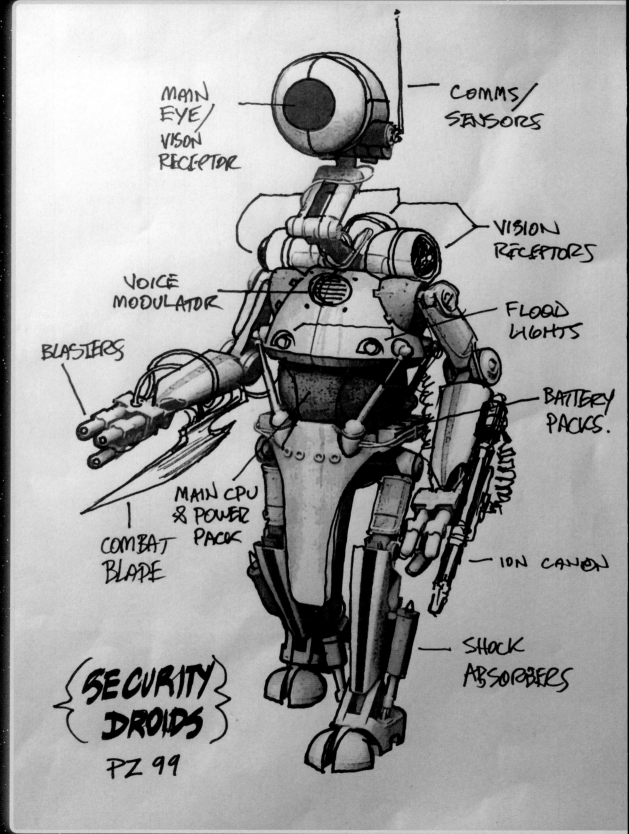

MAIN EYE/ VISION RECEPTOR

COMMS/ SENSORS

VISION RECEPTORS

VOICE MODULATOR

FLOOD LIGHTS

BLASTERS

BATTERY PACKS.

MAIN CPU & POWER PACK

ION CANON

COMBAT BLADE

SHOCK ABSORBERS

{SECURITY} DROIDS

PZ 99

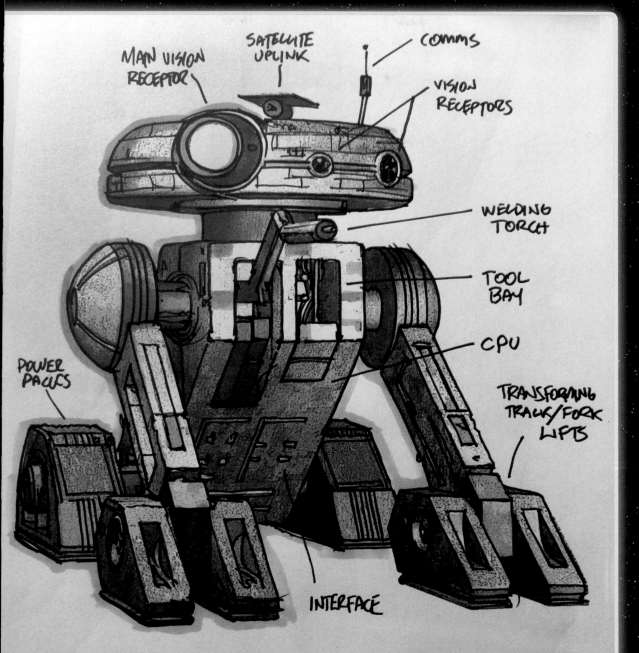

MAIN VISION
RECEPTOR

SATELLITE
UPLINK

COMMS

VISION
RECEPTORS

WELDING
TORCH

TOOL
BAY

CPU

POWER
PACKS

TRANSFORMING
TRACK/FORK
LIFTS

INTERFACE

CO-34

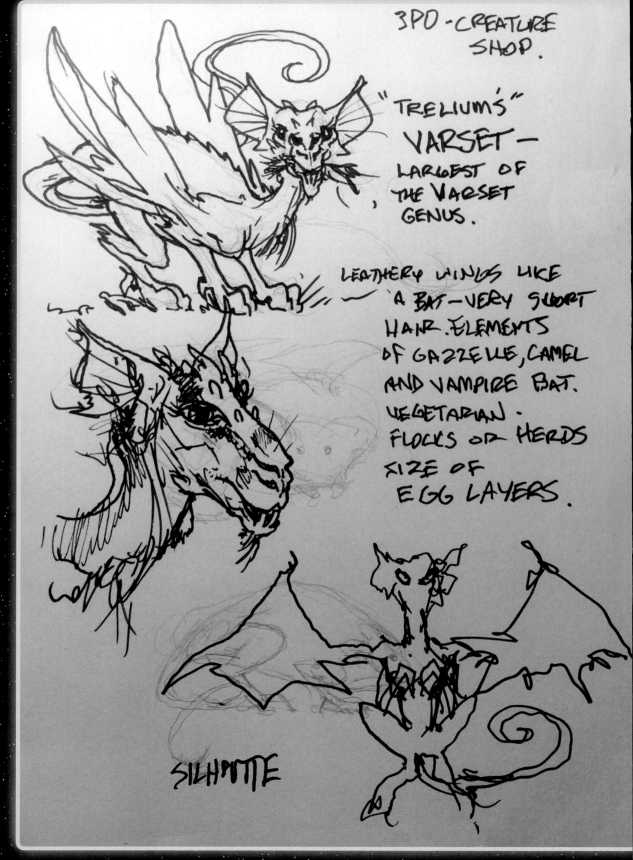

3PO - CREATURE SHOP.

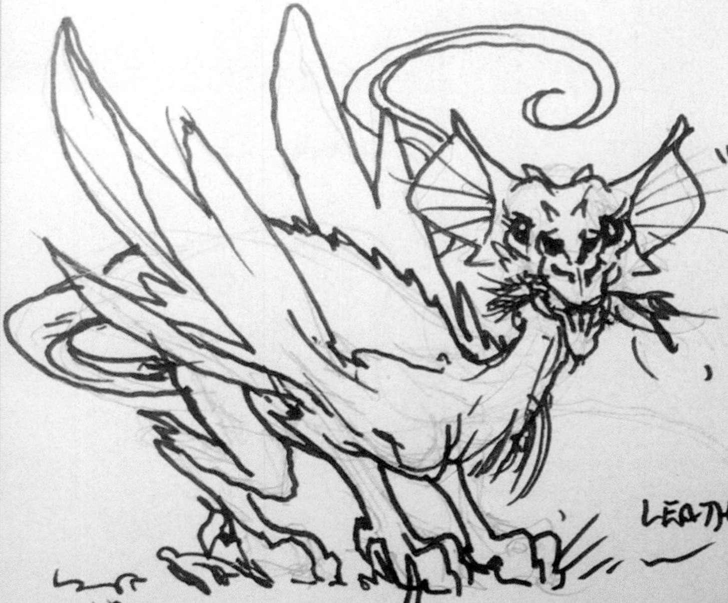

"TRELIUM'S" VARSET — LARGEST OF THE VARSET GENUS.

LEATHERY WINGS LIKE A BAT — VERY SHORT HAIR. ELEMENTS OF GAZZELLE, CAMEL AND VAMPIRE BAT. VEGETARIAN - FLOCKS OR HERDS SIZE OF EGG LAYERS.

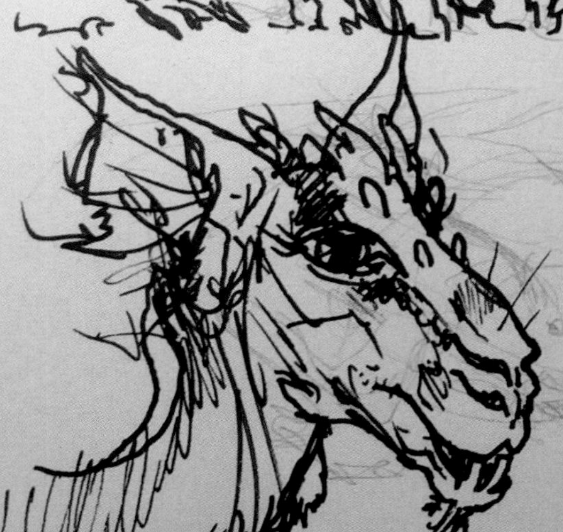

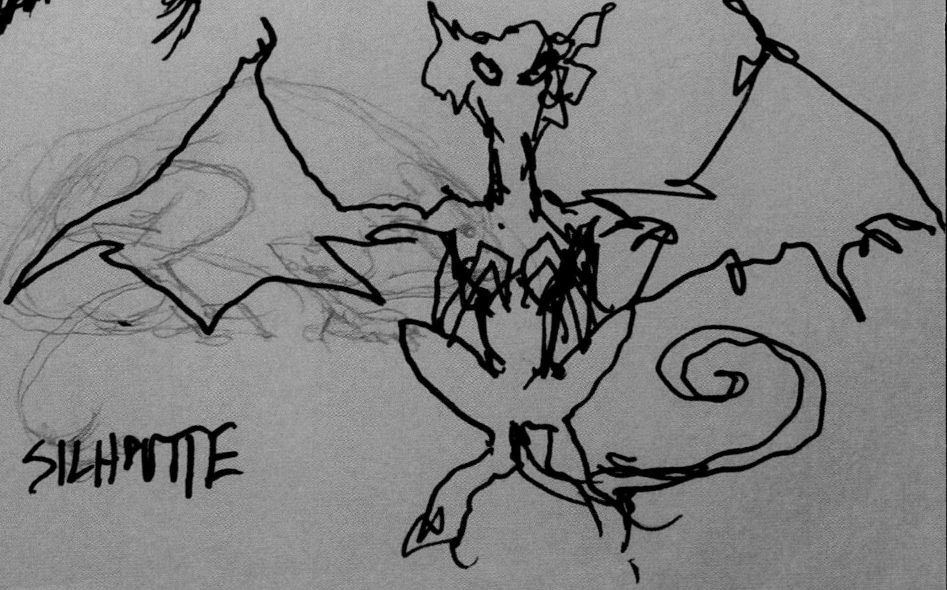

SILHOUTTE

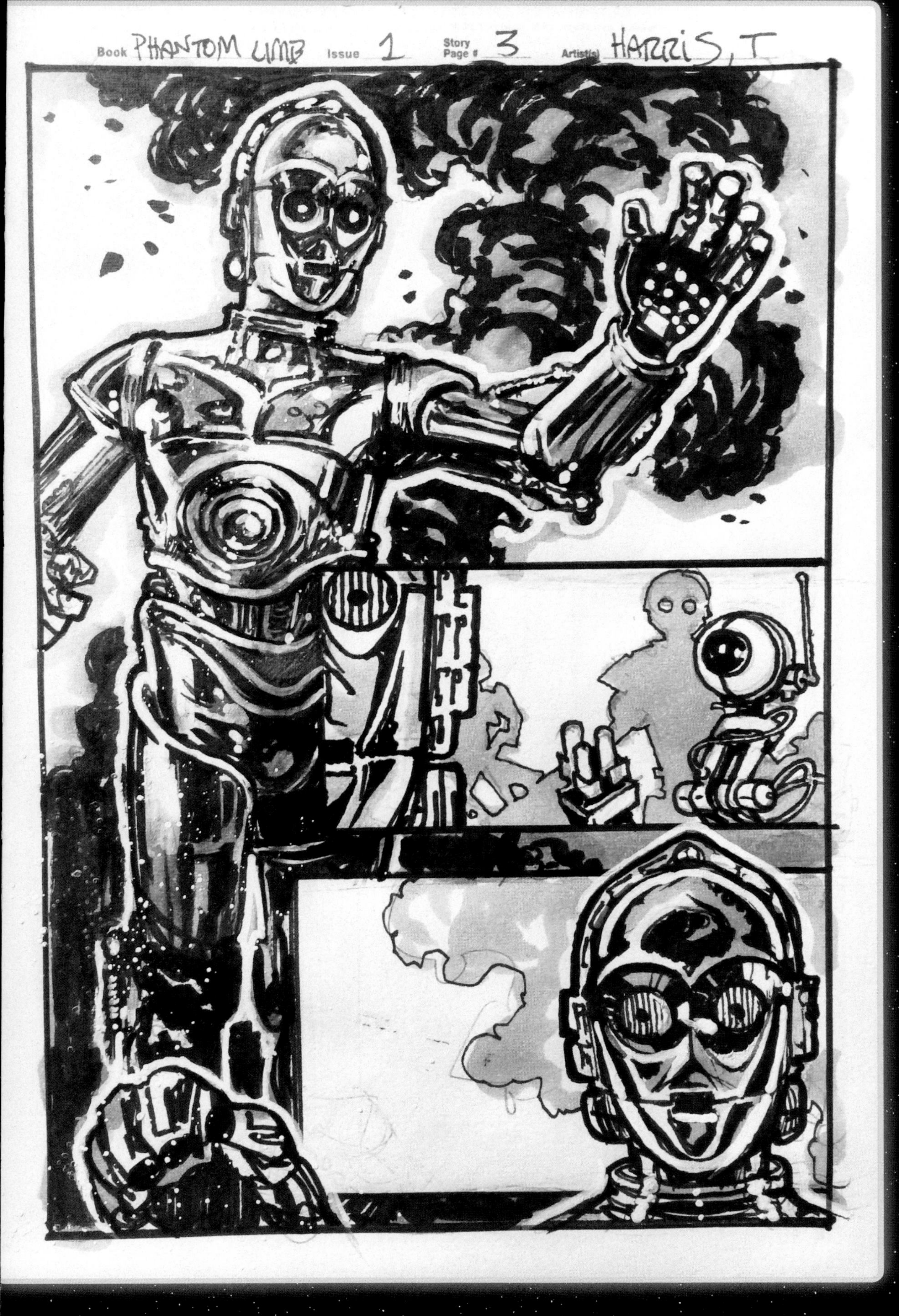
Book PHANTOM LIMB Issue 1 Story Page # 3 Artist(s) HARRIS, T

STAR WAR SPECIAL: C-3PO 1, Page 3 Art

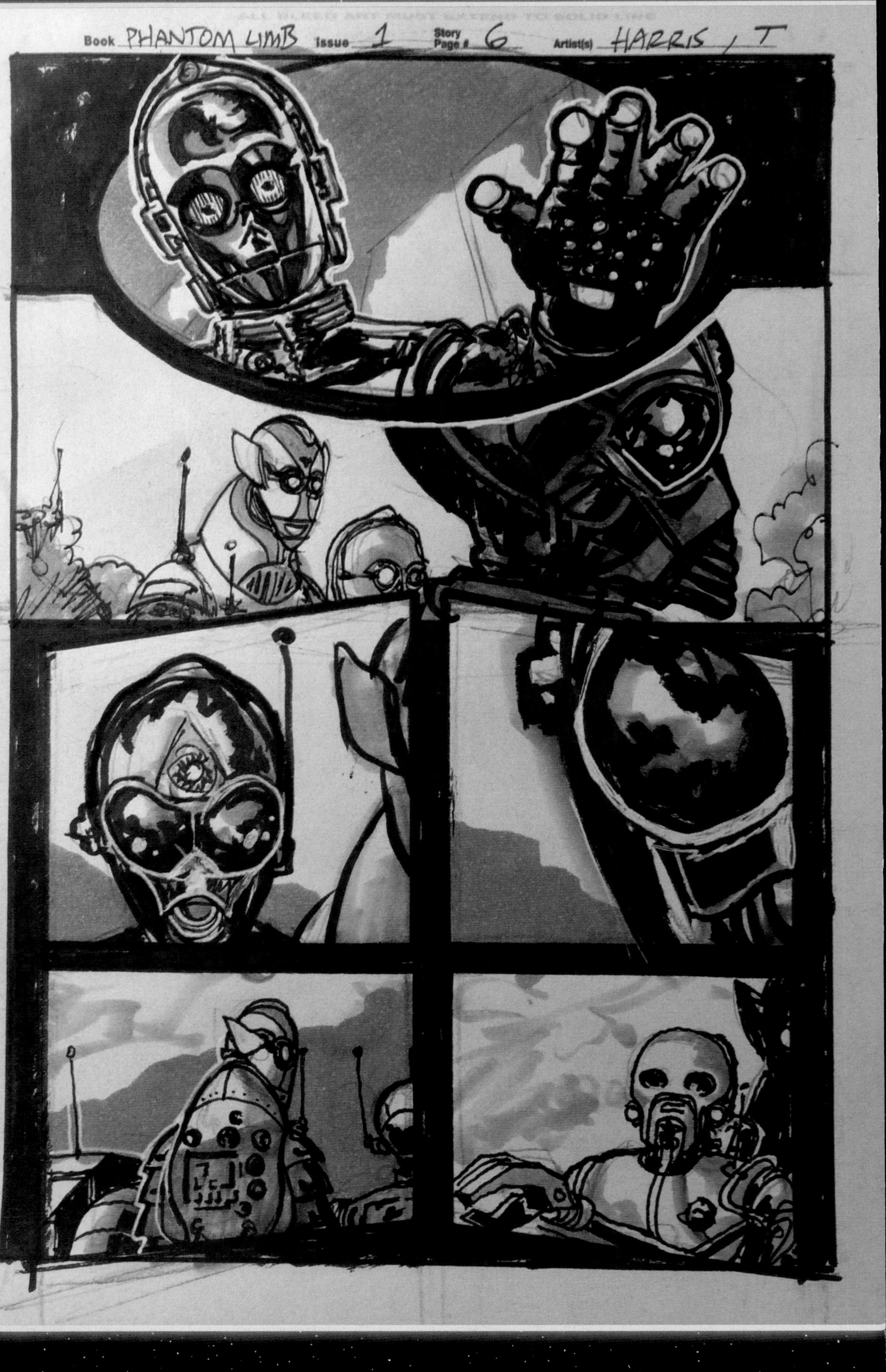
Book PHANTOM LIMB Issue 1 Story Page # 6 Artist(s) HARRIS / T

STAR WAR SPECIAL: C-3PO 1, Page 6 Art

ALL BLEED ART MUST EXTEND TO SOLID LINE

Book PHANTOM LIMB Issue 1 Story Page # 7 Artist(s) HARRIS, T

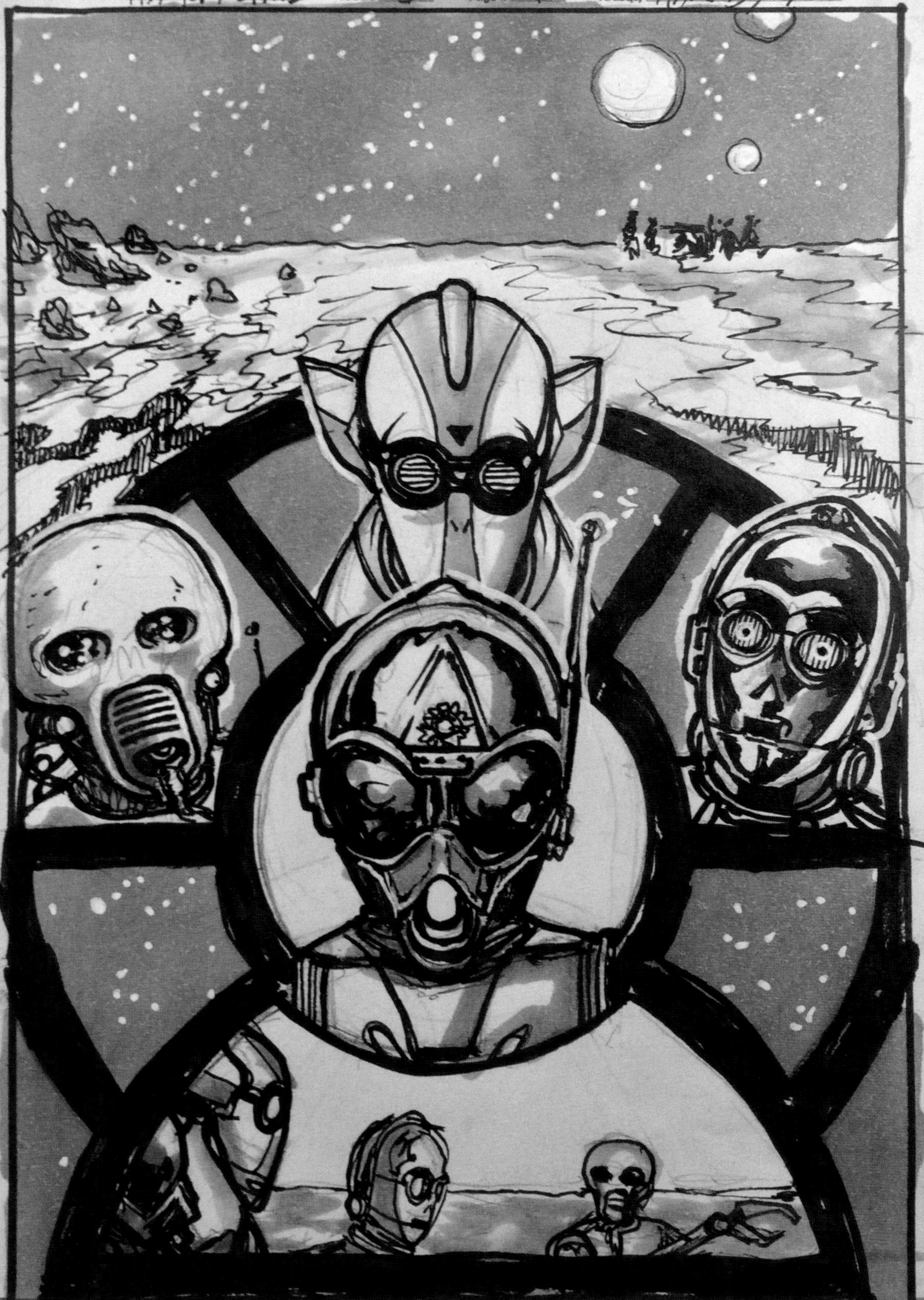

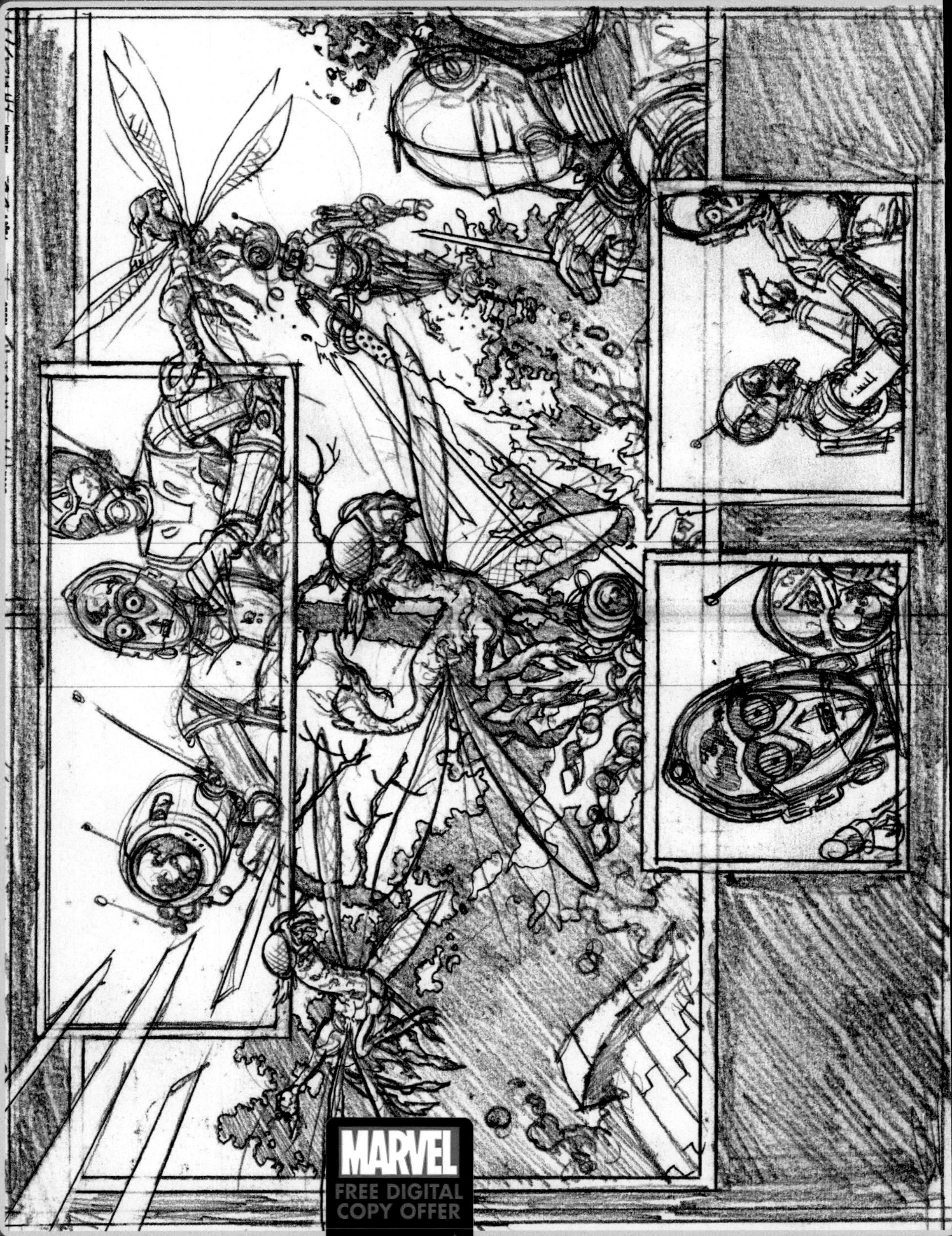